ADAM LOVELADY

CODE OFFICIALS HANDBOOK

A Legal Guide to Administering Building and Property Codes in North Carolina

School of Government

The School of Government at the University of North Carolina at Chapel Hill works to improve the lives of North Carolinians by engaging in practical scholarship that helps public officials and citizens understand and improve state and local government. Established in 1931 as the Institute of Government, the School provides educational, advisory, and research services for state and local governments. The School of Government is also home to a nationally ranked Master of Public Administration program, the North Carolina Judicial College, and specialized centers focused on community and economic development, information technology, and environmental finance.

As the largest university-based local government training, advisory, and research organization in the United States, the School of Government offers up to 200 courses, webinars, and specialized conferences for more than 12,000 public officials each year. In addition, faculty members annually publish approximately 50 books, manuals, reports, articles, bulletins, and other print and online content related to state and local government. The School also produces the *Daily Bulletin Online* each day the General Assembly is in session, reporting on activities for members of the legislature and others who need to follow the course of legislation.

Operating support for the School of Government's programs and activities comes from many sources, including state appropriations, local government membership dues, private contributions, publication sales, course fees, and service contracts.

Visit sog.unc.edu or call 919.966.5381 for more information on the School's courses, publications, programs, and services.

Printed in the United States of America
30 29 28 27 26 1 2 3 4 5
ISBN 978-1-64238-129-0

Contents

Chapter 6
Building Permit Procedures

Chapter 7
Building Code Inspections

Chapter 8
Building Code Enforcement

Chapter 9
Building Code Interpretations and Appeals

Chapter 10
Unsafe Structures

Chapter 11
Commercial Maintenance Code

Chapter 12
Minimum Housing and Abandoned Structures

Acknowledgments

This book is built upon a solid foundation laid by some of the legendary faculty at the UNC Institute of Government (now the School of Government). Phil Green researched and wrote about building codes and development regulations from his arrival in 1949 through his retirement in 1988. His 1987 book, *Legal Aspects of Building Code Enforcement in North Carolina*, was the primary text in the field for years and sets the framework for this book. Rich Ducker's wide-ranging service included decades on the North Carolina Code Officials Qualification Board, training a generation of code officials, and writing about the intricacies of code enforcement. David Owens set the bar for legal scholarship and practical guidance in North Carolina, especially on topics related to development regulations. The School of Government in general, and this book in particular, benefit from their great contributions.

Code Officials Handbook is informed by the guidance and expertise of current School of Government colleagues. Becca Fisher-Gabbard, Jim Joyce, Taylor Morris, Tyler Mulligan, and Jeff Welty each provided careful review and valuable insights to help refine the many technical legal fields.

This book benefits greatly from the dedicated work of public servants. No one knows practical scholarship better than practitioners. Officials from the Office of State Fire Marshal and Department of Insurance, in particular Mike Hejduk and Beth Williams, provided essential knowledge and encouragement to complete the book. Local government officials across North Carolina, including Tony Baker, Les Everett, Shandy Padgett, Matt Pentz, and Michael Slate, significantly improved this work with their expertise and wisdom. Extra thanks to Sofia Hernandez and Chris Young—their ideas and experience shaped the project from the start and refined it to the end.

Note on Statutory Language in this Book

Text quoted directly from the North Carolina General Statutes features a gray bar on the left and is set in a different font, to set it apart from the rest of the book text. See the example below for reference:

> **§ 143-138. North Carolina State Building Code.**
>
> (a) Preparation and Adoption. — The Building Code Council and Residential Code Council may prepare and adopt, in accordance with the provisions of this Article, a North Carolina State Building Code. The Building Code Council shall oversee codes applicable to commercial or multi-family construction and contained in Code volumes, as specified in subdivisions (1) through (9) of this subsection, that apply to commercial and multi-family construction. The Residential Code Council shall oversee codes applicable to residential construction and contained in Code volumes, as specified in subdivisions (1) through (10) of this subsection, that apply to residential construction.

Part 1
Governance and Administration

Code officials operate in a complex area of law and governance. The work is shaped and limited by federal and state constitutions, regulatory rules from all levels of government, and legal requirements for local government departments and public officials. Part 1 introduces the institutional framework for code enforcement, including the history of building code regulation, the governing bodies and documents, and the roles and responsibilities of the inspection department and the code official. These topics are presented in the following chapters:

- **Chapter 1:** Introduction
- **Chapter 2:** Governance
- **Chapter 3:** The Inspection Department
- **Chapter 4:** The Code Official

Chapter 1

Introduction

Regulating Buildings in North Carolina

> It is within the police power of the General Assembly and of a city, when authorized, to establish minimum standards, materials, designs, and construction of buildings for the safety of the occupants, their neighbors, and the public at large.[1]

Public safety is an essential governmental function, and building construction is a critical component of public safety. Building safety includes standards for new construction—technical engineering standards for framing, wiring, plumbing, mechanical systems, and more—as well as standards and remedies for existing structures that may become unsafe over time.

In North Carolina, the state adopts the North Carolina State Building Code, and local inspection departments administer and enforce it. Additionally, the state has enabled local governments to adopt local building regulations to address topics such as unsafe structure orders, commercial maintenance requirements, and minimum housing ordinances.

All of these regulations are rooted in public health and safety, but they also affect private property and personal liberty. While development regulations are a valid exercise of governmental powers, government officials must take care to adhere to state law requirements and ensure constitutional protections.

Contents

This book seeks to clarify the legal framework of building safety regulation in North Carolina—the authorities, procedures, options, and limits for local code enforcement. It is not a technical code book; it does not detail the intricacies of engineering requirements in the North Carolina State Building Code. As the subtitle states, this book is *A Legal Guide to Administering Building and Property Codes in North Carolina.*

1. State v. Walker, 265 N.C. 482, 484, 144 S.E.2d 419, 421 (1965).

The book is divided into three parts. Part 1 explores the governance and administration of code enforcement. Beyond this introductory chapter, it includes Chapter 2 (Governance), Chapter 3 (The Inspection Department), and Chapter 4 (The Code Official).

Part 2 investigates the legal framework for the State Building Code. This includes Chapter 5 (North Carolina State Building Code), Chapter 6 (Building Permit Procedures), Chapter 7 (Building Code Inspections), Chapter 8 (Building Code Enforcement), and Chapter 9 (Building Code Interpretations and Appeals).

Part 3 outlines the legal authority and procedures for existing structures and unsafe situations. This includes Chapter 10 (Unsafe Structures), Chapter 11 (Commercial Maintenance Code), Chapter 12 (Minimum Housing and Abandoned Structures), Chapter 13 (Nuisance Code and Abatement), Chapter 14 (Zoning Enforcement for Existing Structures and Uses), and Chapter 15 (Vacant Building Receivership). The Appendixes include selected North Carolina cases and a wide range of sample materials, including fee schedules, permitting and inspection flowcharts, applications, notices, enforcement documents, and compliance forms.

Laws change. This book is current through October 2025, but state legislation and agency action will continue. For updates on changes to the laws, check the School of Government's annual bulletin, *North Carolina Legislation Related to Planning and Development Regulation*. For updates on applicable building code provisions, check with the Office of State Fire Marshal.

The focus of this book is the legal framework within which building and property codes exist. The key elements are the state and federal constitutions, statutes, and court cases. Of course, the provisions of the State Building Code—especially the procedural rules of the Administrative Code and Policies that are incorporated in the State Building Code—shape the legal framework. This book is going to press as the North Carolina State Building Code is in a state of transition. With that in mind, this book references the 2018 *and* the 2024 versions of the Administrative Code and Policies. Text quoted directly from the North Carolina General Statutes is styled differently to set it apart from the rest of the book.

The 2024 North Carolina State Building Code was intended to take effect on January 1, 2025, but the effective date was delayed until a future date, contingent upon certain criteria being met. The first delay came in the wake of Hurricane Helene. The Disaster Recovery Act of 2024—Part III, S.L. 2024-57, included a provision at Section 1F.3 to postpone the effective date of the State Building Code until July 1, 2025. Subsequently, Section 5.12 of the 2025 Recovery Act, Part V (S.L. 2025-2 (H.B. 47)), further delayed the effective date of the 2024 State Building Code. Under this provision, the 2024 Building Code will become effective twelve months after the first day of the month following the State Fire Marshal's letter certifying that the following events have occurred:

> (1) The Building Code Council and Residential Code Council have completed all of the following publication and distribution requirements:
>
> a. The initial publication and printing of the adopted 2024 North Carolina State Building Code, including all amendments adopted as of the effective date of this act.
>
> b. The distribution of copies of the initially published 2024 North Carolina State Building Code to all state and local officials and departments required to receive copies under G.S. 143-138(g), without the necessity of a written request.
>
> c. The making of copies of the initial publication of the 2024 North Carolina State Building Code available for purchase by members of the general public.
>
> (2) The Residential Code Council is fully constituted in accordance with the membership requirements set forth in G.S. 143-136.1.

State Fire Marshal Brian Taylor issued a letter on March 31, 2025, which addressed the delayed effective date and the interim use of the 2024 North Carolina State Building Code. Regarding the criteria outlined above for triggering the effective date, the Office of State Fire Marshal (OSFM) anticipated that printed and digital copies of the code would be ready by July 1, 2025. However, OSFM does not oversee the appointment and confirmation of members of the Residential Code Council; those responsibilities fall to the governor and the General Assembly.

In the interim, the State Fire Marshal noted that, pursuant to Section 102.5 of the 2018 North Carolina Administrative Code and Policies, "the 2024 Code may be used as an alternate method of construction at the building owner's or his agent's request."

History of Building Codes in North Carolina

The history of building codes is long and closely tracks the history of buildings and construction technology. Aspects of building code regulation appear in ancient legal documents such as the Code of Hammurabi[2] and the Hebrew Scriptures.[3] In the American and North Carolina context, building safety regulations predate the United States. Edenton's charter of 1740 prohibited wooden chimneys.[4] In 1768, Charlotte's charter from King George III required that every grantee of a lot in town erect within three years "one well framed sawed or hewed log house, twenty

2. The Babylonian legal text stated that if a house collapsed and killed the owner, the builder would be put to death.

3. Deuteronomy 22:8 requires that builders put a parapet around a roof.

4. Laws of North Carolina, 1740, ch. 1.

feet in length, and sixteen feet wide, and ten feet high in the clear, with a brick or stone chimney or chimneys. . . ."[5] In 1788, the Town Council of Salem considered, and the Salem Community Conference approved, rules for building permits, land use regulation, building safety, and fire protection.[6]

Through the 1800s, the state of North Carolina authorized specific local regulations to address building safety. These included fire safety measures, establishment of fire limits and regulation of wooden structures, limitations on explosives and flammable materials, inspection of unhealthful conditions, and abatement of such conditions.[7]

Early twentieth-century legislation authorized local governments to regulate building safety. In 1905, the North Carolina General Assembly first adopted statewide regulations for building design and construction.[8] These newly adopted regulations, which applied in cities and towns with populations over 1,000 (and smaller towns that chose to adopt them), included specifications for building construction and materials, requirements for building permits, establishment of fire limits, limitations on wood construction, and provisions for existing structures that appear "especially dangerous." A general grant of power to municipalities in 1917 enabled cities to adopt their own local regulations for building safety, plumbing, electrical systems, explosives, and fire safety.[9]

Early caselaw clarified the legal framework for building permitting. In *State v. Tenant*[10] the state Supreme Court emphasized the need for clear standards in permitting. The City of Asheville required a permit from the city council for any new construction, but the ordinance lacked clear standards for when a permit would be issued or denied. When a property owner challenged the ordinance, the court ruled that "it is unconstitutional and void, because it fails to furnish a uniform rule of action, and leaves the right of property subject to the despotic will of aldermen, who may exercise it so as to give exclusive profits or privileges to particular persons." In *State v. Eubanks*,[11] a property owner obtained a permit from the local inspector, as required by state law. A local ordinance purported to require a separate permit, and the city sought to prevent the construction. The court ruled that the owner obtained the necessary permit and a local ordinance could not make a lawful act illegal. And in *Clinard v. City of Winston-Salem*,[12] the court confirmed that "[t]he exercise of the power to grant or refuse the license to erect a building was a governmental function."

---

5. 9 Geo. III (Nov. 7, 1768); Philip P. Green, Jr., Building Regulation and Inspection in North Carolina 1 (1954).

6. Salem Town Council Minutes (June 1788), reprinted in Luther Lashmit, *Historic Building Regulations of Old Salem, North Carolina*, in Readings in Code Administration, vol. I, History/Philosophy/Law, ch. 3 (Richard L. Sanderson ed., 1974) (excerpted from *BOCA News*, Feb. 1964, at 3, 6–7).

7. *See, e.g.*, N.C. Priv. Laws, 1866, ch. 1, § 66 (Raleigh); N.C. Laws, 1850–51, ch. 334, § 27 (Charlotte); N.C. Pub. Laws, 1879, ch. 117, § 10; Green, *supra* note 5, at 1–2.

8. N.C. Pub. Laws 1905, ch. 506.

9. N.C. Pub. Laws 1917, ch. 136, subch. VIII, § 3.

10. 110 N.C. 609 (1892).

11. 154 N.C. 628 (1911).

12. 173 N.C. 356 (1917).

As such, if a permit was improperly withheld, the city was obligated to issue it, and the court could require issuance by an order (writ of mandamus).

In the 1930s, the state established the foundations for the modern approach to building code enforcement in North Carolina: a statewide code adopted by a state-level council and enforced at the local level. A meeting in November 1931 at North Carolina State College (later University) brought together officials from state organizations interested in the construction industry, as well as fire chiefs, in the interest of establishing a state building code. Speakers included W.G. Geile, Chairman of the Building Code Committee of the North Carolina Society of Engineers, and Sherwood Brockwell, the State Fire Marshal. Over the next two years, that group drafted a proposed building code for North Carolina. In 1933, the General Assembly established the Building Code Council and authorized adoption of a State Building Code.[13] The council reviewed the draft code, and in 1936 submitted it to the Insurance Commissioner, who approved the State Building Code.[14] To resolve lingering questions of authority and delegation, in 1941 the General Assembly "ratified and adopted" the 1936 State Building Code but also clarified the limited scope of the Building Code Council's authority.[15]

During the early twentieth-century period of modernization and authorization, the General Assembly also empowered local governments to address other development regulations. It delegated authority for land use zoning in 1923 (for municipalities), county electrical inspections in 1937, and minimum housing standards in 1939 (for municipalities).[16] In 1957, the General Assembly revised and codified the authority of the Building Code Council and State Building Code as part of Chapter 143 of the North Carolina General Statutes (hereinafter G.S.).[17]

Throughout the 1960s and 1970s, the General Assembly took important steps to empower and professionalize inspections at the local government level. Legislation in 1969 provided comprehensive authority and guidance for local inspection departments in municipalities and counties.[18] In 1977, the General Assembly passed legislation requiring all local governments to provide building code enforcement within their jurisdictions and established the North Carolina Code Officials Qualification Board to oversee education and certification programs for local inspectors.[19]

While the General Assembly has long delegated authority to the Building Code Council (and more recently, the Residential Code Council) to adopt technical building codes, it also has a history of specifying certain code elements in state law. From

---

13. S.L. 1933-392.

14. N.C. Building Code Council, N.C. Building Code, iv–v (1936).

15. N.C. Pub. Laws 1941, ch. 280; Green, *supra* note 5, at 13–17.

16. N.C. Pub. Laws 1923, ch. 250; N.C. Pub. Laws 1939, ch. 287.

17. S.L. 1957-1138; Philip P. Green, Jr., Legal Aspects of Building Code Enforcement in North Carolina 2 (2d ed. 1987).

18. S.L. 1969-1065, -1066; Green, *supra* note 17, at 2.

19. S.L. 1977-531.

the 1990s through the present, the General Assembly has taken regular legislative action to specify technical standards in the State Building Code.[20]

In the 2020s, the General Assembly made major changes to the Building Code Council. In 2023, the legislature established a new council, the Residential Code Council, to oversee the Residential Building Code. And in 2024, the legislature re-composed the Building Code Council. The 2024 changes reduced the membership from seventeen to thirteen and specified certain positions as appointed by the General Assembly and not the governor.

The technical content of the State Building Code has evolved over time. The Building Code Council adopted codes in 1936, 1953, 1958, 1967, 1978, 1991, 1996, 2002, 2006, 2009, 2012, 2018, and 2024. Starting in the 1950s, the council relied on a third-party model code as the basis for the State Building Code and made North Carolina–specific revisions. The 1953 State Building Code was a comprehensive revision based on the National Building Code of the National Board of Fire Underwriters.[21] The council based the 1967 Code on the Standard Building Code, drafted by the Southern Building Code Congress International. In 2002, the council based the State Building Code on the International Code Council (ICC) codes. Because the Building Code Council adopts state-specific revisions, North Carolina has typically been one code cycle behind the ICC model codes (e.g., the 2018 North Carolina Building Codes were based on the 2015 ICC Codes).[22] While the ICC codes are updated on a three-year cycle, North Carolina law limits updates to the Residential Building Code to a six-year cycle.[23]

---

20. The legislative history of G.S. 143-138 reflects frequent technical revisions to the code content through numerous session laws (S.L. 1957-1138; S.L. 1969-567; S.L. 1969-1229, §§ 2–6; S.L. 1971-1100, §§ 1, 2; S.L. 1973-476, §§ 84, 128, 138, 152; S.L. 1973-507, § 5; S.L. 1981-677, § 3; S.L. 1981-713, §§ 1, 2; S.L. 1981-1282, § 20.2D (Reg. Sess., 1982); S.L. 1981-1348, § 1; S.L. 1983-614, § 3; S.L. 1985-576, § 1; S.L. 1985-622, § 2; S.L. 1985-666, § 39; S.L. 1989-25, § 2; S.L. 1989-681, §§ 2, 3, 9, 10, 18, 19; S.L. 1989-727, §§ 157, 158; S.L. 1991-895, § 1 (Reg. Sess., 1992); S.L. 1993-329, §§ 1, 3; S.L. 1993-539, § 1009; S.L. 1994-24, § 14(c) (Ex. Sess.); S.L. 1995-111, § 1; S.L. 1995-242, § 1; S.L. 1995-507, § 27.8(r); S.L. 1995-535, § 30; S.L. 1997-26, §§ 1–3, 5; S.L. 1997-443, §§ 11A.93, 11A.94, 11A.118(a), 11A.119(a); S.L. 1998-57, § 2; S.L. 1998-172, § 1; S.L. 1998-202, § 4(u); S.L. 1999-456, § 40; S.L. 2000-137, § 4(x); S.L. 2000-140, § 93.1(a); S.L. 2001-141, §§ 1, 2, 3, 4; S.L. 2001-421, §§ 1.1, 1.2, 1.5; S.L. 2001-424, § 12.2(b); S.L. 2002-144, § 5; S.L. 2003-221, § 6; S.L. 2003-284, § 22.2; S.L. 2004-124, §§ 21.1, 21.2; S.L. 2005-205, § 6; S.L. 2007-182, §§ 1, 2; S.L. 2007-529, § 1; S.L. 2007-542, § 1; S.L. 2008-176, § 2; S.L. 2008-219, § 1; S.L. 2009-79, § 1(a)-(c); S.L. 2009-243, § 1; S.L. 2009-532, § 1; S.L. 2009-570, § 18; S.L. 2010-97, § 6(b); S.L. 2011-145, § 19.1(mm); S.L. 2011-364, § 1; S.L. 2012-34, § 1; S.L. 2012-187, § 16.1; S.L. 2013-75, § 1; S.L. 2013-118, §§ 2, 3; S.L. 2013-206, § 2; S.L. 2013-265, § 18; S.L. 2013-413, §§ 19(a), 41; S.L. 2014-79, § 5; S.L. 2014-90, § 1; S.L. 2014-115, § 17; S.L. 2014-120, § 22(c); S.L. 2015-145, §§ 4.1, 5.2; S.L. 2015-241, § 14.30(s), (u); S.L. 2015-263, § 34; S.L. 2016-113, § 13(a); S.L. 2017-10, §§ 1.3(b), 1.4; S.L. 2017-108, § 8(b); S.L. 2017-130, § 8(a); S.L. 2017-186, § 2(aaaaaa); S.L. 2017-212, § 8.11; S.L. 2018-65, § 2(a); S.L. 2019-174, § 4; S.L. 2021-121, § 2; S.L. 2021-180, § 19C.9(ttt); S.L. 2021-192, §§ 2(a), (b), 4(b); S.L. 2022-55, § 1; S.L. 2023-91, § 1; S.L. 2023-108, §§ 1(a), 2(c), (d), 4(a); S.L. 2023-137, § 36; S.L. 2023-151, § 11.56; S.L. 2024-1, § 6.4(i); S.L. 2024-49, §§ 2.1, 5.2(c)).

21. Green, *supra* note 5, at 18.

22. North Carolina Construction Law § 13:3 (*Code Adoption and Amendment*, 2024 update).

23. Chapter 143, Section 138(d) of the North Carolina General Statutes.

Chapter 2
Governance

Overview

Building safety is a technical engineering topic that exists within a complex legal framework. Because federal, state, and local governments impact building regulations, code officials must understand the constitutions, statutes, regulations, and codes involved, as well as the many agencies and boards that oversee the activities of inspectors.

This chapter outlines those different laws and governmental bodies involved.

Governance Structure

Federal, State, and Local Government

The United States federal system divides government authority and responsibility between the federal and state governments. Through the United States Constitution, the states granted authority to the federal government to handle certain broad topics like national defense, international affairs, and commerce among the states. State governments are responsible for all of the governmental functions not delegated to the federal government. Those wide-ranging topics include law enforcement, fire protection, parks and recreation, public education, infrastructure, social services, public health, planning and zoning, and, yes, building safety.

Each state divides responsibility for governmental functions between itself and units of local government such as counties and municipalities. Different states structure governance in different ways, so there is variability across the states as to how governmental functions are delegated and managed. In North Carolina, the state remains central to government authority. Local governments may only govern as authorized by the state. In contrast, some states are *home rule* states where the state has granted local governments broad authority to act. North Carolina is not a *home rule* state.

Legislative, Executive, and Judicial Branches

Students learn about the basic separation of powers in high school civics class (and the cartoon *Schoolhouse Rock!*): the legislative branch adopts the laws; the executive branch enforces the laws; and the judicial branch interprets the laws and resolves disputes.

This holds true in the world of building codes. The state legislative body (the North Carolina General Assembly) adopts the laws governing building codes. The executive agencies, like the Office of State Fire Marshal, oversee implementation and enforcement of the building codes. And individuals can appeal disputes into the state court system.

But government actions do not always fit neatly into simple frameworks. There is overlap between the branches. While the General Assembly adopts the laws, it also delegates some of the rulemaking to executive branch boards like the Building Code Council (so the executive branch is writing some of the rules). While some appeals go to court, many appeals are handled within a local inspections department or taken to the Office of State Fire Marshal or a quasi-judicial local board (so the executive branch or local government interprets the rules and resolves disputes). The details of these overlapping roles are explored more later in the book.

Local Government and Development Regulations

Authority

The state of North Carolina has delegated various responsibilities to counties and municipalities. Some responsibilities must be handled by local governments. Counties, for example, are obligated to manage certain governmental functions such as public education, social services, public health, and emergency management. Other responsibilities *may* be handled by local governments, including community development, planning and zoning, parks and recreation, and more.

For building codes, the state adopts the North Carolina State Building Code, and local governments must enforce it. Municipalities and counties are both obligated to enforce the code within their jurisdictions. Some municipalities meet this obligation by contracting with the county, as discussed below.

Beyond building code enforcement, municipalities and counties have authority to adopt and enforce a range of regulations that affect building and land development. These include unsafe structures, minimum housing, public nuisance, land use zoning, land subdivision, and local environmental rules.

Jurisdiction and Extraterritorial Jurisdiction

The geographic scope of local government authority is an important issue for development regulations and building code enforcement. Municipalities are authorized to enforce development regulations within their municipal boundaries and within their extraterritorial jurisdiction (ETJ).[1] The municipal ETJ is an area just outside

1. Chapter 160D, Sections 201 to 204 of the North Carolina General Statutes (hereinafter G.S.).

the municipal boundary. Depending on the population of the jurisdiction and the consent of the county, the ETJ may extend up to three miles beyond the municipal boundary.

State law allows a municipality to exercise all development regulations authorized under Chapter 160D within the ETJ. This includes planning, zoning, subdivision, historic preservation, minimum housing, building code enforcement, and more. A municipality may exercise a power in the ETJ only if it is also exercising that power within its corporate boundaries.[2]

Governing Documents

The legal framework for building codes and development regulations is set by many different governing documents at many different levels of government. These regulations are primarily authorized and limited by the state and local authorities listed below. But federal rules and regulations may also come into play, including the United States Constitution, the United States Code (U.S.C.), the Code of Federal Regulations (C.F.R.).

Here are the primary state and local governing documents applicable to building codes and development regulations:

The **North Carolina Constitution** is the foundational document establishing the governance of the state. It declares the rights of individuals and limits government authority, establishes the structure of the state government (legislative, executive, judicial), and sets broad frameworks for issues such as finance, elections, education, and local government. It is available at www.ncleg.gov/Laws/Constitution. The United States Constitution also sets limits on government authority in areas such as government inspections and the taking of private property. Constitutional protections are discussed further in Chapter 4.

The **North Carolina General Statutes** (G.S.) are the compilation of laws adopted by the state legislative body, the North Carolina General Assembly. The statutes cover a wide range of topics, including court procedures, criminal laws, business regulations, transportation, and environmental protection. The statutes are available at www.ncleg.gov/Laws/GeneralStatutes.

The statutes set forth provisions for the North Carolina Building Code in Chapter 143, starting with Article 9. The rules and authorities for local development regulations, including local enforcement of the State Building Code, are found in Chapter 160D. Additional *municipal* authority is outlined in Chapter 160A, and additional *county* authority is outlined in Chapter 153A.

The **North Carolina Administrative Code** (N.C.A.C.) is the compilation of administrative rules adopted by state agencies and licensing boards and approved

2. For more on local government jurisdiction, see Frayda S. Bluestein & David M. Lawrence, North Carolina Annexation Law (UNC School of Government, 2024).

by the North Carolina Rules Review Commission. These rules provide detailed guidance and regulations used to implement the general laws in the North Carolina General Statutes. The rules for the Engineering and Building Codes Division—including matters of code official certification—are set forth in Title 11, Chapter 8 of the North Carolina Administrative Code. The N.C.A.C. is available at http://reports.oah.state.nc.us/ncac.asp.

The **North Carolina State Building Code** is the compilation of codes covering technical standards for various construction trades, including building, electrical, fire, and more. The State Building Code is adopted by the Residential Code Council (for topics affecting residential construction) and the Building Code Council (for other code topics). The North Carolina State Building Code is available through the International Code Council at codes.iccsafe.org/codes/north-carolina.

The **Administrative Code and Policies** (N.C.A.C.P.) of the North Carolina State Building Code is a portion of the State Building Code and provides important guidance for implementation. Chapter 1 (Administrative Code) contains formal agency rules adopted by the Building Code Council and approved by the Rules Review Commission, comparable to rules in the North Carolina Administrative Code. These provisions are incorporated into the various technical codes. Chapter 2 (Policies) outlines general policies and procedures based on the North Carolina General Statutes. Chapter 3 is a list of N.C. General Statutes Pertaining to the Administration of the North Carolina State Building Code. The Administrative Code and Policies is available through the International Code Council along with the rest of the State Building Code (codes.iccsafe.org/codes/north-carolina).

Local Ordinances are the laws adopted by the governing board of a municipality or county that apply within that particular jurisdiction. Local ordinances may address a range of topics including vehicles and traffic, business regulation, solid waste, local offenses, and more. With regard to land development, local ordinances may address zoning, subdivision, environmental protection, historic preservation, minimum housing, and more. Development regulations may be adopted as stand-alone local ordinances or as part of a unified development ordinance (UDO). Local ordinances are available through local government websites or third-party platforms such as Municode (library.municode.com) and American Legal Publishing (codelibrary.amlegal.com).

State Government Bodies

General Assembly

The General Assembly is the legislative body for the state of North Carolina. It is composed of two chambers: the state House of Representatives, with 120 members, and the state Senate, with 50 members. Members of the General Assembly are elected every two years. If legislation passes both chambers and is signed by the governor, it becomes law for the state. With regard to building safety and land development regulations, the General Assembly has delegated much of the work to state agencies and local governments but regularly refines and revises the scope of delegated authority and technical requirements.

Building Code Council

The Building Code Council is the state body tasked with adopting, amending, and overseeing the North Carolina Building Code.

In 2025, the Building Code Council was reconstituted by the General Assembly.[3] The legislative change, adopted in 2024, reduced the council from seventeen members to thirteen, granted power to the General Assembly to name six of the seats, and altered the council's composition.

The current Building Code Council is composed of thirteen members, with six appointed by the General Assembly (three on the recommendation of the speaker of the House of Representatives and three on the recommendation of the president pro tempore of the Senate) and seven appointed by the governor, subject to senate confirmation.[4] Areas of expertise include multifamily and commercial construction; electrical, mechanical, and structural engineering; trade-specific contracting; inspections, fire code, and the fuel-gas industry; tall building construction; and construction law.

Members serve six-year terms (though terms are staggered at initial appointment to allow for continuity). A member may be removed by their respective appointing body for misfeasance, malfeasance, or nonfeasance. The governor appoints the chair of the council. In making appointments, the governor must ensure that minorities and women are represented on the council.[5]

The Building Code Council has a Building Code Committee tasked with reviewing proposed revisions and amendments to the North Carolina Building Code (including the trade codes), overseeing the process of code revision, and considering any appeal or interpretation of the code. Revisions and amendments may not be considered by the Building Code Council unless recommended by the Building Code Committee.[6]

In addition to handling matters of the Building Code, the Building Code Council is required to study the building laws of North Carolina (statutes and rules) and recommend to the General Assembly changes to "simplify and improve such laws." The council also must study the enforcement procedures of the building laws and recommend improvements to laws and administrative practices.[7]

The council appoints its own officers and adopts rules for the discharge of its duties. It meets regularly (at least every six months) in meetings open to the public.

---

3. S.L. 2024-49 (S.B. 166).
4. G.S. 143-136(a).
5. G.S. 143-136(a1).
6. G.S. 143-136(d).
7. G.S. 143-142(a)–(b).

Staff from the Division of Engineering of the Department of Insurance serve as staff to the council, handling records and correspondence, among other matters. Council funds are managed by the Department of Insurance.[8]

The membership of the Building Code Council includes the following:

1. a general contractor who specializes in multifamily construction (speaker),
2. a professional engineer who specializes in structural engineering (president pro tempore),
3. a general contractor who specializes in commercial construction (speaker),
4. a professional engineer who specializes in electrical engineering (president pro tempore),
5. a design professional such as an architect (speaker),
6. an electrical contractor (president pro tempore),
7. a general contractor who specializes in buildings greater than 75 feet in height (governor),
8. a professional engineer who specializes in mechanical engineering (governor),
9. a plumbing and heating contractor who specializes in plumbing contracting (governor),
10. a plumbing and heating contractor who specializes in mechanical contracting (governor),
11. a level III code-enforcement official employed by a municipality or county (governor),
12. a North Carolina certified level III fire code official (governor), and
13. a representative of the fuel-gas industry (governor).

Residential Code Council

The Residential Code Council is the state body tasked with adopting, amending, and overseeing the North Carolina Residential Code.

The Residential Code Council is composed of thirteen members, with seven appointed by the governor and six appointed by the General Assembly. Membership includes contractors, an engineer, a local government official, a fire official, and a member of the public, with expertise in plumbing, heating, electrical, coastal construction, natural gas, and concrete.[9] Members serve six-year terms (with some planned staggering of terms for initial members). A member may be removed by their respective appointing body for misfeasance, malfeasance, or nonfeasance. The governor appoints the chair of the Council.[10]

---

8. G.S. 143-137.
9. G.S. 143-136.1(a).
10. G.S. 143-136.1(b).

The Residential Code Council is tasked with reviewing and considering proposals for revisions or amendments to the North Carolina Residential Code, including the applicable trade codes as they apply to residential construction. The Residential Code Council decides appeals and interpretations pertaining to the Residential Code.[11]

Like the Building Code Council, the Residential Code Council is required to study the building laws of North Carolina, recommend changes to "simplify and improve such laws," and recommend improvements to enforcement laws and administrative practices.[12]

The Residential Code Council may adopt rules for the discharge of its duties. The council meets regularly (at least every six months) in meetings open to the public. Staff from the Division of Engineering of the Department of Insurance serve as staff to the council, handling records and correspondence, among other things. Council funds are handled by the Department of Insurance.[13]

The membership of the Residential Code Council includes the following:

1. an individual who holds an unlimited general contractor license and specializes in residential construction (speaker),
2. an individual who holds an unlimited or intermediate general contractor license and specializes in residential construction (president pro tempore),
3. an individual who holds a plumbing contractor license and specializes in residential construction (speaker),
4. an individual who holds a heating contractor license and specializes in residential construction (president pro tempore),
5. an individual who holds an unlimited, intermediate, or limited general contractor license and specializes in coastal construction (speaker),
6. an individual who holds an unlimited, intermediate, or limited general contractor license and specializes in residential construction (president pro tempore),
7. an individual who holds an electrical contractor license under Chapter 87 of the General Statutes (governor),
8. an individual who is a licensed professional engineer and specializes in residential construction (governor),
9. an individual who is a level I or level II code-enforcement official employed by a municipality or county (governor),
10. an individual who is a member of the public at large (governor),
11. an individual who is a representative of the natural gas industry (governor),

---

11. G.S. 143-136.1(d).
12. G.S. 143-142(a)–(b).
13. G.S. 143-137.1.

12. an individual who is a fire service representative (governor), and
13. an individual who holds a general contractor license and specializes in residential foundations or concrete placement (governor).

Code Officials Qualification Board

The North Carolina Code Officials Qualification Board is the state body tasked with overseeing training and certification for code-enforcement officials.

The board is tasked with, among other things, establishing minimum standards and certifying individuals as meeting those standards; coordinating with schools for training and establishing standards for instructors; collecting information about code-enforcement officials; and establishing within the Department of Insurance a marketplace pool of qualified code-enforcement officials.[14] The board may make reports to the governor or General Assembly as requested or as the need arises.[15]

The board is composed of twenty members from a variety of backgrounds, including a local government manager, local elected officials, a building inspector, an architect, an engineer, contractors, and representatives from various educational institutions. Members serve staggered four-year terms.[16] The board selects its own officers and meets at least four times per year.[17]

The Division of Engineering and Building Codes in the Department of Insurance provides administrative support to the board, including enforcing rules, recordkeeping, and handling certificates.[18]

The membership of the Code Officials Qualification Board includes the following:

1. a city or county manager;
2. an elected official representing a city over 5,000 population;
3. an elected official representing a city under 5,000 population;
4. an elected official representing a county over 40,000 population;
5. an elected official representing a county under 40,000 population;
6. a municipal building official with responsibility for administering building, plumbing, electrical and heating codes;
7. a county building official with responsibility for administering building, plumbing, electrical and heating codes;
8. a licensed (registered) architect;
9. a licensed (registered) engineer;
10. a licensed general contractor;
11. another licensed general contractor (at least one must specialize in residential construction);
12. a licensed electrical contractor;

14. G.S. 143-151.12.
15. G.S. 143-151.11.
16. G.S. 143-151.9.
17. G.S. 143-151.11.
18. G.S. 143-151.19.

13. a licensed plumbing or heating contractor;
14. an individual selected from the faculty of the North Carolina State University School of Engineering;
15. an individual selected from the faculty of the School of Engineering of North Carolina Agricultural and Technical State University;
16. an individual selected from the faculty of the School of Government at the University of North Carolina at Chapel Hill;
17. an individual selected from the Community Colleges System Office;
18. an individual selected from the Division of Engineering and Building Codes in the Department of Insurance;
19. an individual who is a local government fire prevention inspector; and
20. an individual who is a citizen of the state.

Office of State Fire Marshal

The Office of State Fire Marshal is the state agency office tasked with overseeing the implementation of fire and building safety rules across the state.

In 2023, the North Carolina General Assembly made the Office of State Fire Marshal an independent office supported by clerical and professional services from the Department of Insurance.[19] This change formally shifted many responsibilities from the Commissioner of Insurance to the State Fire Marshal.

The Office of State Fire Marshal is empowered to enforce laws, adopt rules, and conduct investigations and hearings. In addition to responsibility for a variety of fire regulations, the Office of State Fire Marshal is also responsible for

- the Building Code Council and Residential Code Council;[20]
- the North Carolina Manufactured Housing Board—Manufactured Home Warranties;[21]
- the Uniform Standards Code for Manufactured Homes;[22]
- the North Carolina Code Officials Qualification Board;[23]
- the North Carolina Home Inspector Licensure Board;[24]
- the Engineering and Building Codes Division;
- the Risk Management Division; and
- the Community Risk Reduction Division.[25]

The Office of State Fire Marshal and local police and inspectors are authorized to inspect buildings for overcrowding, combustible materials, and dangerous

19. S.L. 2023-151, pt. X.
20. Article 9 of G.S. Chapter 143.
21. Article 9A of G.S. Chapter 143.
22. Article 9B of G.S. Chapter 143.
23. Article 9C of G.S. Chapter 143.
24. Article 9F of G.S. Chapter 143.
25. G.S. 58-78A-1.

conditions, and to issue orders for those conditions to be remedied. The State Fire Marshal hears appeals from such orders.[26]

The Office of State Fire Marshal, through the Engineering Division, has authority "to supervise, administer, and enforce all sections of the North Carolina State Building Code pertaining to plumbing, electrical systems, general building restrictions and regulations, heating and air conditioning, fire protection, and the construction of buildings generally."[27] Additionally, the State Fire Marshal has supervision over local investigators of fires and fire prevention inspectors.[28]

The Office of State Fire Marshal is responsible for fire code inspections of state property.[29] Local governments and school districts must submit plans for any building of 20,000 square feet or more to the State Fire Marshal for review for fire safety.[30] The Administrative Code and Policies set forth additional plans that must be submitted to the Office of State Fire Marshal, as discussed in Chapter 6.

The Office of State Fire Marshal oversees and coordinates the marketplace pool of qualified code-enforcement officials. The State Fire Marshal may set and collect fees and reimbursements for the work of marketplace pool inspectors.[31]

The Division of Engineering and Building Codes provides administrative support to the Office of State Fire Marshal, the Building Code Council, the Residential Code Council, and the Code Officials Qualifications Board.

Related State Departments

Other North Carolina departments and agencies have separate authority related to building safety and land development. The Department of Labor's Bureau of Boiler Inspection, for example, oversees the rules pertaining to boilers.[32] The Department of Labor administers rules for "elevators, moving stairways, and amusement devices such as merry-go-rounds, roller coasters, Ferris wheels, etc."[33] Other related state departments include the Department of Agriculture, the Department of Health and Human Services, the Department of Environmental Quality, the Department of Administration, and a variety of both state agency and occupational licensing boards.

26. G.S. 58-79-20.
27. G.S. 143-139(b).
28. G.S. 58-78A-15.
29. G.S. 58-31-41.
30. *Id.*
31. G.S. 143-151.12(9).
32. G.S. 143-139(c).
33. G.S. 143-139(d).

Local Government Bodies

Governing Board

The local governing board—the town council, board of aldermen, or board of county commissioners—is the local legislative body. It is authorized to adopt ordinances affecting building safety and land development, including zoning, subdivision, minimum housing, and nuisances, among others.

Appointed Boards and Quasi-Judicial Decisions

Local governments commonly have a set of appointed boards tasked with advising on and making decisions about specific topics such as planning and development, parks and recreation, transportation, housing, and more. Certain boards serve as court-like panels to make quasi-judicial decisions. Appeals of certain enforcement actions are quasi-judicial decisions.

Examples of quasi-judicial decisions include the following:

- a governing board hearing an appeal from an inspector's order of corrective action for an unsafe structure,
- a housing appeals board hearing an appeal of housing code violation enforcement, and
- a board of adjustment hearing a request for a variance from the zoning ordinance.

Quasi-judicial decisions require a formal evidentiary hearing. The procedures for the evidentiary hearing are set forth at G.S. 160D-406 and include sworn testimony, formal legal procedures, and a written decision based on the evidence in the record. The governing board may affirm, modify and affirm, or revoke the order. The governing board's decision must be rendered within a reasonable time.

Permitting and Inspections Staff

Local government staff are responsible for the wide array of plan review, permitting, inspections, certification, and enforcement duties related to building safety and land development. Different local governments manage these duties in different ways. The next chapter explores the roles and responsibilities of local permitting and inspections.

Chapter 3

The Inspection Department

Overview

The local inspection department plays a key role in coordinating local building permitting and inspections. This chapter outlines the duties of the inspection department, possible arrangements for staffing and coordination among *local* governments, fees and finances, and recordkeeping.

In some communities, the duties for inspections and enforcement are consolidated into one office or one department. In other communities, the duties for inspections and enforcement may be spread out among several different departments (planning, building inspections, code enforcement, housing, development services, solid waste, etc.). There is some flexibility in state law to allow this variety, but the legal roles and responsibilities must be met regardless of the organizational arrangement.

Duties and Responsibilities

North Carolina state law requires each local government to administer building code permits and inspections, and North Carolina state law authorizes local governments to adopt and enforce other development regulations such as zoning, minimum housing, and nuisance codes.[1] This includes "the authority to enact ordinances, procedures, and fee schedules relating to the administration and the enforcement of this Chapter [Chapter 160D]."[2] To the extent there is any conflict between the general authority in Article 4 of Chapter 160D and the specific authority of other articles, the more specific controls.[3]

---

1. Administration of development regulations is authorized under multiple provisions of Chapter 160D of the North Carolina General Statutes (hereinafter G.S.), including Article 4 (general development regulations), Article 11 (building code enforcement), and Article 12 (minimum housing codes).

2. G.S. 160D-402(b).

3. G.S. 160D-401(b).

Building Code Administration

For building code administration, state law requires that "[e]very local government shall perform the duties and responsibilities" for building permits and inspections.[4] The local governments may perform those duties directly or contract for those duties to be performed, as discussed below.

The local inspection department and inspectors are responsible to enforce, within the applicable jurisdiction, the state and local laws related to the following:

> (1) The construction of buildings and other structures.
> (2) The installation of such facilities as plumbing systems, electrical systems, heating systems, refrigeration systems, and air conditioning systems.
> (3) The maintenance of buildings and other structures in a safe, sanitary, and healthful condition.
> (4) Other matters that may be specified by the governing board.[5]

"The administrative and enforcement provisions related to building permits set forth in [Chapter 160D's Article 11 on Building Code Enforcement] shall be followed for those permits."[6] The local governing board (city council or county commission) may "enact reasonable and appropriate provisions governing the enforcement of those laws."[7] In furtherance of those general duties and responsibilities, the inspection department and inspectors

- receive and decide upon applications for permits,
- make necessary inspections in a timely manner,
- issue or deny certificates of compliance,
- issue orders to correct violations,
- bring judicial actions against actual or threatened violations,
- keep adequate records, and
- take any other actions that may be required in order to adequately enforce those laws.[8]

Local legislation cannot alter the general assignment of building code administration responsibilities. In *City of New Bern v. New Bern-Craven County Board of Education*,[9] legislation shifting building code enforcement was ruled unconstitutional. The General Assembly passed legislation reassigning building code responsibility from New Bern to Craven County for properties of the board of education, community college, and medical center. The court found that the legislation was local legislation, not generally applicable. Under the North Carolina Constitution, local legislation cannot address subjects "[r]elating to health, sanitation, and

4. G.S. 160D-1102(a).
5. G.S. 160D-1104(a).
6. G.S. 160D-402(b).
7. G.S. 160D-1104(b).
8. *Id.*
9. 338 N.C. 430, 450 S.E.2d 735 (1994).

the abatement of nuisances."[10] The court ruled that building code enforcement affects health and sanitation, so it cannot be altered by local legislation.

Additional details of building code administration and enforcement are discussed in Part 2.

Other Development Regulation Administration

Beyond the specifics of building code enforcement, local governments have authority to adopt and administer development regulations generally. The general provisions for administration outlined in Article 4 of Chapter 160D apply "to any other local ordinance that substantially affects land use and development."

The duties to develop, administer, and enforce development regulations may include the following:

- drafting and implementing plans and development regulations;
- determining whether applications for development approvals are complete;
- receiving and processing applications for development approvals;
- providing notices of applications and hearings;
- making decisions and determinations regarding development regulation implementation;
- determining whether applications for development approvals meet applicable standards established by law and local ordinance;
- conducting inspections;
- issuing or denying certificates of compliance or occupancy;
- enforcing development regulations, including issuing notices of violation, orders to correct violations, and recommending judicial actions against actual or threatened violations;
- keeping adequate records; and
- taking any other actions that may be required in order to adequately enforce the laws and development regulations under their jurisdiction.[11]

Those administrative provisions may apply to any ordinance adopted under the general police powers (Article 8 of Chapter 160A and Article 6 of Chapter 153A).[12] As such, if a county does not have zoning but has ordinances *substantially affecting land use and development* (such as a high-impact land use ordinance), the county will follow the provisions of Article 4 for administration, enforcement, and appeals. Additionally, a local government *may* follow the provisions of Article 4 for the administration, enforcement, and appeals of a nuisance code adopted under the general police powers.

Additional details of administration and enforcement of other development regulations are discussed in Part 3.

---

10. N.C. Const. art. II, § 24(a).
11. G.S. 160D-402(b).
12. G.S. 160D-401(a).

Department and Staffing Arrangements

Departments

In order to meet the obligation to provide building code administration and to administer development regulations generally, a local government may

- create a joint inspection department in cooperation with one or more other units of local government,
- contract for staff from one local government to administer the development regulations and/or inspection services within another local government,
- agree for the county to exercise development regulation and/or building code enforcement within a municipality, and
- contract for an individual, company, or regional organization to administer development regulations and/or building code enforcement within the jurisdiction.[13]

State law outlines specific procedural and substantive requirements for these alternative arrangements. For example, if a local government pursues a joint inspection department or a contract for provision of inspection services from another local government, such arrangements are done pursuant to the statutes on Interlocal Cooperation outlined in Part 1 of Article 20 of Chapter 160A of the North Carolina General Statutes (hereinafter G.S.).

Staffing

For building code administration, "[the] local government may create an inspection department and may appoint inspectors who may be given appropriate titles, such as building inspector, electrical inspector, plumbing inspector, housing inspector, zoning inspector, heating and air-conditioning inspector, fire prevention inspector, or deputy or assistant inspector, or another title generally descriptive of the duties assigned."[14]

Individuals hired to enforce the North Carolina Building Code must be properly certified for such work.[15] Local governments may contract with individuals (who are not local government employees) to enforce the building code, but those individuals still must be properly certified under G.S. 160D-1103.[16]

State law requires clearly assigned management of building code enforcement matters: "Every local government shall designate a person responsible for the daily oversight of the local government's duties and responsibilities under G.S. 160D-1104."[17]

---

13. For development regulations generally, see G.S. 160D-402(c). For administration of the building code, see G.S. 160D-1102(a) and -1105.
14. G.S. 160D-1102(a).
15. G.S. 160D-1103.
16. G.S. 160D-1105.
17. G.S. 160D-1102(a).

For development regulations generally (beyond building code enforcement), a local government "may employ any organizational structure, board, commission, or staffing arrangement authorized by [Article 4]."[18] State law authorizes local governments to "appoint administrators, inspectors, enforcement officers, planners, technicians, and other staff to develop, administer, and enforce development regulations."[19]

Mutual Aid

Two or more local governments may enter contracts to provide mutual aid and assistance in the administration and enforcement of the building code. Contracts may specify the scope of aid, reimbursement and indemnification, delegation of authority, and more. Unless stated otherwise in the contract, a code-enforcement official providing aid has the same powers and immunities as the officials of the requesting agency. Under state law, parties to a mutual aid agreement retain discretion about whether to send aid when requested.[20]

Office of State Fire Marshal Intervention

If a local government ceases to provide building code inspection services, the Office of State Fire Marshal must arrange for inspection services. This may be through department personnel or through an arrangement with another local government. In such an event, the Office of State Fire Marshal has the same authority for building inspections as the local government. If the Office of State Fire Marshal has intervened to provide inspections services for a local government, that government may only resume inspection services again with two years' written notice or an earlier agreement by the Office of State Fire Marshal.[21]

Fees and Finances

Authority

A local government may appropriate general funds to support the administration of development regulations. Additionally, a local government has the "power to fix reasonable fees for support, administration, and implementation of programs authorized by this Chapter [160D]."[22] See Appendix B for sample fee documents.

In *Homebuilders Association of Charlotte, Inc. v. City of Charlotte*,[23] the North Carolina Supreme Court made clear that permitting fees must be reasonably related to the cost of administering the permit or inspection.

18. G.S. 160D-401(a).
19. G.S. 160D-402(a).
20. G.S. 160D-1107.
21. G.S. 160D-1102(b).
22. G.S. 160D-402(d).
23. 336 N.C. 37, 442 S.E.2d 45 (1994).

While state law and courts allow for permitting fees, North Carolina courts do not interpret the General Statutes to authorize broad development impact fees, such as school impact fees, unless there is clear statutory authority.[24]

Accounting and Reporting

Building inspection fees must be used for building inspection administration: "All fees collected by a building inspection department for [building code] administration and enforcement . . . shall be used to support the administration and operations of the building inspection department and for no other purposes."[25]

Funds collected must be managed and deposited according to state law. Any money received must be deposited daily with the finance officer or an official depository, or submitted to a properly licensed cash collection service. A local governing board may alter this rule so that money is deposited only once the amount on hand exceeds $500. Prior to deposit, money must be maintained in a secure location. If money is deposited, the official must immediately report to the finance officer with a duplicate deposit ticket. The finance officer may audit at any time any officer or employee who collects or receives money and must conduct such audits at least once a year.

Twice a year, local government finance officers must submit to the secretary of the Local Government Commission a statement of financial information. That statement must include "the total revenues received from building inspections, by source, and the total expenditures paid from all revenues received, by object."[26]

With legislation adopted in 2022, state law requires local governments to make public how they use permitting and inspection fees. "No later than October 1 of 2023, 2024, and 2025, every local government shall publish an annual financial report on how it used fees from the prior fiscal year for the support, administration, and implementation of its building code enforcement program as required by G.S. 160D-402(d)."[27]

Criminal fines must be filed with the county board of education.[28]

Homeowners Recovery Fund

The Homeowners Recovery Fund is administered by the State Licensing Board for General Contractors to reimburse homeowners for losses related to constructing or altering a single-family residential dwelling unit.[29] Funds are provided through permitting fees. For each permit for construction or alteration of a single-family residential dwelling unit, the local inspections department must collect ten dollars. The department forwards nine dollars to the board (funds submitted quarterly), and the local government retains one dollar. The board may suspend collection of funds for any year if it determines the fund is sufficient to meet likely disbursements.

24. *See* Lanvale Properties, LLC v. Cnty. of Cabarrus, 366 N.C. 142, 731 S.E.2d 800 (2012).
25. G.S. 160D-402(d).
26. G.S. 159-33.1(a).
27. G.S. 160D-1102(c).
28. G.S. 14-244.
29. G.S. 87-15.6.

Records

Record and Reporting Requirements

Local governments must keep adequate records for administration of development regulations generally.[30] For building code administration specifically, "[t]he inspection department shall keep complete and accurate records in convenient form of all applications received, permits issued, inspections and reinspections made, defects found, certificates of compliance or occupancy granted, and all other work and activities of the department."[31] Additionally, the inspection department must maintain lien agent information (further discussed in Chapter 6) in the same manner as it maintains building permits.[32]

The inspection department may be required to provide periodic reports "to the governing board and to the State Fire Marshal as they shall by ordinance, rule, or regulation require."[33]

Public Records

Records related to public work are public records and must be made available to the public. The definition is broad and includes physical records (like paper documents), electronic records (like email), and other documentary materials regardless of physical form. If the record was "made or received in the transaction of public business," it is a public record. Limited exceptions apply, but in general a public record will be subject to disclosure upon request.[34]

Records Retention

The Government Records Section of the Department of Natural and Cultural Resources provides retention schedules for local government records management.[35] The retention schedules for development regulations are part of the Program Records Schedule for Local Government Agencies.[36] Standard 12 gives requirements for Code Enforcement and Inspection Records. Standard 15 covers Planning and Regulation of Development Records.

Table 3.1 shows certain standards from the schedule related to development regulations. Notably, under the National Flood Insurance Program (NFIP), floodplain management and development records must be maintained in perpetuity.

30. G.S. 160D-402(b).

31. G.S. 160D-1126.

32. G.S. 160D-1110(g).

33. G.S. 160D-1126.

34. Frayda Bluestein, *Public Records in North Carolina* (UNC School of Government, 2012), https://www.sog.unc.edu/sites/default/files/course_materials/public_records_overview.pdf; David M. Lawrence, Public Records Law for North Carolina Local Governments (UNC School of Government, 2009).

35. G.S. 121-5(c); 132-8.

36. N.C. Dep't of Nat. & Cultural Res., Gov't Rec. Section, *Records Retention and Disposition Schedule: Program Records Schedule: Local Government Agencies* (Oct. 1, 2021), https://archives.ncdcr.gov/program-records-schedule-local-government-agencies/open.

Table 3.1. Selected Standards from the Local Government Records Schedule

Standard	Records Series Title	Disposition Instructions
12.03	**BUILDING AND ROAD PERMITTING AND INSPECTION RECORDS** Records documenting applications for permits from property owners to erect new structures or manufactured homes, or to make structural modifications, demolition, fire permits, or the installation of plumbing, electrical, or mechanical systems. Includes permits, inspection reports, inspector's worksheets, inspection requests, denial reports, sketches, correspondence (including e-mail), and contractor change forms.	a) Destroy in office permits, applications, and inspection reports (or worksheets) 6 years after Certificate of Occupancy is issued or project is complete (inactive). b) Destroy in office Certificate of Occupancy 6 years after permit is expired. c) Destroy in office remaining records, including applications for which a permit was never issued, when reference value ends.± Agency Policy: Destroy in office after ________________
12.12	**INSPECTIONS** Inspections conducted by local government agencies concerning enforcement of state and local laws, codes, and ordinances.	Destroy in office after 6 years.*
12.15	**PERMITS: CONSTRUCTION** Records documenting applications and permits regarding sign installation, fencing, swimming pools, driveways, or similar activity required by local ordinance. **SEE ALSO: GENERAL RECORDS SCHEDULE: LOCAL GOVERNMENT AGENCIES, Miscellaneous (Non-Building) Applications, Licenses, and Permits (STANDARD 1: ADMINISTRATION AND MANAGEMENT RECORDS)**	a) Destroy in office 3 years after completion of project. b) Destroy in office applications for which a permit was never issued when reference value ends.± Agency Policy: Destroy in office after ________________
12.17	**RECREATIONAL VEHICLE REGISTRATION RECORDS** Records concerning issuance of registrations/decals for recreational vehicles. Includes, but is not limited to, golf carts, canoes, and mopeds as well as proof of insurance and renewals.	Destroy in office 1 year after expiration.*
12.20	**VIOLATIONS: BUILDING AND HOUSING** Records documenting violations of building and fire code, minimum housing, and erosion and sediment control. Includes complaints, summons, notices, appeals, and other information created or compiled during the course of investigation and resolution of each alleged violation. **SEE ALSO: Water Analysis.**	a) Destroy building code violations in office 6 years after verification of correction. b) Destroy remaining records in office 3 years after verification of correction.

Standard	Records Series Title	Disposition Instructions
15.09	**PERMITS: ZONING COMPLIANCE** For residential uses, non-residential uses, and accessory structures.	a) Retain in office permits concerning subdivision, historical structure, major commercial or industrial development, or capital construction, where county or municipality is lead agency, permanently. b) Destroy in office permits concerning subdivision, historic structures, major commercial or industrial development, or capital construction, where county or municipality is not lead agency, 6 years after last entry. c) Destroy in office any other permits and related records 6 years after last entry.
15.11	**PLANNING REVIEW CASE FILE** For required review of site plan, zoning variance, special permit, change of zoning, subdivision creation or enlargement, municipal or county planning action, or other required review; including, but not limited to, maps, plans, sketches, photographs, engineering reports, environmental impact statement and studies, copies of zoning records, project narrative, correspondence (including e-mail), and record of final determination.	a) Retain plan reviews and related records containing subdivision, historical structure, major commercial or industrial development, or capital construction, where county or municipality is lead agency, permanently. b) Destroy in office plan reviews and related records containing subdivision, historic structures, major commercial or industrial development, or capital construction, where county or municipality is not lead agency, 6 years after last entry. c) Destroy in office any other mandatory reviews and related records 6 years after last entry.
15.15	**VIOLATIONS: ZONING** Records concerning notices of zoning violations.	Destroy in office after 6 years.*

* No destruction of records may take place if audits or litigation are pending or reasonably anticipated. See AUDITS, LITIGATION, AND OTHER OFFICIAL ACTION, page A-5.

± The agency hereby agrees that it will establish and enforce internal policies setting minimum retention periods for the records that Natural and Cultural Resources has scheduled with the disposition instruction "destroy when reference value ends." Please use the space provided.

Chapter 4

The Code Official

Overview

The local code official is a public official exercising governmental powers. Accordingly, the position carries certain authorities but is also subject to an array of legal limitations. Constitutional limits, criminal statutes, and conflicts of interest requirements apply equally to code officials whether they are handling building code, housing code, nuisance code, or other regulations. This chapter broadly outlines the roles and responsibilities of code officials, including building code officials, housing code officials, nuisance code officials, and others. Officials administering the State Building Code must have certification from the North Carolina Code Officials Qualification Board. These requirements are summarized at the end of the chapter.

Public Service and Customer Service

Public officials represent more than themselves. They represent the government agency and the public at large. They bear high expectations of professionalism and courtesy. Additionally, many code enforcement tasks are performed for particular individuals (like customers). When a permitting official works with an applicant, and when a building inspector visits a site, they are serving the broader public, yes, but they are also serving a particular customer.

With all of that in mind, the code official must be aware that their public service is also customer service. Here are a few reminders for bringing a customer service mindset to public service work:

- **Be respectful.** Treat individuals with respect. Listen to their concerns. Apply the rules fairly and evenly. "Yes, ma'am," "No, sir," "Please," and "Thank you" go a long way.
- **Be clear.** Communicate with coworkers and community members clearly and regularly. Be kind, but direct about violations and issues. Be humble and open about what you don't know: "I'll have to check on that" may be the best answer.

- **Be diligent.** Follow the applicable rules and policies. Be thorough in reviewing applications and performing inspections. Be creative in looking for solutions to problems.
- **Be efficient.** Time is money for the local government and the customer. Provide timely responses. Provide warm handoffs to other departments when necessary. Look for opportunities to improve systems and processes.
- **Be understanding.** Members of the community come from all walks of life. They may be having a tough day, month, or year. Consider the situation from their perspective.

Code Official as Public Official

The law classifies a code official as a public official. With regard to building code enforcement, the state laws governing the North Carolina Code Officials Qualification Board define a "Qualified Code-enforcement official" as "[a] person qualified under this Article to engage in the practice of Code enforcement."[1] Article 11 of Chapter 160D of the North Carolina General Statutes (hereinafter G.S.) sets forth the authority for "Building Code Enforcement." The law also defines "Public officer" to "[i]nclude the officer or officers who are authorized by regulations adopted hereunder to exercise the powers prescribed by the regulations and by this Article."[2]

With regard to housing codes and commercial maintenance codes, the statutory authority requires the local government to designate a public officer to administer and enforce the codes. Similarly, for zoning codes and nuisance codes, the local government typically designates an officer (or officers) to administer and enforce the codes.

North Carolina courts have concluded that the chief building inspector and other building inspectors are public officials for purposes of public official immunity.[3]

As a public official, a code official must take an oath "before entering on the duties of the office."[4]

Under the North Carolina Constitution and statutes, an individual may hold two—but no more than two—appointed or elected public offices concurrently.[5]

---

1. Chapter 143, Section 151.8 of the North Carolina General Statutes (hereinafter G.S.).
2. G.S. 160D-1101.
3. Wiggins v. City of Monroe, 73 N.C. App. 44, 49 (1985); Pigott v. City of Wilmington, 50 N.C. App. 401, 405 (1981); Woodard v. Cleveland Cnty., 202 N.C. App. 586 (2010) (unpublished); McCoy v. Coker, 174 N.C. App. 311, 319 (2005).
4. G.S. 128-5.
5. G.S. 128-1.1.

Bond

State law requires individuals in certain public offices to secure a public official bond.[6] In particular, local government finance law requires that any local government officer, employee, or agent who handles more than $100 in public funds must "give a faithful performance bond with sufficient sureties payable to the local government or public authority."[7] Typically, a local government maintains insurance providing blanket faithful performance bonding for all applicable officers, employees, and agents, as allowed by state law.

Constitutional Limits

A foundational element of the United States constitutional system is the protection of individuals against government overreach. Building code regulations and related property codes inherently involve government action that may infringe on individual liberties: regulations limit property rights; inspections typically require a government officer to enter private property; and enforcement actions may include fines, criminal punishment, or even the removal of a private building by the public agency. These types of actions raise the risk for government overreach, so constitutional protections are essential.

In general, an individual must bring legal challenges through the standard appeal processes and timelines (i.e., administrative remedies). However, where the standard process does not afford an adequate remedy for the alleged constitutional violation, the individual may bring those constitutional claims even if they did not exhaust their administrative remedies.[8]

Due Process and Equal Protection

Two principles are foundational to our North Carolinian and United States systems of governance: (1) if an individual's property rights are impacted, the government must take extra precautions to ensure that legal procedures are sufficient (due process); and (2) the law must be applied evenhandedly (equal protection).

The North Carolina Constitution's Declaration of Rights outlines these principles in the Law of the Land Clause:

> **Sec. 19. Law of the land; equal protection of the laws.**
> No person shall be taken, imprisoned, or disseized of his freehold, liberties, or privileges, or outlawed, or exiled, or in any manner deprived

---

6. G.S. 58-72-10 ("Every treasurer, sheriff, coroner, register of deeds, surveyor, and every other officer of the several counties who is required by law to give a bond for the faithful performance of the duties of his office, shall give a bond for the term of the office to which such officer is chosen.")

7. G.S. 159-29.

8. Askew v. City of Kinston, 386 N.C. 286, 902 S.E.2d 722 (2024).

> of his life, liberty, or property, but by the law of the land. No person shall be denied the equal protection of the laws; nor shall any person be subjected to discrimination by the State because of race, color, religion, or national origin.

In the U.S. Constitution, the Fifth Amendment and the Fourteenth Amendment provide similar protections of due process and equal protection.

The Fifth Amendment provides that "[n]o person shall . . . be deprived of life, liberty, or property, without due process of law." This Due Process Clause, like the Law of the Land provision in the North Carolina Constitution (above), touches on broad aspects of law, but in practice it often serves as a straightforward requirement for basic fairness in property regulation. It ensures that the following elements are met. "Procedural due process simply ensures a fair process before the government may deprive a person of life, liberty, or property, but does not require certain results,"[9] The elements of a fair process may include:

- clear legal standards,
- adequate notice,
- opportunity to be heard,
- impartial decision-makers, and
- the right to appeal.

The Fourteenth Amendment to the U.S. Constitution, like Section 19 of North Carolina's Declaration of Rights, provides protection and equal treatment for individuals: "[N]or shall any State deprive any person of life, liberty, or property, without due process of law; nor deny to any person within its jurisdiction the equal protection of the laws." In the context of building codes and development regulations, equal protection requires that enforcement be evenhanded and fair. It must not target particular areas or individuals based on race, ethnicity, religion, or other personal characteristics. Even beyond classifications like race and religion, when local regulations distinguish between categories of uses or activities, there must be a reasonable rationale for the different treatment. "The equal protection clauses of the United States and North Carolina Constitutions impose upon law-making bodies the requirements that any legislative classification 'be based on differences that are reasonably related to the purposes of the Act in which it is found.'"[10]

Eminent Domain and Taking Private Property

The Fifth Amendment to the United States Constitution provides, in part: "nor shall private property be taken for public use, without just compensation." Under this Takings Clause, the government has the authority to take private property for

9. Sansotta v. Town of Nags Head, 724 F.3d 533, 540 (4th Cir. 2013) (citations and quotations omitted).

10. State v. Greenwood, 280 N.C. 651, 656, 187 S.E.2d 8, 11 (1972).

public use (such as a public highway or public park), but only if it pays the owner a fair price for the property.

Private property owners may argue that regulations are a "taking," but it is rare for a regulation to rise to that level. Regulations such as building codes, zoning, and other development regulations may limit the use of a property. They may even reduce the value of a property. But that does not amount to a taking unless it goes too far and effectively eliminates all economically beneficial uses of the property.[11]

North Carolina courts have affirmed that in the context of condemnation and demolition, if a property is determined to be a nuisance threatening public health and safety, removal is a proper exercise of the police power, and no compensation is required under the Takings Clause.[12] (To be clear, condemnation and demolition may violate other laws or constitutional rights even if they do not amount to a taking.)

Exactions are a closely related legal topic that may arise in the development process (more commonly in planning and zoning approvals). An exaction occurs when a government agency requires a property owner to dedicate property to the public as a condition of obtaining development approval (such as requiring a developer to build roads in a new subdivision and dedicate them to the public). Exactions are a matter of balancing. They are permissible to address the impacts expected from the development, but if exactions go too far (beyond what is necessitated by the development), they run afoul of the Takings Clause.[13]

Fourth Amendment Protections Against Unreasonable Searches

A code official is a government agent and must honor an individual's reasonable expectations of privacy. The Fourth Amendment to the United States Constitution protects individuals from government intrusion into private spaces and matters.

> The right of the people to be secure in their persons, houses, papers, and effects, against unreasonable searches and seizures, shall not be violated, and no Warrants shall issue but upon probable cause, supported by Oath or affirmation, and particularly describing the place to be searched, and the persons and things to be seized.[14]

---

11. Pennsylvania Coal v. Mahon, 260 U.S. 393 (1922); Lucas v. South Carolina Coastal Council, 505 U.S. 1003 (1992); Finch v. City of Durham, 325 N.C. 352 (1989).

12. Hillsboro Partners, LLC v. City of Fayetteville, 226 N.C. App. 30, 738 S.E.2d 819, *review denied*, 367 N.C. 236, 748 S.E.2d 544 (2013).

13. Sheetz v. Cnty. of El Dorado, California, 601 U.S. 267 (2024); Anderson Creek Partners, L.P. v. County of Harnett, 382 N.C. 1 (2022); Dolan v. City of Tigard, 512 U.S. 374 (1994); Nollan v. California Coastal Comm'n, 483 U.S. 825 (1987).

14. U.S. Const. amend. IV.

This section explores the basics of Fourth Amendment jurisprudence. For a more complete discussion, see Robert L. Farb and Christopher Tyner, *Arrest, Search, and Investigation in North Carolina*, 6th ed. (2021).

Context matters. An individual's reasonable expectation of privacy depends on the context. For residential property, the Fourth Amendment protects the interior of the house and the "curtilage." Curtilage is the area immediately surrounding the house. A government official may be in areas beyond the curtilage without violating the Fourth Amendment, but the official may still be violating state criminal trespass laws. To determine the curtilage, courts look to these specific factors:

- proximity to the home,
- whether the area is enclosed with a fence or other enclosure,
- nature and use of the area, and
- steps taken by the resident to protect the area from observation by passers-by.[15]

For commercial property, the reasonable expectation of privacy is different. There is an expectation of privacy for private offices, closed storerooms, and other areas closed off to the public. For areas where the public is generally invited, there is not an expectation of privacy. So a government official could be in the lobby of an office building, the shopping area of a store, or the merchandise area of a gas station without violating the Fourth Amendment.[16]

Reasonable approach. A code official may make a reasonable approach to a property. They may walk up to the front porch of a conventional home or enter the reception lobby or sales area of a commercial property where the public is generally invited. In contrast, if a property is clearly marked with "No Trespassing" signs and clearly fenced to prevent any approach, a reasonable approach will be limited or prohibited. Each situation is context-specific, so officials must be sensitive to the facts on the ground.

A simple rule of thumb is the so-called Girl Scout Rule: If a Girl Scout would be comfortable approaching a building to sell cookies, then a government official may make a reasonable approach along that path.[17]

Consent. An individual may consent to a government search despite Fourth Amendment protections. In the case of construction projects and building code inspections, the individual generally wants the inspector on the property, so consent is common. (There are important limitations on requiring consent through a permit application, noted below.) In the case of existing buildings, however, inspections may be prompted by complaints, and tenants or owners may be less inclined

---

15. United States v. Dunn, 480 U.S. 294 (1987).

16. For a discussion of how a reasonable expectation of privacy may be determined in the context of commercial premises, see *United States v. Lewis*, 864 F.3d 937 (8th Cir. 2017).

17. A recent Supreme Court case exploring this issue is *Florida v. Jardines*, 569 U.S. 1 (2013). A case endorsing the Girl Scout Rule is *State v. Falls*, 275 N.C. App. 239 (2020).

to grant consent. Either way, there are important considerations for obtaining appropriate consent.

- Consent must come from the individual whose privacy rights are affected. For example, a tenant can consent to a search of their private space, but a landlord cannot consent to an inspection of the tenant's private space. Similarly, a roommate can consent to a search of a common space but not to their roommate's private space.
- Consent must come from an individual with the authority or capacity to grant it. A resident adult can consent to an inspection of a residential space, but a young child cannot. A shift manager may consent to an inspection of a commercial space, but a low-level clerk might not have the same authority.
- Consent must be given voluntarily. An individual cannot be coerced into waiving their constitutional rights.
- Consent may be oral, but it is prudent to obtain written consent. If there is a dispute later about whether consent was granted, documentation is key.
- Consent may be limited. An individual may grant consent to search some areas of the property but not others.
- Consent may be revoked. An individual may initially allow a search to proceed and later decide to revoke consent. The inspector must respect that revocation or risk violating the individual's rights.

With regard to permit applications, a local government may seek consent, but it must be limited to the area of work. G.S. 160D-403 notes that even for inspections of works in progress, inspectors must ensure that "appropriate consent has been given for inspection of areas not open to the public or an appropriate inspection warrant has been secured." While an application form may request consent to inspect areas of work, an application may not be used to require broad consent to inspections. "Administrative staff are prohibited from requiring unrestricted written consent from a permit applicant to enter any premises or areas not open to the public as a condition to accepting an application for, or the issuance of, development approvals."[18] Even with prior written consent, if the property owner withdraws or denies consent when the inspector arrives, the inspector must discontinue the inspection. Consent remains revocable, and the prior written consent would be trumped by the current refusal to consent.

Plain view. Wherever a government officer is lawfully located, the officer may observe things in *plain view* without it being a "search" under the Fourth Amendment. This is known as the plain view doctrine. For example, if an officer is making a reasonable approach to a residence (such as walking up the walkway to the front porch) and observes a building code violation, that is not a search, and the

18. G.S. 160D-403.

information may be used to initiate an enforcement action. Similarly, an inspector lawfully present in the public area of a commercial building may observe a violation. An inspector driving down a public road in a department truck or standing on the sidewalk within the public right-of-way may also observe a violation. Such observation is not a search because the violation is in plain view.[19]

There is one major limitation to the plain view doctrine. When performing an inspection pursuant to an administrative inspection warrant (discussed below), the inspection is limited to the subject of the warrant. Evidence of other violations is inadmissible in any court or administrative proceeding, even if that evidence was in plain view.

Consequences of Fourth Amendment violation. Government officers are sworn to uphold the Constitution, so there is a basic obligation to honor the Fourth Amendment. Additionally, a violation may lead to several possible consequences, including the following:

- A civil lawsuit against the government officer and the employing agency.
- The exclusion of evidence obtained as a result of the Fourth Amendment violation from later court proceedings.
- Disciplinary action against the government officer by the officer's employing agency.
- Criminal prosecution of the government officer.

Administrative Search and Inspection Warrant

When there is evidence of a building violation but an individual refuses consent to a search, an administrative inspection warrant may be necessary. Administrative inspection warrants are authorized at G.S. 15-27.2 and have been approved by the Supreme Court.[20] They may be issued by a magistrate, judge, or clerk of court (including assistant and deputy clerks) of the court with jurisdiction over the property.

In order to issue a warrant, the court official must determine that the following conditions are met:

- The official seeking the warrant has established, under oath, that either (1) the property is to be inspected or searched as part of a legally authorized program of inspection or (2) there is probable cause to believe there is a violation.
- The official seeking the warrant has signed an affidavit under oath establishing the grounds for the warrant.
- The court official must examine the official seeking the warrant to verify the accuracy of the affidavit.

---

19. *See generally* State v. Mitchell, 300 N.C. 305 (1980) (discussing the plain view doctrine).
20. *See* Camara v. Mun. Ct., 387 U.S. 523 (1967).

The North Carolina Administrative Office of the Courts provides many legal forms, including the *Affidavit To Obtain Administrative Inspection Warrant for Periodic Inspection* (AOC-CR-914M, Rev. 7/2000), and the *Affidavit To Obtain Administrative Inspection Warrant For Particular Condition Or Activity* (AOC-CR-913M, Rev. 7/01).[21]

An administrative inspection warrant is valid for only twenty-four hours after issuance. It must be personally served on the owner or possessor of the property between the hours of 8:00 a.m. and 8:00 p.m. It must be returned within forty-eight hours. If the owner or possessor is not present at the time of the inspection and reasonable efforts to locate them have failed, a copy of the warrant may be affixed to the property and has the effect of personal service on the owner or possessor.

Evidence obtained during an administrative inspection warrant is limited to the subject for which the warrant was obtained. Evidence of other violations or criminal activity may not be used in civil, criminal, or administrative actions, nor as the basis for obtaining an additional warrant.

Fourth Amendment Summary

The Fourth Amendment protects individuals from government intrusion into private spaces and matters. A code official is a government official and must respect the individual privacy protections of the Fourth Amendment.

- **Context matters.** At a residential property, a resident has a reasonable expectation of privacy inside the home and within the curtilage (the area immediately surrounding the home). An inspector may not enter those areas without consent or a warrant. At a commercial property, individuals have a reasonable expectation of privacy in closed offices and back rooms but not in lobbies or sales areas open to the public.
- **An inspector may make a reasonable approach.** Unless the walkway is blocked or clearly marked otherwise, an inspector may walk from the sidewalk up the walkway to the porch of a house. Similarly, an inspector may enter a business lobby or sales area where the public is generally invited.
- **Obtain consent.** An inspector should request consent from an authorized individual before performing the inspection.
- **Plain view matters.** Evidence that is in plain view—clearly visible from a place where an inspector is lawfully allowed to be—may be used in an enforcement action. If an inspector sees a violation from a public road, while making a reasonable approach, or while performing an inspection with consent, the inspector may use the observed evidence.

21. North Carolina Judicial Branch, *Forms*, available at https://www.nccourts.gov/documents/forms.

- **Warrants are available.** If there is evidence of a violation but an owner or resident refuses to consent to an inspection, the code official may obtain an administrative search and inspection warrant to conduct the search.

Liability and Immunity

Local government liability and immunity are broad and complex concepts. What follows is a brief summary of these topics as they relate to code enforcement and inspections in North Carolina. For a more in-depth analysis of local government liability and immunity, see Trey Allen's *Local Government Immunity to Lawsuits in North Carolina* (UNC School of Government, 2018).

Governmental Immunity

In North Carolina, governmental immunity protects local governments from liability for negligence and other tort claims against the local government when the claim arises from the performance of a governmental function and the local government has not waived immunity through the purchase of insurance or other means.

"The doctrine of sovereign [or governmental] immunity cannot stand as a barrier to North Carolina citizens who seek to remedy violations of their rights guaranteed by the Declaration of Rights."[22] Therefore, a claim of constitutional violation is not barred by governmental immunity.

A key issue in determining whether governmental immunity applies is this: Was the action a core governmental function like law enforcement, or a proprietary function like operating a public arena? Governmental immunity covers governmental but not proprietary functions.

The public duty doctrine is a related legal defense that limits governmental liability in very limited instances. It protects local governments from liability for negligent failure by their law enforcement agencies to prevent harm to certain individuals caused by third parties. At the local government level, North Carolina courts have declined to extend the public duty doctrine beyond law enforcement. For a time, North Carolina courts applied the public duty doctrine to building inspections, but that line of cases was overruled.[23] The public duty doctrine does not shield a local government or its inspectors from claims of negligence in inspections.

Public Official Immunity

Another derivative of governmental immunity shields public officers from liability for tort claims in certain circumstances. If an individual or entity sues a public official or employee, the extent of immunity depends on several factors: Is the individual a "public official" or a "public employee"? Is the lawsuit against the individual

---

22. Corum v. Univ. of N.C., 330 N.C. 761, 785–86, 413 S.E.2d 276, 291 (1992).

23. Thompson v. Waters, 351 N.C. 462, 526 S.E.2d 650 (2000); Lovelace v. City of Shelby, 351 N.C. 458, 526 S.E.2d 652 (2000).

in their "official capacity" or their "individual capacity"? And was the action subject to the lawsuit within the scope of their public duties?

Public official v. public employee. Public official immunity provides a defense for "public officials" from personal liability for conduct within the scope of their official duties. The immunity does not extend to a public official acting maliciously or corruptly. Public employees who are not public officials are not protected by this immunity.

To determine if a position is a public official or public employee, courts look to certain factors: (1) Is the position created by state law? (2) Do the duties of the position require the use of discretion? (3) Does the position exercise a portion of the state's sovereign power? (4) Courts have sometimes looked at whether an individual took an oath of office as a factor in determining public official status, but the lack of an oath is not dispositive.[24]

North Carolina courts have held that the chief building inspector and other building inspectors are public officials for purposes of public official immunity.[25] Other staff within the inspections department, however, may be treated as public employees rather than public officials, so immunity may not be available to them.

Official capacity v. individual capacity. To sue a public worker "in their official capacity" is to sue the formal office or the local government unit itself, not really the person as an individual. And as such, if a public official or employee is sued in their official capacity, governmental immunity may apply and may be a defense against the claims. A lawsuit against someone "in their individual capacity" is not a lawsuit against the government, but is a lawsuit against that person as an individual.[26] Current caselaw provides that governmental immunity does not protect individuals sued in their individual capacity from liability for tort claims. That said, public official immunity may apply for officers.

Scope of duties. Public official immunity applies to the acts, omissions, and duties of the public official that are within the scope of the official job. Intentional wrongdoing is generally outside the scope of duties. For example, if an inspector physically assaults a property owner during a building inspection, that conduct is outside the scope of the inspector's authority, and the inspector may be personally liable without any public official immunity (as well as potentially subject to criminal liability).

---

24. Isenhour v. Hutto, 350 N.C. 601, 610 (1999); Trey Allen, *Do Intentional Tort Claims Always Defeat Public Official Immunity?*, LOCAL GOV'T L. BULL. No. 139 (UNC School of Government, Sept. 2016), https://www.sog.unc.edu/publications/bulletins/do-intentional-tort-claims-always-defeat-public-official-immunity.

25. Wiggins v. City of Monroe, 73 N.C. App. 44, 49 (1985); Pigott v. City of Wilmington, 50 N.C. App. 401, 405 (1981); Woodard v. Cleveland Cnty., 202 N.C. App. 586 (2010) (unpublished); McCoy v. Coker, 174 N.C. App. 311, 319 (2005).

26. *See, e.g.*, Meyer v. Walls, 347 N.C. 97, 110 (1997) ("A suit against a defendant in his individual capacity means that the plaintiff seeks recovery from the defendant directly; a suit against a defendant in his official capacity means that the plaintiff seeks recovery from the entity of which the public servant defendant is an agent.").

Limited Liability for Actions by Third Parties

As the state has authorized more inspection activities by third parties, it has also limited local government liability for the actions of those parties. For third-party plan review in commercial construction, for example, "A local government and inspection department are discharged and released from any liabilities, duties, and responsibilities imposed by this Article, or in common law, from any claim arising out of, or attributed to, plans subject to a third-party independent review pursuant to subsection (e) of this section." In addition, when inspections are performed by a marketplace pool inspector, any claim of negligence is a claim against the state, and the local inspection department and inspectors are released from liability.[27]

Conflicts of Interest

State law establishes certain conflict of interest standards specifically for local government staff handling development decisions. Local policies may address additional conflicts of interest and professional ethics.

Financial Interest or Close Relationship

A staff member may not decide a permit, perform an inspection, or make other development decisions "if the outcome of that decision would have a direct, substantial, and readily identifiable financial impact on the staff member."[28]

Similarly, a staff member may not be the decision-maker for a permit, inspection, or other development decision "if the applicant or other person subject to that decision is a person with whom the staff member has a close familial, business, or other associational relationship."[29]

If either type of conflict of interest exists, the decision must be assigned to another staff person.[30]

Employment in Development-Related Work

No staff member may be "financially interested or employed by a business that is financially interested in a development" within the jurisdiction of the local government's development regulations.[31] State law concerning building code enforcement provides more specificity. An inspection department staff member may not have a financial or employment interest in a business "that is financially interested in the furnishing of labor, material, or appliances for the construction, alteration, or maintenance of any building within the local government's planning and development

27. G.S. 143-139.4.
28. G.S. 160D-109(c); *see also* G.S. 160D-1108(3).
29. G.S. 160D-109(c); *see also* G.S. 160D-1108(2).
30. G.S. 160D-109(c).
31. *Id.*

regulation jurisdiction or any part or system thereof, or in the making of plans or specifications therefor."[32]

The state law on conflicts of interest also looks back to prior employment. If, within the last two years, a staff member worked for the owner, developer, contractor, or project manager of the project to be inspected, that staff member has a conflict of interest, and another staff member must provide the permitting and/or inspection services.[33]

There are limited exceptions. A staff member may still own land and buildings within the jurisdiction and seek permits for development.[34] However, the staff member cannot approve the permits or perform inspections of their own property, as discussed above.

Another exception applies to firefighters. A firefighter whose primary duties are fire suppression and rescue may engage in fire inspection activities as a secondary responsibility of their employment. However, "no firefighter may inspect any work actually done, or materials or appliances supplied, by the firefighter or the firefighter's business within the preceding six years."[35]

Local Policies

State law provides that inspections staff must not "engage in any work that is inconsistent with his or her duties or with the interest of the local government, as determined by the local government."[36] Local policies may give additional guidance and parameters for staff conflicts of interest.

Criminal Limits

A code official making poor choices could face an array of criminal consequences. The crimes highlighted below provide an instructive but not exhaustive list.

Acting as an Officer

An individual without a valid certificate may not represent themselves as a qualified code-enforcement official. Moreover, an individual may not practice code enforcement at levels higher than those for which they are certified. Doing so constitutes a Class 1 misdemeanor, and the Code Officials Qualification Board may seek an injunction from superior court to prevent such a violation.

More broadly, an individual may not begin the duties of a public office before they take and file the oath of office and provide any necessary bonds.[37]

---

32. *Id.*
33. G.S. 160D-1108.
34. G.S. 160D, §§ 109(c), 1108.
35. G.S. 160D-1108.
36. G.S. 160D-109(c); *see also* G.S. 160D-1108.
37. G.S. 14-229 (acting as officer before qualifying as such).

Failure to Perform Duties

Public officials are obligated to perform the duties of their office and failing to do so is a crime. Various laws address this responsibility.

Specifically, for members of inspection departments, it is a Class 1 misdemeanor to do any of the following:

- fail to perform the duties required by law,
- improperly issue a building permit,
- give a certificate of compliance without first making the inspections required by law, or
- improperly issue a certificate of compliance.[38]

Note that there is an exception for accepting a signed, written document of compliance from an architect or engineer pursuant to G.S. 160D-1104(d).

More generally, state law provides that if a court determines that an officer failed to discharge duties or violated their oath of office, the court may remove the officer from office during sentencing.[39] Additional laws[40] specify other failures of officers punishable as crimes, including

- failure to make, file, or publish a report, as required,
- failure to deliver books and property of the office to their successor,
- failure to deliver moneys as required,
- swearing falsely to a report or statement, and
- failure to file reports of fines or penalties to the county board of education, if required.

Personal Benefit

State law puts significant rules in place to prevent improper personal benefit from public official work. Public officers may not benefit from public contracts, except for very limited exceptions.[41] Individuals may not misuse confidential information obtained during their work for the public.[42] Public officers may not financially benefit from their public position.[43] And there are limits on local public officials approving contracts that benefit a nonprofit with which the official is associated.[44]

Public Funds

A public official must take great care with public funds. The criminal laws set forth a variety of crimes for misuse of public funds.

---

38. G.S. 160D-1109.
39. G.S. 14-230 (willfully failing to discharge duties).
40. G.S. 14, §§ 231 (failing to make reports and discharge other duties), 232 (swearing falsely to official reports), 244 (failing to file report of fines or penalties).
41. G.S. 14-234 (public officers or employees benefiting from public contracts; exceptions).
42. G.S. 14-234.1 (misuse of confidential information).
43. G.S. 14-234.2 (public officers or employees financially benefiting from public position).
44. G.S. 14-234.3 (local public officials participating in contracts benefiting nonprofits with which associated).

Embezzlement is the illegal act of taking money or property that has been entrusted into someone's care. Article 18 of Chapter 14 of the North Carolina General Statutes (hereinafter G.S.) sets forth the punishments for embezzlement. In particular, G.S. 14-91 and -92 state that it is a felony for any officer, agent, or employee of the state or a local government to embezzle money or property from the public.

Public funds must be kept separate from personal funds. The Local Government Commission is obligated to report to the local district attorney any knowledge of an officer commingling funds. Such violation is a Class 1 misdemeanor.[45]

Vehicles

State law specifies improper actions related to vehicles and public duties. It is unlawful for any public official, agent, or employee to use a public vehicle for a private purpose.[46] An individual may drive a public vehicle between their official work station and their home. Additionally, it is unlawful for any official, agent, or employee to have a private vehicle repaired at a public garage.[47]

Bribery

It is illegal for a public officer to receive something of value or personal advantage for performing or neglecting to perform an official duty.[48] Bribery is punishable as a felony.

Trespass

An inspector may obtain permission to be on private property, but such permission may be revoked. Without permission, an inspector may be liable for trespass.[49]

Certification for Building Code Officials

Certification Types and Levels

An individual must be properly certified to enforce the State Building Code, and a local government may not employ an inspector to enforce the code who is not certified.[50] For other enforcement activities, such as housing code enforcement, nuisance code enforcement, or zoning enforcement, state law does not require certification for enforcement officers. Some local governments require certification

45. G.S. 128, §§ 11 (trust funds to be kept separate), 12 (violations to be reported; misdemeanors).

46. G.S. 14, §§ 247 (private use of publicly owned vehicle), 252 (applying §§ 247–251 to cities and towns).

47. G.S. 14-248 (obtaining repairs and supplies for private vehicle at expense of state).

48. G.S. 14-217 (bribery of officials).

49. G.S. 14, §§ 159.12 (first degree trespass—misdemeanor), 159.13 (second degree trespass—misdemeanor).

50. G.S. 160D-1103; 143-151.13.

such as the Certified Zoning Official designation through the North Carolina Association of Zoning Officials.

For building code official certification, the North Carolina Code Officials Qualification Board (the board) primarily issues two types of certificates attesting to an inspector's qualifications: standard certificates and probationary certificates.[51]

These certificates are issued across three levels (I, II, and III) in the following trade categories:

> (1) Building inspector.
> (2) Electrical inspector.
> (3) Mechanical inspector.
> (4) Plumbing inspector.
> (5) Fire inspector.
> (6) Residential changeout inspector.[52]

For promotion to a new position requiring a higher-level certificate, an inspector must first obtain a standard or probationary certificate appropriate for that position.

For a standard certificate, the individual must pass a board examination based on the State Building Code. Standard certificates are issued by trade and level. "The holder of a standard certificate may practice Code enforcement only within the inspection area and level described upon the certificate issued by the Board."[53]

A probationary certificate is a certificate issued to an individual who is newly hired or newly promoted and does not yet have the necessary standard certificate. The board may issue probationary certificates for one to three years, as specified in the board's rules.[54] Probationary certificates may include conditions related to the place of employment, supervision, or other matters.[55]

The board adjusted the levels for standard certificates in 2025.[56] Previously, the levels for trade inspector certificates were based on occupancy, number of stories, and square footage per story. Now, levels correspond to the applicable code: Level I for residential, Level II for commercial up to four stories, and Level III for all others.

Fire inspector levels are still related to building occupancy, with Level III inspectors handling higher-risk buildings such as high-rise buildings, hazardous materials, and institutional buildings.

Finally, limited certificates were issued in the 1970s and 1980s to assist with the transition to modern certification requirements for building code officials. These certificates allowed then-current inspectors to continue working within their jurisdiction while completing in-service training by a certain deadline.[57]

---

51. *Id.*
52. G.S. 143-151.13.
53. *Id.*
54. *See also* Title 11, Chapter 8, Sections .0600 and .0700 of the North Carolina Administrative Code (hereinafter N.C.A.C.).
55. G.S. 143-151.13.
56. 11 N.C.A.C. 08, § .0706.
57. G.S. 160D-1103; 143-151.13.

"Code Enforcement"

An individual must be properly certified to perform code enforcement. With regard to the State Building Code, code enforcement is defined as follows:

> Code enforcement. — The examination and approval of plans and specifications, the inspection of the manner of construction, workmanship, and materials for construction of buildings and structures and their components, or the enforcement of fire code regulations by any of the following, to assure compliance with the State Building Code and related local building rules:
>
> a. An employee of the State or local government, except an employee of the State Department of Labor engaged in the administration and enforcement of sections of the Code that pertain to boilers and elevators.
>
> b. An employee of a federally recognized Indian Tribe employed to perform inspections on tribal lands.
>
> c. An individual contracting with the State, a local government, or a federally recognized Indian Tribe to perform inspections on tribal lands.
>
> d. An individual who is employed by a company contracting with a county or a city to conduct inspections.
>
> e. A person who is contracting with a local government to perform third-party plan review under G.S. 160D-1110.1(d).
>
> f. A person who is contracting with a permit applicant to perform third-party plan review under G.S. 160D-1110.1(e).[58]

Comity

The board is authorized to grant a standard certificate to an individual who is certified as a code official in good standing by another state, district, or territory, or by the International Code Council. Such certificate expires after three years unless the certificate holder completes a prescribed short course.[59]

Session Law 2025-61 required occupational licensing boards and state agency licensing boards to issue a license, certification, or registration to individuals licensed in nearby states who meet certain criteria (establish residency in North Carolina, be licensed in certain nearby states for at least one year, be in good standing, demonstrate competency as determined by the licensing board, and more). This provision applies to a wide range of licensing boards, including the Code Officials Qualification Board, which oversees building inspector licensing. As such, building inspectors licensed in neighboring states may be licensed in North Carolina if they meet the criteria.

Other Licensed Professionals

Certain licensed professionals can obtain a standard certificate after completing a board-prescribed short course. These professionals include licensed general

58. G.S. 143-151.8.
59. G.S. 143-151.14; 11 N.C.A.C. 08, § .0707.

contractors; licensed plumbing or heating contractors; licensed electrical contractors; licensed architects; and licensed professional engineers. Engineers and architects with a standard certificate and who are not employed by the state or local government may qualify to perform third-party plan review.[60]

Certificate Maintenance

A certificate is valid as long as the holder maintains it and is employed as a code-enforcement official by the State of North Carolina, a North Carolina local government, or a federally recognized tribe. If the person leaves such employment, the individual returns the certificate to the board. If an official obtains such employment again, the board may reissue the certificate.[61] Certificates are either *active* or *inactive* depending upon employment by a jurisdiction.

An individual must pay an application fee for each certification, and certificates must be renewed annually. If an individual fails to renew a certificate for two consecutive years, the board may require the individual to take and pass the applicable exam before renewal.[62]

The board may further require professional development to renew a certificate. The required number of credit hours is set by the board, not to exceed six hours per trade per twelve-month period. The board may require professional development as a condition of reactivating a standard or limited certificate.[63]

Board Discipline

The board may investigate and "suspend, revoke, demote to a lower level, or refuse to grant a certificate" to any person for the following reasons:

> (1) Has been convicted of a felony against this State or the United States, or convicted of a felony in another state that would also be a felony if it had been committed in this State.
>
> (2) Has obtained certification through fraud, deceit, or perjury.
>
> (3) Has knowingly aided or abetted any person practicing contrary to the provisions of this Article or the State Building Code or any building codes adopted by a federally recognized Indian Tribe.
>
> (4) Has defrauded the public or attempted to do so.
>
> (5) Has affixed his or her signature to a report of inspection or other instrument of service if no inspection has been made by him or her or under his or her immediate and responsible direction.
>
> (6) Has been guilty of willful misconduct, gross negligence, or gross incompetence.[64]

---

60. G.S. 143-151.13(f)–(g); 11 N.C.A.C. 08, § .0707.
61. G.S. 143-151.15.
62. G.S. 143-151.16; 11 N.C.A.C. 08, § .0709.
63. G.S. 143-151.13A; 11 N.C.A.C. 08, § .0712–.0733.
64. G.S. 143-151.17. For disciplinary procedures, see also 11 N.C.A.C. 08, § .0800.

Investigations and actions must follow the procedures set forth in Chapter 150B of the General Statutes, the Administrative Procedure Act.

Notably, misconduct is defined to require accurate and even-handed code enforcement. "[W]illful misconduct, gross negligence, or gross incompetence," which is listed above as a reason for discipline, is defined to include the following:

> (1) Enforcing a Code requirement in areas or circumstances not specified in the requirement.
> (2) Refusing to accept an alternative design or construction method that has been appealed under G.S. 143-140.1 and found by the Office of the State Fire Marshal to comply with the Code under the conditions or circumstances set forth in the Office of the State Fire Marshal's decision for that appeal.
> (3) Refusing to allow an alternative construction method currently included in the Building Code under the conditions or circumstances set forth in the Code for that alternative method.
> (4) Enforcing a requirement that is more stringent than or otherwise exceeds the Code requirement.
> (5) Refusing to implement or adhere to an interpretation of the Building Code issued by the Building Code Council or the Office of the State Fire Marshal.
> (6) Habitually failing to provide requested inspections in a timely manner.
> (7) Enforcing a Code official's preference in the method or manner of installation of heating ventilation and air-conditioning units, appliances, or equipment if it is not required by the State Building Code and is in contradiction of a manufacturer's installation instructions or specifications.[65]

Permit Technician Certification

In 2024, the General Assembly passed legislation for the Code Officials Qualification Board to develop a North Carolina State Building Code Permit Technician Certification Program and certificate.[66] Certification must be based on an exam covering the State Building Code, administrative procedures applicable to permit administration, and relevant topics in support of code-enforcement officials and local inspection departments. The Board will set professional development standards for certificate renewal.

The law allows an individual possessing a building inspector standard certificate to obtain a permit technician certificate without an examination. The statute also allows comity for certificates from another jurisdiction or the International Code Council.

---

65. G.S. 143-151.8.
66. G.S. 143-151.22.

Part 2
State Building Code

The State Building Code is a set of technical codes situated within a complex legal framework of multiple levels of government. Part 2 seeks to clarify that legal framework by addressing the following specific topics of building code administration:

- **Chapter 5:** North Carolina State Building Code
- **Chapter 6:** Building Permit Procedures
- **Chapter 7:** Building Code Inspections
- **Chapter 8:** Building Code Enforcement
- **Chapter 9:** Building Code Interpretations and Appeals

Chapter 5

North Carolina State Building Code

Overview

The North Carolina State Building Code is a set of technical codes for building safety adopted by the applicable council, either the Building Code Council or Residential Code Council. Local authority to modify the State Building Code is limited, and there are specific procedures for alternative design, methods, and materials. This chapter outlines the scope, adoption, and modification of the State Building Code. Subsequent chapters address the details of permitting, inspections, enforcement, and appeals.

Scope

The North Carolina State Building Code regulates the construction, installation, alteration, or repair of "every type of building or structure, wherever it might be situated in the State," except in the limited circumstances and exceptions discussed below.[1]

State law sets forth the framework for the building code—the broad policy foundations and the nitty-gritty details of standards. For the broad policy foundations, the North Carolina General Statutes (hereinafter G.S.) provide this:

> All regulations contained in the North Carolina State Building Code shall have a reasonable and substantial connection with the public health and safety, and their provisions shall be construed reasonably to those ends. Requirements of the Code shall conform to good engineering practice.[2]

1. Chapter 143, Section 138(b3) of the North Carolina General Statutes (hereinafter G.S.).
2. G.S. 143-138(c).

The scope of delegated authority has been a subject of dispute through the decades. One example is *Carolinas-Virginias Ass'n of Bldg. Owners and Managers v. Ingram.*[3] In the 1970s, the Building Code Council adopted building code requirements applicable to existing high-rise buildings. Building owners challenged the regulations as beyond the council's delegated authority. Analyzing the text of the statutory grant of power for the council to adopt the State Building Code, the court found that the express grant was for rules for the construction of new buildings and structures (and reconstruction and altered uses), not for existing buildings. Separately, the General Assembly had passed legislation requiring sprinkler systems in existing buildings, but that legislation was a specific grant of authority. The court found no such grant of authority for broader building code requirements for existing buildings. Subsequently, the General Assembly adopted the high-rise standards directly as G.S. 143-138(i).

The regulations of the Building Code are matters of public health and safety. As noted by the North Carolina Supreme Court:

> [B]oth the legislature's directions for the creation of the Code and the Building Code Council's stated purposes for the different inspections under the Code evince an intent to protect the health of the general public. The Code regulates plumbing in an effort to maintain sanitary conditions in the buildings and structures of this state and thus directly involves sanitation, and consequently the protection of the health of those who use the buildings. The enforcement of the fire regulations protects lives from fire, explosion and health hazards. We find the conclusion that inspections pursuant to the Code affect health and sanitation inescapable.[4]

Technical Codes

The North Carolina State Building Code is a broad term encompassing many technical standards for specific construction trades, including the following:[5]

1. North Carolina Administrative Code and Policies, setting forth the authority and rules for implementation of the Building Code.
2. North Carolina Building Code, applicable to "the construction, alteration, repair, equipment, use and occupancy, location, movement to another site, removal and demolition, or any appurtenances connected or attached to every building or structure, other than [structures subject to the Residential Code]."

---

3. 39 N.C. App. 688, 251 S.E.2d 910 (1979).

4. City of New Bern v. New Bern-Craven Cnty. Bd. of Educ., 338 N.C. 430, 440, 450 S.E.2d 735, 741 (1994).

5. G.S. 143-138(a); Section 101.3.2 of the 2018 North Carolina Administrative Code and Policies (hereinafter N.C.A.C.P.) (2024 N.C.A.C.P. 101.3.2).

3. North Carolina Electrical Code, applicable to "the installation of electrical systems, including alterations, repairs, replacement, equipment, appliances, fixtures, fittings, and appurtenances."
4. North Carolina Energy Conservation Code, applicable to "the thermal envelope of the building and installation of energy systems, including alterations, repairs, replacement, equipment, appliances, fixtures, fittings and appurtenances, ventilating, heating, cooling, air-conditioning and refrigeration systems, incinerators, and other energy-related systems."
5. North Carolina Existing Building Code, applicable to "[a]ll work on any building that undergoes alterations, repairs, replacement, rehabilitation or change of occupancy."
6. North Carolina Fire Code, applicable to "the minimum fire safety requirements to all new and existing buildings, facilities, storage, and processes, except for one- or two-family dwellings and townhouses. The Fire Prevention Code provides a total approach of controlling hazards in all regulated buildings and sites, regardless of the hazard being indoors or outdoors."
7. North Carolina Fuel Gas Code, applicable to "the installation of gas piping systems extending from the point of delivery to the inlet connections of equipment served, and the installation and operation of residential and commercial gas appliances and related accessories."
8. North Carolina Mechanical Code, applicable to "the installation of mechanical systems, including alterations, repairs, replacement, equipment, appliances, fixtures, fittings, and appurtenances, including ventilating, heating, cooling, air-conditioning and refrigeration systems, incinerators, and other energy-related systems."
9. North Carolina Plumbing Code, applicable to "every plumbing installation, including alterations, repairs, replacement, equipment, appliances, fixtures, fittings, and appurtenances."
10. North Carolina Residential Code, applicable to "the construction, alteration, movement, enlargement, replacement, repair, equipment, use and occupancy, location, removal, and demolition of [one-, two-, three-, and four-family dwellings]."

Referenced Standards

The Building Code references a variety of third-party standards. As noted in the N.C. Administrative Code and Policies, these referenced standards "shall be considered an integral part of the codes." If only a portion of a third-party standard is cited in the code text, then only that portion is enforced. If there is a conflict between the code and a referenced standard, the code provision is enforced. And if a referenced standard has permissive or advisory provisions, those are not enforced as mandatory.[6]

Appendixes

The Building Code includes certain appendixes of rules from other state agencies. According to state law, these appendixes are informational only. If the Building Code specifically incorporates such a rule into the technical code, then it may be enforced as part of the Building Code; otherwise, it is merely for convenience. Rules from other agencies are informational only and not part of, nor do they supersede, the Building Code.

The appendixes include the following:

- rules governing boilers adopted by the Board of Boiler and Pressure Vessel Rules;
- rules for elevators adopted by the Commissioner of Labor;
- rules for sanitation adopted by the Commission for Public Health; and
- other rules that may be useful to persons using the code, such as rules from the Medical Care Commission and the Department of Public Instruction.[7]

Workmanship

As noted in the N.C. Administrative Code and Policies, "[w]orkmanship is not within the purview of the technical codes unless specifically stated within the code."[8]

Adoption and Amendment

The Building Code Council and the Residential Code Council have authority to prepare and adopt the Building Code. In adopting codes, certain standards apply. Regulations must "have a reasonable and substantial connection with the public health and safety, and their provisions shall be construed reasonably to those ends." Requirements must conform to good engineering practice. The statutes allow the Building Code Council and the Residential Code Council to use as guidance third-party model codes such as the International Building Code of the International Code Council, the National Electric Code, and the Fire Prevention Code of the National Fire Protection Association.[9]

The Residential Code Council handles the North Carolina Residential Code, including the applicable trade codes, and the Building Code Council handles the

---

6. 2018 N.C.A.C.P. 101.3.5 (2024 N.C.A.C.P. 101.3.5).
7. G.S. 143-138(b7); 2018 N.C.A.C.P. 101.3.4 (2024 N.C.A.C.P. 101.3.4).
8. 2018 N.C.A.C.P. 101.3.3 (2024 N.C.A.C.P. 101.3.3).
9. G.S. 143-138(c).

rest of the Building Code. The applicable council must hold at least one public hearing with proper advance notice published "in the North Carolina Register at least 15 days before the date of the hearing," and follow the procedures of the Administrative Procedures Act outlined in Article 2A of Chapter 150B of the General Statutes.[10]

The Building Code Council and the Residential Code Council may periodically revise and amend the Building Code. Such amendment may be on the motion of the applicable council or upon application by a citizen, state agency, or local government. The Residential Code Council must perform a comprehensive revision of the Residential Code only every six years, with the first revision effective January 1, 2031.[11] Section 102 of the N.C. Administrative Code and Policies outlines the process for amendment, including petitions for rulemaking, records, effective dates, and more.

The responsible council must ask the Office of State Budget and Management to prepare a fiscal note for any proposed Code change "that has a substantial economic impact, as defined in G.S. 150B-21.4(b1), or that increases the cost of residential housing by eighty dollars ($80.00) or more per housing unit." For any changes to the Energy Conservation Code, the responsible council must conduct (or request) a cost-benefit analysis of the change.[12]

Local Modifications

The State Building Code applies throughout the state, with limited local authority for local modifications for floodplain management and fire prevention.

The North Carolina Supreme Court addressed local modification in *Greene v. City of Winston-Salem*.[13] Builders challenged a local ordinance requiring sprinklers in high-rise buildings. The city argued that the ordinance was allowed under its general police powers to protect public health and safety. The court ruled that the building code statutes establish a "complete and integrated regulatory scheme" for building safety, including sprinklers. As such, the state has preempted the field. Local modification is not allowed without express authority from the state.

Statutory provisions allow limited local modification. For floodplain management, "[l]ocal floodplain regulations may regulate all types and uses of buildings or structures located in flood hazard areas identified by local, State, and federal agencies." Such regulations may address improvements, floor elevation, mechanical and electrical systems, foundation construction, flood resistance, and other

10. G.S. 143-138(a).
11. G.S. 143-138(d).
12. G.S. 143-138(a1).
13. 287 N.C. 66, 71, 213 S.E.2d 231, 234 (1975).

measures deemed necessary. Floodplain modifications do not require approval by the Building Code Council or Residential Code Council.[14]

For fire prevention, a few statutory provisions outline possible modifications and their limits. A local government may adopt limited modifications under G.S. 160D-1128 authorizing local fire limits. That section authorizes county and municipal fire limits, permit requirements for wood buildings, and "additional regulations for the prevention, extinguishment, or mitigation of fires within the primary fire limit."

Notably, local fire prevention code provisions may not require anything not prescriptively required by the North Carolina Residential Code for structures subject to that code.[15] And, beyond the allowances in G.S. 160D-1128, any local modification of the fire code must be "officially approved by the responsible Code Council as providing adequate minimum standards to preserve and protect health and safety."[16] G.S. 143-138(b1) states that the code's provisions on fire protection "shall be considered the minimum standards necessary to preserve and protect public health and safety," and that, with approval from the council, a local government may adopt more stringent provisions.

Alternative Design, Methods, and Materials

The Building Code Council and Residential Code Council set forth "rules, procedures, and policies for the approval of alternative designs and construction that follow the North Carolina State Building Code."[17]

As set forth in the Administrative Code and Policies, a local official may allow an alternative material, design, or method if the official finds that the alternative complies with the intent and provisions of the technical code.[18] The 2024 version of the Administrative Code and Policies provides more detail. Under the 2024 rules, a local official may allow an alternative material, design, or method where the alternative demonstrates that it is equal to or safer than the methods required by the technical codes, using either the prescriptive method or the performance method.[19] As noted in the commentary to Section 105.2.2 of the Administrative Code and Policies:

> "Prescriptive method" refers to sections of the technical codes that indicate a specific material or method. An example would be the requirement in the NC Residential Code that a pier footing for a

14. G.S. 143-138(e).
15. *Id.*
16. *Id.*
17. G.S. 143-140.1.
18. 2018 N.C.A.C.P. 105.1.
19. 2024 N.C.A.C.P. 105.2.

> one-story house be 1'4" x 2'0" x 8". That would be the minimum footing size if the footing is designed prescriptively.
>
> "Performance method" refers to sections of the technical codes that indicate minimum design value. The footing for the same pier as described above could be designed to a lesser size if the performance requirements of the NC Residential Code are met. An example could be that the loads of the structure supported by the pier are less than expected by the code or the soil capacity is greater than 2,000 psf. Any of these factors could reduce the size of the footing to less than that required prescriptively in the NC Residential Code.[20]

Additionally, when there is insufficient evidence of compliance, the code official may require testing.[21]

The local inspections department and fire marshal must have a documented, published process for reviewing proposals for alternative materials, designs, or methods. This procedure must provide a written decision within ten business days of receiving the request.[22] The decision must include the evidence and technical codes considered, as well as the conclusions drawn from them. If a designer or owner's representative disputes a decision by a local authority, they may appeal that decision to the Engineering and Building Codes Division of the Department of Insurance, which shall issue a decision within ten business days.[23]

Appeals are discussed more fully in Chapter 9.

20. 2024 N.C.A.C.P. 105.2.2 (original italics omitted).
21. 2024 N.C.A.C.P. 105.2.3.
22. 2024 N.C.A.C.P. 105.3.
23. G.S. 143-140.1.

Chapter 6

Building Permit Procedures

Overview

State law sets certain requirements and procedures for building permit application, review, and decision. It includes specifics for application forms and fees. Drawings are required for some permits, but not all. State law also establishes timelines for review of certain applications and includes special provisions and exceptions for a range of development types. This chapter explores the various rules governing building permit procedures. For more on the best practices of building permitting and inspections in North Carolina, see Obed Pasha, *Promising Practices for Timely Completion of Building Inspections in North Carolina* (UNC School of Government, Oct. 2025). Permitting and inspections flowcharts are included in Appendix C.

Applicability

As required by state law, a person must first secure "all permits required by the North Carolina State Building Code and any other State or local laws applicable to any of the following activities" before commencing the construction, installation, alteration, or repair of a building, structure, plumbing system, heating or cooling system, or any electrical wiring, devices, appliances, or equipment.[1] Notably, however, many exemptions and carveouts apply, as discussed below.

Application and Review, Generally

Application

The local inspection department establishes the standard form for building permit applications. (Sample residential and nonresidential building permit application forms are provided in Appendix D of this handbook.) This form is based on Appendix A of the Administrative Code and Policies. Appendix A, titled *Permit*

1. Chapter 160D, Section 1110 of the North Carolina General Statutes (hereinafter G.S.).

Application Information Sheet, outlines the information required on all permit applications. As stated in Appendix A, "[a]dditional information may be included to ensure that all state and local laws are complied with."[2]

With regard to Appendix B and building code summary information, state law provides that "a local government shall not require a permit applicant to complete Appendix B with a set of plans submitted for review."[3] This legislation is reflected in Section 106.3 of the 2018 Administrative Code and Policies and further explained in the 2024 version as follows:

> A local government shall not require a permit applicant to complete an Appendix B with a set of plans submitted for review. A local government shall only request specific building code summary information from a permit applicant it deems relevant in performing a complete plan review. An inspection department's full and partial building code summary forms shall be in the exact format as, and contain only the information in, Appendix B of the *Administrative Code and Policies*, as relevant to the specific form created. An inspection department shall only modify its full and partial building code summary forms as set forth in Section 103.6, Modifications, or as necessary to reflect any changes by the North Carolina Office of State Fire Marshal to Appendix B that have been approved by the Building Code Council.[4]

Decision

The inspections department has a duty to review and decide on applications for building permits.[5] "A building permit shall be in writing and shall contain a provision that the work done shall comply with the North Carolina State Building Code and all other applicable State and local laws."[6]

If the work proposed in the application meets the technical requirements of the Building Code and other pertinent laws and ordinances, the inspections department must approve the permit. If the application does not meet these requirements, it must be "returned to the applicant with the reasons for refusal stated."[7]

When an applicant meets the objective standards for a permit, they have "a clear legal right to the building permit sought by them, and the [local government] ha[s] no discretionary power to withhold it."[8]

---

2. Section 106.3.1 of the 2018 North Carolina Administrative Code and Policies (hereinafter N.C.A.C.P.); 2018 N.C.A.C.P. App. A. (Permit Application Information Sheet).
3. S.L. 2023-108.
4. 2024 N.C.A.C.P. 106.3.
5. G.S. 160D-1104(a).
6. G.S. 160D-1110(b).
7. 2018 N.C.A.C.P. 204.5.1 (2024 N.C.A.C.P. 204.5.1).
8. Mitchell v. Barfield, 232 N.C. 325, 326, 59 S.E.2d 810, 811 (1950).

Application Fees

A local government has the "power to fix reasonable fees for support, administration, and implementation of programs authorized by this Chapter [160D]."[9] Permitting fees must be reasonably related to the cost of administering the permit or inspection.[10] (See Appendix B for sample fee schedules.)

For certain projects, state law limits permit fees. For the installation of appliances in an existing structure, for example, an inspections department may only require one building permit and "[t]he cost of the building permit for this work shall not exceed the cost of any one individual trade permit issued by that local government."[11]

Related Requirements

Erosion and Sedimentation Control Plan

State law requires that a building permit not be issued unless an erosion and sedimentation control plan has been approved for the site.[12]

General Contractor License and Workers Compensation

For construction costing more than $40,000, the individual seeking a permit must provide proof of licensure as a general contractor and proof of Workers' Compensation insurance as required by Chapter 97 of the North Carolina General Statutes (hereinafter G.S.).[13]

If the individual seeking the permit claims an exemption from licensure, they must execute a verified affidavit attesting to the following:

> a. That the applicant is the owner of the property on which the building is being constructed and, if the applicant is a firm or corporation, that the person submitting the application is an owner, officer, or member of the firm or corporation that owns the property.
>
> b. That the applicant will personally superintend and manage all aspects of the construction of the building and that the duty will not be delegated to any other person not licensed under this Article.
>
> c. That the applicant will be personally present for all inspections required by the North Carolina State Building Code, unless the plans for the building were drawn and sealed by an architect licensed pursuant to Chapter 83A of the General Statutes.[14]

---

9. G.S. 160D-402(d).

10. Homebuilders Ass'n of Charlotte, Inc. v. City of Charlotte, 336 N.C. 37, 442 S.E.2d 45 (1994).

11. G.S. 160D-1110(d)(1).

12. G.S. 160D-1110(e).

13. G.S. 87-14.

14. *Id.*

Additionally, state law requires that an individual claiming an exemption from licensure occupy the building for twelve months following completion; therefore, many forms require this attestation as well.[15] The inspections department must transmit the affidavit to the State Licensing Board for General Contractors to verify that the person is entitled to an exemption. If they are not, the inspections department must revoke the permit.

Lien Agent

For work costing more than $40,000, the project must have a designated lien agent. For these projects, "the name, physical and mailing address, telephone number, facsimile number, and email address of the lien agent designated by the owner pursuant to G.S. 44A-11.1(a) [must be] conspicuously set forth in the permit or in an attachment to the permit."[16]

The lien agent requirements do not apply "to improvements to an existing single-family residential dwelling unit as defined in G.S. 87-15.5 that the owner occupies as a residence or to the addition of an accessory building or accessory structure as defined in the North Carolina Residential Code, the use of which is incidental to that residential dwelling unit."[17]

In determining the need for lien agents for work involving a manufactured home, "the purchase price of the manufactured home is excluded in determining whether the cost of the work is forty thousand dollars ($40,000) or more."[18]

Construction Site Signage

The permit applicant must post the 911 emergency site address at the active jobsite at the commencement of work under the Building Code. Signage may be permanent or temporary. Signage meeting the requirements of the International Residential Code and International Building Code is deemed acceptable as permanent signage. If permanent street signs for the development or subdivision are not present, the permit applicant must provide "a permit placard, an address written on job box, yard signage or other *approved* temporary street name markers." Temporary signage must be placed so that it is legible from the street at all times during construction.[19]

Plan Review, Generally

Building plans are generally required for commercial buildings (with specific exceptions) and may be required for residential buildings. Any plans and specifications

15. G.S. 87-1.
16. G.S. 160D-1110(g).
17. *Id.*
18. *Id.*
19. 2018 N.C.A.C.P. 106.4 (2024 N.C.A.C.P. 106.4).

must be drawn to scale and provide sufficient clarity and detail to indicate the nature and character of the work. Additionally, plans must include the name, address, and signature of the person responsible for the design.[20] The local inspection department may request additional information.

When approving a permit, the local inspection department must "approve, in writing or by stamp, all sets of drawings and specifications 'Reviewed for Code Compliance.'"[21] The 2024 Administrative Code and Policies also provides that applicants and local departments may choose to use the Building Information Modeling—Integrated Project Delivery Process (BIM-IPD process) for plan review and approval.[22]

Plan review requirements and timelines for residential and commercial construction are discussed further in sections below.

For plans that must be prepared by an architect or engineer, no permit may be issued unless the plans and specifications bear the seal of a licensed architect or engineer. For work required by state law or local regulation to be done by a licensed specialty contractor, no building permit may be issued unless the work is to be performed by a licensed contractor.[23]

A local government must not require residential building plans to be sealed by an engineer or architect unless required by the Building Code.[24]

Residential Plan Review and Permits

Singular Permit

Local governments must require no more than "one building permit for simultaneous projects at the time of the application located at the same address and subject to the North Carolina Residential Code."[25]

Time Limits for Residential Plan Review and Concurrent Review

Pursuant to G.S. 160D-1110, residential plans are not required by the State Building Code, and local governments are not required to review residential building plans for structures built under the North Carolina Residential Code, although they may choose to do so. If a local government chooses to review residential building plans, "all initial reviews for the building permit shall be performed within 15 business days of submission of the plans."[26]

---

20. G.S. 160D-1110(b); 2018 N.C.A.C.P. 106.2 (2024 N.C.A.C.P. 106.2).
21. 2018 N.C.A.C.P. 106.2.3 (2018 N.C.A.C.P. 106.2.3).
22. 2024 N.C.A.C.P. 106.2.3.
23. G.S. 160D-1110(b).
24. *Id.*
25. G.S. 160D-1110(d)(2).
26. G.S. 160D-1110(b).

If initial review of the residential building plan is not performed within twenty business days of submission, the local government must refund 10 percent of the application fee for each business day the review is delayed, up to ten business days.

Local governments must perform residential plan review concurrently with other applicable permit reviews: "A local government that reviews residential building plans for the purpose of building permit issuance shall perform its initial review concurrently with processes for project development approvals required from other State, federal, and local agencies."[27]

Commercial and Multifamily Plan Review and Permits

Presubmittal Meeting

For commercial and multifamily buildings, a local government must provide the option for a presubmittal meeting. Presubmittal meetings are held "to discuss a building project and to determine whether the permit applicant possesses necessary plans and sufficient information the local government would require for building permit plan review." The meeting must be scheduled within five business days of the request.

An applicant is eligible to request a presubmittal meeting under the following circumstances:

> (1) The project plans and specifications for a building project are complete and sealed for construction, as applicable, by a professional engineer licensed under Chapter 89C of the General Statutes or an architect licensed under Chapter 83A of the General Statutes.
>
> (2) The project plans and specifications for a building project are substantially identical to those that the permit applicant would submit with the building permit application.
>
> (3) The building permit applicant has made best efforts to compile and prepare documents required by a local government, and other State or federal agencies, for the building project.
>
> (4) The building permit applicant has determined whether an at-risk permit option will be utilized in accordance with subsection (h) of this section.[28]

At-Risk Permits

If an applicant completes a presubmittal meeting for an eligible development, they may request certain permits as at-risk building permits.

An applicant may request an at-risk building foundation permit at the time of general-permit application. The local government must issue the at-risk building

27. *Id.*
28. G.S. 160D-1110.1(b)(4).

foundation permit if the applicant has (1) submitted all necessary plans and information, as discussed at the presubmittal meeting, and (2) received all approvals necessary to lay the foundation ("notwithstanding that other development approvals from the local government, or other State or federal agencies, for the project have not yet been obtained"). The "approvals necessary" include approval of an erosion and sedimentation control plan for land-disturbing activity, but the applicant is not obligated to have obtained other development approvals that may be necessary for the overall project.[29]

An applicant may request an at-risk building structure permit once the applicant has obtained the at-risk foundation permit. A local government may issue an at-risk building structure permit if the applicant has (1) submitted all necessary plans and information and (2) received all approvals necessary to build the structure ("notwithstanding that other development approvals from the local government, or other State or federal agencies, for the project have not yet been obtained"). An at-risk building structure permit is for "the erection and installation of structural or framing members for exterior walls and roof assemblies."[30]

For at-risk permits, the applicant assumes all liability and the local government is released from liability for review, approval, and construction pursuant to the at-risk permit. An at-risk permit does not count as an "initial development permit" for purposes of vesting and multiple permits under G.S. 160D-108(e).

If a local government requires manufacturer specifications or engineering information for an element, component, or fixture, it may not delay or deny issuance of a building permit based on the receipt of that information.

Time Limits for Commercial Plan Review

For commercial and multifamily buildings that are eligible for a presubmittal meeting (as discussed above), the local government must complete its review and issue a decision within forty-five days of submission, unless the applicant and local government agree to additional time. If the local government receives, at its request, additional information or a resubmitted plan, it then "has up to 10 additional days to issue a building permit decision."[31]

If the local government has issued an at-risk permit (discussed below), the deadline for issuing the building permit is extended to sixty days.

Third-Party Plan Review

Licensed engineers and architects who are certified under G.S. 143-151.13(f) may, in certain circumstances, provide independent third-party review of commercial and multifamily construction plans.

29. G.S. 160D-1110.1(h)(1).
30. G.S. 160D-1110.1(h)(2).
31. G.S. 160D-1110.1(c).

G.S. 143-151.13(f) provides that the North Carolina Code Officials Qualification Board shall issue a standard certificate for building code enforcement to certain licensed professionals who complete a required short course on the State Building Code and code-enforcement administration. These professionals include licensed architects, licensed professional engineers, and certain licensed contractors. G.S. 143-151.13(g) states that architects and engineers certified under subsection (f) may provide third-party plan review for commercial and multifamily building projects.

Under G.S. 160D-1110.1, local governments may contract with a licensed engineer or architect certified under G.S. 143-151.13(f) to perform independent third-party plan review of commercial and multifamily development. The third-party review must still comply with applicable timelines for review.

If a local government begins a plan review but fails to complete it within the time required (either because the deadline has passed or the local government has determined it cannot meet the timeline), a permit applicant may elect to contract for an independent third-party plan review by a licensed engineer or architect certified under G.S. 143-151.13(f).

The local government must create a certification form for use by third-party reviewers. When an applicant opts for third-party review, they must submit to the local government a written certification signed by the reviewer.

Third-party plan reviewers must not have conflicts of interest. Conflicts include any financial interest or employment relationship with the project or any involvement in creating the plans under review.

> [A] plan reviewer having any financial interest in, or being employed, other than as a plan reviewer under this section, by a business that has a financial interest in the furnishing of labor, material, or appliances for the construction, alteration, or maintenance of, or any involvement in the making of plans or specifications for, the project subject to plan review.[32]

Plan Review by the Office of State Fire Marshal

Plans for certain buildings (see Table 6.1) must be reviewed by the state before a local inspections department may issue a permit. Alternatively, a local inspections department may request that the Building Code Council grant it authority to review such buildings locally. To receive this authority, the local inspections department must be adequately staffed to perform such reviews and must attest that it can conduct inspections within two business days, as required by G.S. 143-139.4.

32. G.S. 160D-1110.1(g).

Table 6.1 North Carolina Office of State Fire Marshal, Engineering and Building Codes Division Document Approval for New Construction and Additions

Occupancy Group	Building Plans to Be Approved
Section 403—High Rise[a]	All buildings
Section 402—Covered Mall Buildings[a]	All buildings
City/county-owned	All buildings 20,000 sq. ft. or greater as required by N.C.G.S. 58-78A-16
Group A[a,b]	Occupant load over 1,000
Group E[a]	Over 2 stories or over 20,000 sq. ft./story
Group H[a]	Occupant load over 100
Group I[a]	Over 3 stories or over 10,000 sq. ft./story
Group R[a]	Over 4 stories or over 100 units/building

For SI: 1 square foot=0.0929 m^2.

a. Plans and specifications are not required to be reviewed or approved by the Engineering and Building Codes Division for buildings that are located in a city or county inspection jurisdiction approved to perform plans review by the NC Building Code Council, except city/county-owned buildings are not exempt.

b. Except temporary bleachers.

Source: This table is taken from Section 104.1 of the 2024 North Carolina Administrative Code and Policies.

After Permit Approval

Changes

After a building permit is issued, changes or deviations from the approved permit are only allowed if "clearly permissible under the North Carolina State Building Code" or if approved by the inspections department with "specific written approval of proposed changes or deviations."[33]

Expiration

Building permits are valid for six months from the date of issuance (or a shorter period, if set by ordinance). If the applicant has not commenced work within six months, the permit expires. After work begins, if the applicant discontinues work for twelve months, the permit also expires. Once a permit has expired, no work may be performed until a new permit is secured.[34]

In special circumstances North Carolina courts have allowed that "work" may include actions beyond on-site construction. *Morris Communications Corp. v. City*

33. G.S. 160D-1112.
34. G.S. 160D-1111.

of Bessemer City Zoning Board of Adjustment[35] arose from a dispute over a local sign ordinance and the expiration of a sign permit, but the language was similar to the statutory language for building permit expiration and may be instructive. The North Carolina Supreme Court ruled that local officials were overly restrictive in requiring on-site construction as the only acceptable evidence that "work" had commenced. The court allowed that other evidence—such as negotiations with the N.C. Department of Transportation and the landowner during the permit period—could indicate that "work" had commenced. The court noted that common law vested rights caselaw allows off-site effort and expenditures to count as "work." Notably, the holding was "limited to the unusual facts of this case," in which the billboard was forcibly relocated because of a road-widening project.

Permit Choice

The permit choice rule provides this: If an applicant submits a permit application for development, and after submission—but before a decision is made—a rule or ordinance is amended, the applicant may choose whether the former or amended version of the rule or ordinance applies to the application and use of land.[36]

The statutes set certain procedural protections for applicants. If the applicant chooses the former rule, the local government cannot require the applicant to wait for final action on the proposed change. If an applicant challenges a permit denial and it is later determined that the permit was wrongfully denied or that a condition was illegally imposed, the applicant may choose whether the application will be reviewed under the rules in effect at the time of application or under the rules as subsequently amended.

If a permit application is on hold for six consecutive months, the permit choice rule is waived. This may occur if the applicant voluntarily places the application on hold or fails to respond to comments or reasonable requests for additional information for six months. If an applicant resumes the application after six months of discontinuation, the rules in effect at the time of resuming consideration will apply.

Vested Rights

A vested right is the right to continue a permitted development as approved despite subsequent changes to development regulations. North Carolina recognizes *common law vested rights* (established by courts) and *statutory vested rights* (created by state law). A statutory vested right functions as a validity period for a particular development approval. While the approval remains valid, subsequent changes to local development regulations do not apply to the approved development. Different development permits have different periods of validity during which the developer must substantially commence construction. For example, building permits expire after six months, or a shorter period if set by local ordinance, if work has

---

35. 365 N.C. 152, 712 S.E.2d 868 (2011).
36. G.S. 143-755; 160D-108.

not begun. If work begins but is discontinued for twelve months, the permit also expires. However, this period of discontinuance is tolled during appeals or litigation related to the development.

Common law vested rights are similar rights established by courts, not statutes. A property owner may establish a common law vested right when each of the following four tests are met: (1) the owner made substantial expenditures; (2) the expenditures were made in good faith; (3) the expenditures were made in good faith reliance on a valid governmental approval, if required; and (4) the owner would be harmed without a vested right.[37]

A vested right is not a free pass. The development must still comply with the standards, conditions, and requirements of the approval and any applicable regulations. G.S. 160D-108(g) authorizes the local government to conduct inspections and reviews to ensure compliance with applicable land development regulations.

Additionally, while vested rights protect developments from most local regulation changes, state law allows an exception when "a change in State or federal law mandating local government enforcement occurs after the development application is submitted that has a fundamental and retroactive effect on the development or use."[38]

Exemptions and Limitations for Building Permits

As a general rule, a building permit is required before starting construction. However, there are many carve-outs, exemptions, and special provisions. G.S. 143-138, for example, sets forth exemptions and special provisions regarding the applicability of the State Building Code to items such as cisterns, movie sets, hydraulic lifts, and more. The statute also provides exemptions from the Energy Conservation Code for specific buildings and uses.

This section explores those exemptions and limitations.

Dollar Amount

No permit is required for work done in accordance with applicable codes and costing less than $40,000.[39] However, a permit is still required for the following:

- changes to load bearing structures (but not for replacing windows, doors, and certain other elements);
- changes to the design of plumbing (unless there is no change in size or capacity);

37. Browning-Ferris Indus. of S. Atl., Inc. v. Guilford Cnty. Bd. of Adjustment, 126 N.C. App. 168 (1997).
38. G.S. 160D-108(c).
39. G.S. 143-138(b5); 160D-1110(c).

- changes to the design of heating, air conditioning, electrical wiring, appliances, or equipment (but not for like-kind replacements of electrical devices and lighting fixtures);
- the use of materials not permitted by the Building Code;
- the addition of roofing (but not for replacement); and
- changes subject to the Fire Code.

Note that the General Assembly has adopted local legislation to alter these state requirements for certain communities.[40]

Residential Permits, Appliances, and Water Heaters

A local government must not require more than one building permit for simultaneous projects at the same address subject to the Residential Code.[41]

A local government must not require more than one building permit "for the complete installation or replacement of any natural gas, propane gas, or electrical appliance on an existing structure" when the installer is properly licensed under G.S. 87-21 or G.S. 87-43. Moreover, the permit fee must not exceed the cost of any one trade permit issued by that local government.[42]

No permit is required for replacement water heaters in residences if the work is performed by a properly licensed installer under G.S. 87-21 or G.S. 87-43; the energy use rate or thermal input is not greater, and the fuel, location, piping, and venting remain the same; and the installation complies with the Building Code.[43]

No permit is required "for the repair or replacement of dishwashers, disposals, water heaters, electrical devices, or lighting fixtures in residential or commercial structures," provided there is no relocation of electric wiring, the installer is licensed, and the work meets the Building Code.[44]

A local government may not adopt local regulations that prohibit particular types of energy service or appliances based on energy type.[45] For example, a local ordinance may not prohibit natural gas stoves or water heaters.

Manufactured Homes and Modular Construction

Building safety regulations for manufactured homes and modular construction involve a mix of in-factory certification by label and in-field certification by the local inspector. State and federal standards apply to components and units constructed in the factory. Such components and units must bear a label or seal certifying compliance and are presumed to meet the State Building Code without inspection

40. *See* S.L. 1989-611 (Wrightsville Beach Charter allowing permits for construction of smaller dollar amounts). *See also* S.L. 1993-381, S.L. 1995-732, and S.L. 1997-63 (giving various jurisdictions authority to require permits for roof replacement).
41. G.S. 160D-1110(d)(2).
42. G.S. 160D-1110(d)(1).
43. G.S. 143-138(b10); 160D-1110(a)(2), (a)(4).
44. G.S. 143-138(b16).
45. G.S. 160A-203.3.

or fee. The local inspector still inspects and charges fees "as may be required for the enforcement of the Code relative to the connection of units and components and enforcement of local ordinances governing zoning, utility connections, and foundations permits."[46]

North Carolina was an early adopter of standardized approvals for manufactured homes. In 1969, the General Assembly set up a system whereby the state would adopt regulations for manufactured homes (based on standards from a national organization) and would license testing agencies to approve plans, inspect homes during manufacture, and affix a label of compliance. By 1974, the federal government adopted a similar program and preempted the field.[47]

The basic system remains in place. New manufactured homes must be built to standards set by the U.S. Department of Housing and Urban Development (HUD) and bear a HUD label confirming compliance with minimum standards.

While some aspects of manufactured homes are inspected and certified according to HUD processes, the setup and installation of a manufactured home must still comply with the Building Code and related regulations. "Permits shall be required for the installation, connection of units, foundations, utility connections or alterations of buildings or components manufactured off the site and labeled by a third-party agency accredited and listed by the Building Code Council."[48]

New manufactured homes must be installed according to the manufacturer's installation manual. Used manufactured homes must be installed according to the State of North Carolina Regulations for Manufactured Homes.

Beyond Building Code requirements, state law limits local development regulations for manufactured homes.[49] A local government may not exclude manufactured homes from its jurisdiction or regulate them based on age. However, local governments may enforce appearance and dimensional standards and use zoning to regulate the location of manufactured homes and parks. They may also require that manufactured homes be installed according to state standards but "shall not require a masonry curtain wall or masonry skirting for manufactured homes located on land leased to the homeowner."[50]

Utilities, Gas, and Machinery

Public Utility Facilities

Building Code rules do not extend to "equipment or facilities, other than buildings, of a public utility, as defined in G.S. 62-3, a cable television company, or an

---

46. G.S. 143-139.1.

47. S.L. 1969-961; G.S. Ch. 143, Art. 9A and 9B; Philip P. Green, Jr., Legal Aspects of Building Code Enforcement in North Carolina 3 (UNC Institute of Government, 2d ed. 1987).

48. 2018 N.C.A.C.P. 204.4.2 (2024 N.C.A.C.P. 204.5.2).

49. G.S. 160D-910.

50. *Id.*

electric or telephone membership corporation, including without limitation poles, towers, and other structures supporting electric, cable television, or communication lines."[51]

A building permit is not required "for the installation, maintenance, or replacement of any load control device or equipment by an electric power supplier," provided that the work is in accordance with approval from the North Carolina Utilities Commission or a comparable approval by a municipal electric service provider.[52]

Liquefied Petroleum Facilities

Building code rules do not extend to equipment for liquefied petroleum gases, anhydrous ammonia, or other liquid fertilizers. However, specific petroleum equipment within buildings is subject to the Building Code: "liquefied petroleum gas from the outlet of the first stage pressure regulator to and including each liquefied petroleum gas utilization device within a building or structure covered by the Code."[53]

Additionally, no permit is required "for routine maintenance on fuel dispensing pumps and other dispensing devices," including repair and replacement of hoses, O-rings, nozzles, or emergency breakaways.[54]

Industrial Machinery

Industrial machinery is not subject to the Building Code.[55] If an electrical inspector has concerns about the electrical safety of industrial machinery, the inspector may refer the matter to the Occupational Safety and Health Division of the North Carolina Department of Labor. Notably, the inspector may not withhold a certificate of occupancy or require third-party testing based on the concern.

Governmental Property

Federal Property

While the federal government may coordinate with state and local officials on federal construction projects, federal buildings are not subject to state or local building codes. However, federal law does require that federal buildings comply with the latest edition of one of the "nationally recognized model building codes."[56] Private buildings that happen to be leased by the federal government must meet the requirements of the State Building Code.[57]

---

51. G.S. 143-138(b8).
52. G.S. 160D-1110(a).
53. G.S. 143-138(b8).
54. G.S. 143-138(b14).
55. G.S. 143-138(b9).
56. Public Buildings Amendments of 1988, Pub. L. No. 100-678, 102 Stat. 4049 (codified at 40 U.S.C. § 3312).
57. 41 C.F.R. 102-80.85.

State Property

The state administers its own building code enforcement; local inspection offices do not oversee state buildings. The Office of State Construction within the Department of Administration is responsible for enforcing the Building Code for state buildings.[58]

Buildings constructed by the state or by the University of North Carolina system "shall not be subject to inspection by any county or municipal authorities and shall not be subject to county or municipal building codes and requirements."[59] Local governments may request to review plans and specifications for state projects but may not charge inspection fees. If needed, the state may request local inspection services and pay the appropriate fees. Beyond State Building Code enforcement, "local government zoning and development regulations are applicable to the erection, construction, and use of buildings by the State of North Carolina and its political subdivisions."[60] So, while local building inspectors may not be inspecting state buildings for compliance with the State Building Code, local zoning still applies.

School Inspections

Local inspections departments conduct regular inspections of schools for fire hazards, as outlined in G.S. 115C-525. State law also allows schools to use special locking mechanisms for seclusion rooms.[61]

Farm Buildings and Building Permits

Overview

Farm buildings are exempt from some applicable building rules. This section outlines those exemptions. There are general provisions that apply across farm buildings as well as specific exemptions for certain types of farm buildings and uses. As described below, the extent to which building rules apply or do not apply depends on a range of factors.

Here is a list of key questions for evaluating whether certain regulations apply to a farm building:

- Is the property a bona fide farm? Is the building used for a bona fide farm activity?
- What is the applicable jurisdiction? County jurisdiction, municipal jurisdiction, or municipal extraterritorial jurisdiction (ETJ)?

58. G.S. 143-139(e).
59. G.S. 143-135.1(a).
60. G.S. 160D-913.
61. G.S. 143-138(b11).

- Is the building residential or nonresidential?
- Is the activity among those with special protection?
- What regulation is in question? Building code, electrical code, fire code, zoning, or another?

In addition to the building rules exemption, there are other special rules about the applicability of local zoning to bona fide farm activities outside of municipal corporate limits. That is discussed briefly below.

Building Rules

Building rules do not apply to certain farm buildings. The definition of *farm building* is broad, and state law provides many detailed caveats about what is or is not considered a farm building. Those details are outlined below. The phrase *building rules* requires some interpretation and application.

A 2016 appeal of a stop work order to the Department of Insurance concerned whether an event building on a farm required building permits.[62] The appeal decision noted that under the law at the time building rules did not apply to farm buildings, and the event building qualified as a farm building. Notably, the decision stated that "G.S. 143-138 extends only the 'building rules,'" but does not extend to overall safety of the occupancy. Imminent life safety hazards can be identified and cited in accordance with G.S. 153A-365 [now 160D-1118] due to the public nature of the venue."[63]

In 2019, the Department of Insurance issued a Guidance Paper on Wedding Venues and Farm Buildings,[64] based on an advisory letter from Special Deputy Attorney General Daniel Johnson.[65] That Guidance Paper advised that an event venue on a farm is agritourism and thus exempt from the Building Code, but is still subject to the electrical code. In particular, the advisory letter pointed to G.S. 143-143.2 regarding the applicability of electrical code requirements for farm buildings.

Therefore, a nonresidential farm building is exempt from core building code requirements ("building rules"), but electrical code requirements still apply.

Farm Buildings

Building rules do not apply to certain farm buildings, including (1) nonresidential farm buildings in the county jurisdiction (outside of municipality and ETJ);

62. N.C. Dep't of Ins., Office of State Fire Marshal, Eng'g Div., *Jonczak Appeal of the August 2, 2016 Stop Work Order issued by Surry County* (160816 Jonczak NCDOI Decision—Farm Building), Aug. 16, 2016.

63. *Id.*

64. N.C. Dep't of Ins., Office of State Fire Marshal, Eng'g Div., *Guidance Paper: Wedding Venues and Farm Buildings*, Mar. 5, 2019, https://www.ncosfm.gov/guidance-papers/gs-143-138-wedding-venues-and-farm-buildings/open.

65. Special Deputy Attorney Daniel S. Johnson, Advisory Letter to N.C. Dep't of Ins. (Mar. 5, 2019) (attached to *Guidance Paper, supra* note 64).

(2) greenhouses and therapeutic equine facilities within municipal jurisdiction (including ETJ); (3) primitive camps; and (4) primitive farm buildings.[66] State law provides specific definitions of such farm buildings.

Nonresidential Farm Buildings in County Jurisdiction

Building rules do not apply to a farm building in county jurisdiction. *Farm building* is defined as any nonresidential building used for bona fide farm purposes as defined at G.S. 160D-903(a) (discussed more below).

Hosting events does not negate *farm building* status. A *farm building* shall not lose its status as a farm building because it is used for public or private events, including, but not limited to, weddings, receptions, meetings, demonstrations of farm activities, meals, and other events that are taking place on the farm because of its farm or rural setting."[67]

Particular farm structures and activities have particular provisions. The following are exempt as farm buildings with specified conditions:

- "Any structure used or associated with equine activities . . ." but state law allows an "annual safety inspection by the applicable city or county building inspection department of any grandstand, bleachers, or other spectator-seating structures in the farm building."[68]
- Certified Roadside Farm Markets used to display and sell produce, less than 1,000 square feet, open no more than 180 days per year, and certified by the Department of Agriculture and Consumer Services.[69]
- Unoccupied structures on state land used for forestry or agricultural production and research by the North Carolina Department of Agriculture and Consumer Services or North Carolina State University.[70]
- A building used primarily for storage of agriculture commodities, products, or materials, provided there are at least 60 feet of public ways and yards surrounding the building, and the owner posts a 24 inches x 24 inches red and white reflective placard stating "Ag. Exempt" in 12-inch letters.[71]

---

66. G.S. 143-138.
67. G.S. 143-138(b4)(1a).
68. G.S. 143-138(b4)(1)a.
69. G.S. 143-138(b4)(1)b.
70. G.S. 143-138(b4)(1)c.
71. G.S. 143-138(b4)(1)d.

Greenhouses and Therapeutic Equine Facilities Within Municipal Jurisdiction

Building rules do not apply to greenhouses and therapeutic equine facilities located within municipal jurisdiction for building rules.

A *greenhouse* is defined as: "a structure that has a glass or plastic roof, has one or more glass or plastic walls, has an area over ninety-five percent (95%) of which is used to grow or cultivate plants, is built in accordance with the National Greenhouse Manufacturers Association Structural Design manual, and is not used for retail sales." The statute allows that "[a]dditional provisions addressing distinct life safety hazards shall be approved by the local building-rules jurisdiction."[72]

A *therapeutic equine facility* is defined as "an equine facility . . . operated by an organization exempt from federal income tax under section 501(c)(3) of the Internal Revenue Code that provides therapeutic equine-related activities for persons who are physically, intellectually, or emotionally challenged."[73]

Primitive Camps and Primitive Farm Buildings

A primitive camp or primitive farm building is exempt from building rules, whether it is in county or municipal jurisdiction.

A *primitive camp* is defined to include any structure—not greater than 4,000 square feet and not intended to be occupied for more than twenty-four hours consecutively—"primarily used or associated with outdoor camping activities, including structures used for educational, instructional, or recreational purposes for campers and for management training." These include shelters, cabins, tents, and other structures.[74]

A *primitive farm building* is defined to be "any structure used for activities, instruction, training, or reenactment of traditional or heritage farming practices." These include sheds, barns, outhouses, and other structures.[75]

Definition of *Bona Fide Farm Purposes*

The exemptions depend on the wide-ranging yet detailed definition of *bona fide farm purposes*. Understanding that definition is essential to understanding the scope of the exemptions. The phrase is established and defined by G.S. 160D-903 with cross-reference to G.S. 106-581.1.

The key provisions that determine bona fide farm purposes are listed below.

Broad Definition

"[B]ona fide farm purposes include the production and activities relating or incidental to the production of crops, grains, fruits, vegetables, ornamental and flowering plants, dairy, livestock, poultry, and all other forms of agriculture, as defined in

72. G.S. 143-138(b4)(2).
73. G.S. 143-138(b4)(2a).
74. G.S. 143-138(b4)(4).
75. G.S. 143-138(b4)(5).

G.S. 106-581.1."[76] G.S. 106-581.1, in turn, lists many activities as agriculture, including timber management, aquaculture, agritourism, grain warehousing, and more.

Certain Storage Facilities

"A building or structure that is used solely for storage of cotton, peanuts, or sweet potatoes, or any byproduct of those commodities, is a bona fide farm purpose, including a building or structure on a property that does not have the documentation listed in subdivisions (1) through (4) of this subsection."[77]

Turkey Brooder Facilities

"[A] facility that receives used turkey brooder litter from brooder farms and recycles the used litter by means of a drying process to reduce the moisture content of the litter sufficient to send the recycled litter to a turkey grow-out farm for reuse is a bona fide farm purpose."[78]

Agritourism

Agritourism is part of the definition of *agriculture* at G.S. 106-581.1, so agritourism is a bona fide farm purpose. "A building or structure that is used for agritourism is a bona fide farm purpose if the building or structure is located on a property that (i) is owned by a person who holds a qualifying farm sales tax exemption certificate from the Department of Revenue pursuant to G.S. 105-164.13E(a) or (ii) is enrolled in the present-use value program pursuant to G.S. 105-277.3."[79]

The statutes give additional guidance on determining what activities count as agritourism: It is "any activity carried out on a farm or ranch that allows members of the general public, for recreational, entertainment, or educational purposes, to view or enjoy rural activities, including farming, ranching, historic, cultural, harvest-your-own activities, hunting, fishing, equestrian activities, or natural activities and attractions. A building or structure used for agritourism includes any building or structure used for public or private events, including, but not limited to, weddings, receptions, meetings, demonstrations of farm activities, meals, and other events that are taking place on the farm because of its farm or rural setting."[80]

---

76. G.S. 160D-903.
77. *Id.*
78. *Id.*
79. *Id.*
80. *Id.*

State law outlines specific documentation that is sufficient to establish that a property is being used for bona fide farm purposes (other evidence may also be considered):

> (1) A farm sales tax exemption certificate issued by the Department of Revenue.
> (2) A copy of the property tax listing showing that the property is eligible for participation in the present-use value program pursuant to G.S. 105-277.3.
> (3) A copy of the farm owner's or operator's Schedule F from the owner's or operator's most recent federal income tax return.
> (4) A forest management plan.[81]

Zoning

Beyond the building rules exemption, bona fide farm activities are exempt from county zoning (and municipal zoning in the extraterritorial jurisdiction). "County zoning regulations may not affect property used for bona fide farm purposes."[82] Notably, this is not a free pass for anything and everything to occur on a farm. Zoning still applies to non-farm activities even if those activities occur on a farm. There are two key questions for determining bona fide farm activity: Is the property a farm? And is the activity for a farm purpose? For the first question—is the property a farm?—state law sets forth specific documents that can be produced to provide sufficient evidence that the property is a farm (as listed above: sales tax exemption, present-use value program, Schedule F, or forest management plan).

The second question can be more difficult: Is the activity for a farm purpose? Some activities are clearly agricultural, some are clearly not, and many fall somewhere in between. The definition of *bona fide farm purposes*, discussed above, is key. As noted, state law incorporates the broad definition of *agriculture* from G.S. 106-581.1. This includes production and harvesting of crops, planting and production of timber, raising and management of livestock, and aquaculture. It also includes construction and maintenance of land and buildings incident to the farming operation, processing and packing items produced on the farm, marketing and selling agricultural products, certain grain warehouse operations, and agritourism.

Additionally, G.S. 160D-903 offers a broad definition of *agritourism*: "any activity carried out on a farm or ranch that allows members of the general public, for recreational, entertainment, or educational purposes, to view or enjoy rural activities, including farming, ranching, historic, cultural, harvest-your-own activities, hunting, fishing, equestrian activities, or natural activities and attractions." These broad definitions mean that questions about the applicability of the bona fide farm exemption may arise in an array of scenarios: wedding venues, shooting ranges, fall festivals, and more.

---

81. *Id.*
82. *Id.*

If an activity qualifies as a bona fide farm activity, it is exempt from county zoning rules and municipal zoning rules within municipal extraterritorial jurisdiction.

Special Provisions for Residential Buildings and Uses on Farm Property

The Building Code exemption applies only to nonresidential buildings, so residential buildings remain subject to Building Code requirements. Beyond Building Code matters, there are other special provisions for housing on farms.

Migrant Housing

Migrant housing is exempt from Fire Code requirements for automatic sprinkler systems if the housing has one floor and meets certain state and federal requirements for migrant housing.[83]

Housing for the Farm Owner or Operator

G.S. 160D-903(a) includes a specific provision related to housing for the owner or operator of the farm. "Activities incident to the farm include existing or new residences constructed to the applicable residential building code situated on the farm occupied by the owner, lessee, or operator of the farm and other buildings or structures sheltering or supporting the farm use and operation." This provision includes key criteria for the housing to be "incident to the farm" and thus exempt from zoning. To qualify for exemption, the housing must be

- a residence constructed to the applicable residential building code;
- situated on the farm; *and*
- occupied by the owner, lessee, or operator of the farm.

If a residence meets these criteria, it is exempt from zoning, but not from everything. The Building Code still applies, the land subdivision ordinance may apply, and other development regulations may also apply. Notably, a change in occupancy may mean that the home is no longer exempt from zoning. Housing unrelated to the farm does not get special exemption from zoning. At the time of construction and building permits, it is prudent for local governments to communicate to the owner the risk of future enforcement if the home is occupied by someone other than the owner, lessee, or operator of the farm.

---

83. G.S. 143-138(b13).

Chapter 7
Building Code Inspections

Overview

Building code inspections raise important practical issues and complex legal questions. This chapter attempts to illuminate the necessary tasks and duties of inspections as well as highlight the legal limitations and obligations.

Inspections occur in many different contexts—inspections related to a validly permitted construction project, periodic inspections of unsafe situations, inspections in response to complaints or evidence, and more. This chapter is focused on inspections related to permitted construction under the State Building Code. Later chapters outline the authority, procedures, and limits for inspections related to unsafe structures, minimum housing codes, and more. (See Appendix C for sample permitting and inspections flowcharts.)

Inspection Duties

Throughout the building process, the permit holder requests, and the inspector must perform, the necessary inspections. For inspections required by the North Carolina Residential Code, an inspector may not require an affidavit of code compliance in lieu of conducting the inspection.[1]

After inspection, the inspector must inform the permit holder of any instances in which the work fails to meet the requirements of the North Carolina State Building Code.[2] Additionally, an inspector has a duty to notify an owner or occupant if the inspector finds

- defects in the building,
- construction that does not comply with applicable state and local laws,
- conditions that make a building dangerous or pose fire hazards, or
- any other failures to comply with the law.[3]

---

1. Chapter 160D, Section 1104(c) of the North Carolina General Statutes (hereinafter G.S.).
2. G.S. 160D-1104(c).
3. G.S. 160D-1118.

The owner or occupant then has an obligation to remedy the defects, hazardous conditions, or violations of the law. (See Appendix E for sample stop work order documents.)

> **Fourth Amendment Reminder**
>
> For a detailed discussion of Fourth Amendment limits on inspections, see Chapter 4. In brief, code officials must honor constitutional privacy protections, obtain consent or a warrant when needed, and rely only on observations made lawfully.

Inspection of Works in Progress

As work progresses under a building permit, local inspectors "shall make as many inspections thereof as may be necessary to satisfy them that the work is being done according to the provisions of any applicable State and local laws and of the terms of the permit."[4]

In order to perform such inspections, an inspector may enter any premises within the department's jurisdiction during reasonable hours and upon presenting proper credentials for inspection or other enforcement action. If a project is exempt from the requirement for a general contractor under Chapter 87, Section 1(b)(2) of the North Carolina General Statutes (hereinafter G.S.), the owner must be present for any inspection unless the plans were drawn and sealed by a North Carolina licensed architect.[5]

G.S. 160D-403 notes that even for inspections of works in progress, inspectors must ensure that "appropriate consent has been given for inspection of areas not open to the public or an appropriate inspection warrant has been secured." While an application form may request consent to inspect areas of work, an application may not be used to require broad consent to inspections. "Administrative staff are prohibited from requiring unrestricted written consent from a permit applicant to enter any premises or areas not open to the public as a condition to accepting an application for, or the issuance of, development approvals."[6] Even with prior written consent, if the property owner withdraws or denies consent when the inspector arrives, the inspector must discontinue the inspection. Consent remains revocable, and the prior written consent is trumped by the current refusal to consent.

4. G.S. 160D-1113.
5. *Id.*
6. G.S. 160D-1104(e).

The Administrative Code and Policies calls for the following inspections. Each is described in more detail in Section 107.1 of the code.

1. Footing
2. Under slab, as appropriate
3. Foundation
4. Building framing
5. Rough-in
6. Insulation
7. Fire protection
8. Final

For inspections under the Residential Code, the inspector must conduct all inspections requested by the permit holder for the scheduled inspection.[7]

When work is ready for inspection, the permit holder (or agent) must notify the code official and "provide access to and means for inspection of the work."[8] Work may not be done beyond the inspection point without approval. Upon the request for inspection, the code official must make the requested inspection and inform the permit holder "of instances in which the work inspected is incomplete or otherwise fails to meet the requirements of the North Carolina Residential Code or the North Carolina State Building Code."[9] The inspector must identify code violations and, if requested, must identify the specific code sections violated.[10]

Noncompliant work must be corrected and may not be covered until authorized by the inspector.[11] On reinspection, if the inspector identifies additional violations on items already approved by the inspections department, such violations shall not delay a temporary certificate of occupancy, and the inspections department may not charge a fee for reinspection on such violations.[12]

If inspections are not performed within two business days, the requestor may seek inspection from the state pool of inspectors discussed below.

Periodic Inspections

In addition to inspections of works in progress, the inspections department is authorized to make periodic inspections "for unsafe, unsanitary, or otherwise hazardous and unlawful conditions in buildings or structures within its planning and development regulation jurisdiction."[13] Such inspections must be conducted

---

7. G.S. 160D-1104(d).

8. Section 107.2 of the 2018 North Carolina Administrative Code and Policies (hereinafter N.C.A.C.P.) (2024 N.C.A.C.P. 107.3).

9. G.S. 160D-1104(d); 2018 N.C.A.C.P. 107.3 (2024 N.C.A.C.P. 107.3).

10. 2018 N.C.A.C.P. 107.3 (2024 N.C.A.C.P. 107.3).

11. *Id.*

12. G.S. 160D-1104(d).

13. G.S. 160D-1117.

during reasonable hours and upon presentation of proper credentials. As always, these inspections may be limited by constitutional protections against unreasonable searches. For areas not open to the public, the inspector must have proper consent or an inspection warrant. Additionally, state law limits periodic inspections of dwellings.

The authority for and processes of inspections for Unsafe Structures (Chapter 10), Commercial Maintenance Code (Chapter 11), and Minimum Housing and Abandoned Structures (Chapter 12) are discussed in those chapters.

Fire Code Periodic Inspections

Fire code officials must make certain periodic inspections. The North Carolina Fire Code sets the fire inspection intervals based on occupancy use and hazard.

State statutes also specify certain fire code inspections. The fire code official must inspect public school buildings for removal of hazards at least two times during the calendar year (at least 120 days apart).[14]

The fire code official must inspect new and existing lodging establishments at least annually for installation and maintenance of carbon monoxide alarms and detectors.[15]

Limits on Residential Inspections

In general, for buildings or structures built under the Residential Code, a local government may not require regular, routine inspections beyond what is required by the Building Code without approval from the Residential Code Council.[16] There are exceptions. A local government may "require inspections upon unforeseen or unique circumstances that require immediate action."[17] Additionally, the inspection department may only make periodic inspections of residential buildings or structures "when there is reasonable cause to believe that unsafe, unsanitary, or otherwise hazardous or unlawful conditions may exist," as defined in state law.[18]

The limits and exceptions for periodic inspections of residential property are discussed further in Chapter 12.

Limits on Sheathing Inspections

The Building Code must not require routine exterior sheathing inspections in regions where the ultimate wind speed is less than 140 miles per hour.[19] Additionally, a local government may not adopt a local ordinance or policy requiring such inspections in those regions.[20]

---

14. G.S. 115C-525(b); 2024 N.C.A.C.P. 204.3.
15. G.S. 143-138(b2); 2024 N.C.A.C.P. 204.3.
16. G.S. 160D-1104(d).
17. *Id.*
18. G.S. 160D-1207.
19. G.S. 143-138(b23).
20. G.S. 160D-1104(d).

Inspection Personnel

Generally, inspections are performed by personnel from the local inspections department. State law, however, allows for other inspection arrangements under certain circumstances.

Third-Party Inspections

State law allows for a local government to contract with an individual or employer for inspections to be performed by an individual who is not a local government employee but who holds an applicable certificate under G.S. 160D-1103.[21]

State Pool of Inspectors

If a local inspections department fails to provide timely inspections, the state may assign a code official from the marketplace pool to perform the necessary inspections.[22] When that happens, the local government must "promptly return to the permit holder the fee collected by the local government for such inspection."[23]

The following process is set forth in state law at G.S. 143-139.4:

- The local inspection department informs the permit holder that an inspection has not been, or will not be, conducted within two business days after the initial request.
- The permit holder submits a request (on a form provided by the State Fire Marshal) for the State Fire Marshal to assign personnel to conduct the inspection.
- The local inspection department maintains a record of each inspection request, including the date and time, type of inspection requested, address of the property, person to whom the request is directed, and name of requestor (inspection requests received after 12:00 noon are deemed to be received the next business day).
- The State Fire Marshal verifies the necessary information, including the permit holder's desire for the inspection to be completed, confirmation that the local inspection department received the request and that the inspection has not been completed, including the reason for the delay, and any other relevant information.
- The State Fire Marshal decides whether to assign personnel. If personnel is assigned, the State Fire Marshal notifies the local inspection department. The State Fire Marshal shall charge a fee to the permit holder (due within thirty days after completion of the requested inspection).

---

21. G.S. 160D-1105.
22. G.S. 143-139(b)(2).
23. G.S. 160D-402(d).

- The local inspection department provides the State Fire Marshal with information about the relevant outstanding permits and prior inspections, as well as information about other properties where the permit holder has outstanding permits and inspections.
- Personnel assigned by the State Fire Marshal begin conducting inspections within two business days after assignment and provide a report to the State Fire Marshal.
- Within one business day of receiving the report, the State Fire Marshal provides the report to the local inspection department, the permit holder, and the requestor (if different from the permit holder).

When inspections are performed by a marketplace pool inspector, any claim of negligence is a claim against the state, and the local inspection department and inspectors are released from liability.[24]

Component or Element Inspections by Design Professionals

An inspections department must accept and approve a design or proposal for a "component" or "element" from a licensed architect or engineer, provided the following apply:[25]

- The submission is under the valid seal of the architect or engineer, if required.
- Field inspection of the component or element is performed by a licensed architect or engineer, or a person under the direct supervision of a licensed architect or engineer.
- The licensed architect or engineer who oversaw the inspection provides a signed written Design Professional Inspection Form (in Appendix G)[26] to certify the component or element. The inspections department must promptly acknowledge receipt of the form.

A "component" is "[a]ny assembly, subassembly, or combination of elements designed to be combined with other components to form part of a building or structure. Examples of a component include an excavated footing trench containing no concrete, a foundation, and a prepared underslab with slab related materials without concrete. The term does not include a system." An "element" is "[a] combination of products designed to be combined with other elements to form all or part of a building component. The term does not include a system."[27]

---

24. G.S. 143-139.4.
25. G.S. 160D-1106; 2018 N.C.A.C.P. 107.6 (2024 N.C.A.C.P. 107.6).
26. 2018 N.C.A.C.P. App. G (Design Professional Inspection Form) (2024 N.C.A.C.P. App. G), https://codes.iccsafe.org/content/NCAPC2018P2/appendix-g-design-professional-inspection-form.
27. G.S. 160D-1106(d).

Upon acceptance and approval, the local government is discharged from any liability or responsibility related to the component or element.

The 2024 N.C. Administrative Code and Policies provides guidance, stating that a code official may authorize a licensed or registered design professional to inspect the following types of structural work:[28]

1. The excavation of soil and/or forming of footings with the associated placement of reinforcing steel prior to pouring concrete; and
2. The forming of floors, columns, beams and other structural members, including the placement of reinforcing steel prior to pouring concrete.

For such inspection, the permit holder continues to schedule inspections with the inspections department. The registered design professional must provide weekly reports with their professional seal indicating if the construction does or does not comply with approved permit documents. Any change from the permit documents must be approved by the code official, and the permit holder must inform the official if the permit holder ends the relationship with the registered design professional.

Remote Inspections

The State Fire Marshal, through the Division of Engineering, is tasked to "[d]evelop eligibility criteria for and procedures to conduct certain inspections required by the North Carolina State Building Code as remote inspections." Remote inspection includes real-time audio and video communication with a permit holder or review of an electronic video submitted by the permit holder.[29]

Under state law a local inspection department must implement remote inspection procedures in accordance with state criteria and procedures. The local department must, at the time of permit issuance, specify the extent to which a project is eligible for remote inspection and allow permit holders to elect remote inspection.[30]

Certificates

In state caselaw and common practice the terms "certificate of compliance" and "certificate of occupancy" are sometimes used interchangeably.[31] Indeed, the court of appeals seemed to use them interchangeably in *First American Federal Savings*

28. 2024 N.C.A.C.P. 107.4.
29. G.S. 143-139(b)(3).
30. G.S. 160D-1104.1.
31. *See* First Am. Fed. Sav. & Loan Ass'n v. Royall, 77 N.C. App. 131, 334 S.E.2d 792 (1985); Boor v. Spectrum Homes, 196 N.C. App. 699 (2009).

& Loan Association v. Royall. That said, there are important distinctions between these terms.

No building or portion of a building may be occupied without proper certificates. Occupancy of a building—or allowing occupancy of a building—prior to issuance of a certificate of compliance or temporary certificate of occupancy is a Class 1 misdemeanor.[32]

Trade-Specific Certificate of Compliance

A certificate of compliance is a trade-specific approval by the "appropriate inspector" that the work for a particular trade complies with applicable requirements. "At the conclusion of all work done under a building permit, the appropriate inspector shall make a final inspection, and, if the completed work complies with all applicable State and local laws and with the terms of the permit, the inspector shall issue a certificate of compliance."[33]

The certificate of compliance certifies that the structure or system is complete. For some trades, the certificate of compliance serves as permission to connect to a utility system.[34]

Certificate of Occupancy or General Certificate of Compliance

Beyond the trade-specific certificate of compliance, a local government may make an overall certification at the conclusion of a development. This may be a certificate of compliance or occupancy. "A local government may, upon completion of work or activity undertaken pursuant to a development approval, make final inspections and issue a certificate of compliance or occupancy if staff finds that the completed work complies with all applicable State and local laws and with the terms of the approval."[35]

Temporary Certificate of Occupancy

"A [building] permit holder may request and be issued a temporary certificate of occupancy if the conditions and requirements of the North Carolina State Building Code are met."[36] A temporary certificate of occupancy may be issued for a stated period of time and may be for the whole building or a specified portion of the building.

32. G.S. 160D, §§ 403, 1116.
33. G.S. 160D-1116.
34. 2018 N.C.A.C.P. 204.9.1 (2024 N.C.A.C.P. 204.9.2).
35. G.S. 160D-403(g).
36. G.S. 160D-1116(b).

Limits on Withholding Permits and Certificates

As outlined at G.S. 160D-1116 and 160D-403, a local government may withhold a certificate of compliance or certificate of occupancy if the completed work fails to comply with all applicable state and local laws and with the terms of the permit.[37]

Building permits and certificates of occupancy may not be withheld to compel compliance on another property or parcel except for public safety issues.[38] Additionally, state law specifies that building permits and certificates of occupancy may not be withheld to compel compliance with the following:

> (1) Landscaping around dwellings subject to the North Carolina Residential Code within individual lots.
> (2) Landscaping within common areas within a subdivision development.
> (3) Street lighting fixtures within common areas of a subdivision development.[39]

If a developer has not completed these site improvements, they must submit to the local government "a signed affidavit detailing the reasons why the required site improvements are not complete, the expected date of completion and compliance, and a statement promising to complete the required site improvements."[40]

A local government may not withhold a building permit where a project does not propose to increase the daily flow or wastewater strength of the existing system. The property owner must submit an on-site wastewater existing system inspection exemption affidavit and affirm that any modifications will meet applicable wastewater system setback requirements as required at G.S. 130A-335.[41]

---

37. *See also* First Am. Fed. Sav. & Loan Ass'n v. Royall, 77 N.C. App. 131, 334 S.E.2d 792 (1985).

38. G.S. 160D-1110.

39. G.S. 160D-1110(h).

40. *Id.*

41. G.S. 160D-1110(h1).

Chapter 8

Building Code Enforcement

Overview

Building code violations may arise in many different ways, and the North Carolina General Statutes (hereinafter G.S.) outline many paths for enforcement. These include stop-work orders, notices of violation, withholding or revoking permits, criminal enforcement, and court action. This section focuses on building code enforcement, but a violation may also trigger zoning, subdivision, minimum housing, or nuisance code violations, so other enforcement actions may be available.[1] (See Appendix E for sample enforcement notices.)

Enforcement Authority

The local code official or the State Fire Marshal may "institute any appropriate action or proceeding to: (i) prevent the unlawful maintenance, erection, construction, or reconstruction or alteration of purpose, or overcrowding, (ii) restrain, correct, or abate the violation, or (iii) prevent the occupancy or use of the building, structure, or land until the violation is corrected."[2]

The State Fire Marshal, through the Division of Engineering, has general authority to supervise, administer, and enforce the Building Code. To that end, the Division of Engineering is tasked with cooperating with local inspection departments.[3]

A local government may enforce new building code requirements, even if existing structures are allowed to continue as lawful nonconformities. In *State v. Martin*, the city enforced requirements against the owner of newly installed manufactured homes. The owner claimed that other properties with trailers were not being enforced against, but "[i]t is no defense to a criminal charge nor to one of this type that others have not been penalized or the law enforced as to them."[4]

---

1. Chapter 160A, Section 175 and Chapter 153A, Section 123 of the North Carolina General Statutes (hereinafter G.S.) provide a range of enforcement options for local ordinances. Other sections authorize specific enforcement.
2. G.S. 143-139(b1).
3. G.S. 143-139(b).
4. 7 N.C. App. 18, 21, 171 S.E.2d 115, 117 (1969).

Duty to Inspect

North Carolina courts have ruled that the local inspector is obligated to perform an investigation when there is a valid complaint of violation (investigation is a ministerial duty). After the investigation, there is some room for discretion in bringing an enforcement action.[5]

Notice of Violation

When local government staff determines that work or activity is in violation of state or local law, staff may issue a notice of violation. The notices must be written and delivered to the holder of the applicable development approval and property owner by personal delivery, email, or first-class mail. The notice may also be sent to the occupant (if different from owner and permit holder) and posted on the site. The staff person issuing the notice must certify to the local government that the notice was provided.[6]

Stop Work Order

If work "is undertaken in substantial violation of any State or local law, or in a manner that endangers life or property, staff may order the specific part of the work or activity that is in violation or presents such a hazard to be immediately stopped."[7] A stop work order must be in writing, state the specific work to be stopped and the reasons for stopping, and outline actions necessary to resume work. The order must be directed at the person doing the work, and a copy may be delivered to the owner of the property by personal delivery, email, or first-class mail. The staff person issuing the notice must also certify to the local government that the notice was provided.

---

5. Midgette v. Pate, 94 N.C. App. 498, 380 S.E.2d 572 (1989) ("Though the zoning administrator may exercise discretion in assessing the alleged violations, this does not lessen the duty to investigate the charges of a plaintiff who has legal right to have the duty enforced." 94 N.C. App. at 503–04, 380 S.E.2d at 576).

6. G.S. 160D-404(a).

7. G.S. 160D-404(b).

Permit Revocation

The inspections department shall revoke a building permit for any of the following reasons:

- significant deviations from the approved application, plans, or specifications;
- refusal or failure to comply with the applicable state or local laws; or
- providing false statements or misrepresentations made in securing the permit.[8]

Additionally the inspections department may revoke a permit that was mistakenly issued in violation of applicable state or local law.[9] In exercising this discretion, the administrator must weigh factors such as the following to balance the value of enforcement against the detriment to the individual who relied on the mistakenly issued permit.

- Was it a clear error? Revoking a clear error is more defensible than revoking a permit issued based on a judgment call or close interpretation.
- How long has the owner relied on the permit? The longer the mistake, the less defensible the revocation.
- How much has the owner relied on the permit? The more money and effort the owner has expended on the mistakenly issued permit, the less defensible a revocation will be.

To revoke a permit, the appropriate inspector must "notify the permit holder in writing stating the reason for the revocation."[10] A revoked permit does not establish vested rights because vested rights require a valid governmental permit.[11]

Withhold Electrical Connection

For newly erected buildings, state law requires that the electrical inspector or inspection department inspect and certify the electrical wiring of the building before an electric utility can turn on the electrical current for the new building.[12]

---

8. G.S. 160D-1115.

9. *Id.*; E. Outdoor, Inc. v. Bd. of Adjustment of Johnston Cnty., 150 N.C. App. 516, 564 S.E.2d 78 (2002), *aff'd*, 357 N.C. 501, 586 S.E.2d 90 (2003).

10. G.S. 160D-1115.

11. Mecklenburg Cnty. v. Westbery, 32 N.C. App. 630, 233 S.E.2d 658 (1977).

12. G.S. 143-143.2.

Withhold Certificates

Certificates of compliance and certificates of occupancy were discussed more fully in the previous chapter with regard to the inspection process. But certificates are also a topic for enforcement. The whole point of a certificate, either compliance or occupancy, is confirmation that a building meets applicable standards. If the project does not meet standards, the certificate is withheld.

Criminal Enforcement

Criminal enforcement is available for building code violations. Table 8.1 outlines the authority, violations, and penalties as authorized in state law.

Civil Penalties

A civil penalty is a monetary penalty for a violation of a local ordinance. Civil penalties are generally authorized for enforcing local ordinances. Civil penalties are not explicitly authorized for building code enforcement generally, but they are explicitly authorized for fire code violations as outlined at G.S. 143-139(b1). If the penalty is not paid within a reasonable time, the jurisdiction may institute a civil action.

The underlying purpose of civil penalties is to secure compliance, cover administrative costs for enforcement, and seek equity with those who are complying with applicable rules. Civil penalties are not intended for revenue generation. Civil penalties commonly are used in conjunction with a notice of violation when a violator has not complied. The local ordinance may establish that each day's continuing violation is a separate and distinct offense, so civil penalties may accrue over time, with another charge each day of noncompliance.[13]

While the statutes do not set a maximum or minimum amount for civil penalties, a civil penalty likely should not exceed the maximum for criminal penalties. With regard to misdemeanor violations of local ordinances, G.S. 14-4 sets a presumption that fines are $50 or less but allows fines up to $500 if expressly stated in the ordinance. Using the limits on criminal fines as a gauge, civil penalties should not exceed $500 per day.

Given the accruing nature, amounts owed for civil penalties may be substantial. Importantly, the maximum amount of the penalty may not exceed the amount reasonably related to the harm of the violation and the cost to the local government to secure compliance. Courts may cap the amount to be recovered accordingly.

While civil penalties may be assessed from the time the violation began, the local government should give notice to the violator that civil penalties are accruing.

---

13. G.S. 160A-175(g); 153A-123(g).

Table 8.1. Statutory Violations and Penalties

Statute	Violation	Penalty
G.S. 14-68. Failure of owner of property to comply with orders of public authorities.	"If the owner or occupant of any building or premises shall fail to comply with the duly authorized orders of the chief of the fire department, or of the State Fire Marshal, or of any municipal or county inspector of buildings or of particular features, facilities, or installations of buildings,"	"he shall be guilty of a Class 3 misdemeanor, and punished only by a fine of not less than ten ($10.00) nor more than fifty dollars ($50.00) for each day's neglect, failure, or refusal to obey such orders."
G.S. 160D-1110. Building permits.	"Violation of this section [setting requirements and limitations on building permits]"	"is a Class 1 misdemeanor."
G.S. 160D-404(b). Enforcement.	"Violation of a stop work order . . ."	". . . shall constitute a Class 1 misdemeanor."
G.S. 143-138(h). North Carolina State Building Code.	"Any person who shall be adjudged to have violated this Article or the North Carolina State Building Code, except for violations of occupancy limits established by either,"	"shall be guilty of a Class 3 misdemeanor and shall upon conviction only be liable to a fine, not to exceed fifty dollars ($50.00), for each offense. Each 30 days that such violation continues shall constitute a separate and distinct offense."
G.S. 143-138(h). North Carolina State Building Code.	"Violation of occupancy limits established pursuant to the North Carolina State Building Code . . ."	"shall be a Class 3 misdemeanor."
G.S. 160D-1116. Certificates of compliance; temporary certificates of occupancy.	"Any person who owns, leases, or controls a building and occupies or allows the occupancy of the building or a part of the building before a certificate of compliance or temporary certificate of occupancy has been issued pursuant to subsection (a) or (b) of this . . .	". . . section is guilty of a Class 1 misdemeanor."

Generally, civil penalties begin with the notice of violation or after allowing a specified time for compliance.

A civil penalty is treated as a debt owed to the local government. While the civil penalty is not an automatic lien against the property, the local government may bring a civil action in court to recover the penalty as a debt.[14]

14. G.S. 160A-175(c); 153A-123(c).

Court Action

A local government may take a violator to court to secure compliance.

Specific to building code enforcement, if a violation is listed as a misdemeanor, the local government may "initiate any appropriate action or proceedings to prevent, restrain, correct, or abate the violation or to prevent the occupancy of the building or structure involved."[15]

For development regulations, under G.S. 160D-404(c)(1), a local government "may institute any appropriate action or proceedings to prevent the unlawful erection, construction, reconstruction, alteration, repair, conversion, maintenance, use, or development; to restrain, correct or abate the violation; to prevent occupancy of the building, structure, or land; or to prevent any illegal act, conduct, business, or use in or about the premises."

Local government general enforcement authority may also apply. G.S. 160A-175 and G.S. 153A-123 authorize a local government to bring a civil action against a violator to address violations of land development regulations. In such actions, the court may issue remedial orders, such as "mandatory or prohibitory injunction and order of abatement commanding the defendant to correct the unlawful condition upon or cease the unlawful use of the property." With regard to judicial orders of abatement, if the violator fails to comply, they may be cited for contempt of court, the local government may execute the court's order of abatement, and the local government may have a lien on the property for the costs of abatement.

15. G.S. 160D-1125.

Chapter 9

Building Code Interpretations and Appeals

Overview

Given the breadth and depth of the technical standards across the Building Code, there are many questions, interpretations, and potential disputes. This chapter outlines the procedures for interpretation and appeal.

State law calls for interpretation to center on public health and safety: "All regulations contained in the North Carolina State Building Code shall have a reasonable and substantial connection with the public health and safety, and their provisions shall be construed reasonably to those ends."[1]

Note that this chapter is specific to interpretations of the State Building Code and appeals of those decisions. Appeals of housing code decisions, zoning enforcement, and other local ordinances are discussed separately in Part 3.

Internal Review

Each local inspection department must have a process for informal internal review of decisions by the department's inspectors. The process must include (1) initial review by the supervisor of the inspector, (2) notice on each permit of the availability of internal review and supervisor contact information, and (3) procedures for internal review when requested.[2]

Technical Interpretation

Upon request, the Engineering Division provides informal and formal interpretations on technical topics. Informal interpretations may be accepted by the local

1. Chapter 143, Section 138(c) of the North Carolina General Statutes (hereinafter G.S.).
2. G.S. 160D-1104.

code official or the party requesting the interpretation, and either party may request a formal interpretation.[3]

Any person may request a formal technical interpretation of the North Carolina State Building Code.[4] Such requests must be in writing, be specific, and reference the technical code section(s) in question. The Chief Code Consultant is tasked with issuing formal interpretations. Interpretations must be issued in writing within a reasonable time and set forth the facts found, the decision reached, and the reasons for the decision. Formal interpretations include Appendix E[5] as a cover document. If a formal interpretation is general in nature, it may be posted to the Office of State Fire Marshal website.

Formal interpretations are binding on all parties unless appealed. They may be appealed to the Building Code Council, the Residential Code Council, or superior court as provided in Chapter 143, Section 141 of the North Carolina General Statutes (hereinafter G.S.).

If an interpretation of a code provision from the Office of State Fire Marshal changes after a building permit is issued, "the permit applicant may choose which version of the interpretation will apply to the permit, unless such a choice would cause harm to life or property."[6]

While agency interpretations can guide a court's review, they do not override clear statutory law: "An administrative interpretation of a statute, acquiesced in over a long period of time, is properly considered in the construction of the statute by the courts. But an administrative interpretation can never be considered when in direct conflict with the intent and purpose of the act, or when in conflict with the interpretation of the courts."[7]

Appeal to the Office of State Fire Marshal

An appeal of an order, decision, or determination by a member of an inspection department relating to the Building Code is taken to the State Fire Marshal or designee.[8] An individual seeking an appeal must file written notice to the chief engineer and the relevant inspection department within ten days after the order, decision, or determination is issued.

3. Section 203.2.1 of the 2018 North Carolina Administrative Code and Policies (hereinafter N.C.A.C.P.) (2024 N.C.A.C.P. 203.2.1).

4. G.S. 143-140; 2018 N.C.A.C.P. 203.2.1.2 (2024 N.C.A.C.P. 203.2.1.2).

5. N.C. Office of State Fire Marshal, *Appendix E: Formal Interpretation and Appeals*, https://www.ncosfm.gov/appeals-and-formal-interpretations/open.

6. G.S. 143-140.

7. Petty v. Owen, 140 N.C. App. 494, 500, 537 S.E.2d 216, 220 (2000) (citations and quotations omitted).

8. G.S. 160D-1127.

The policies of the Administrative Code and Policies state that "[t]he appeal shall contain the type and size of the building in question, the location of the building and shall reference the technical code sections in question." The decision by the chief engineer shall be written and set forth the facts found. For a decision concerning alternate material, design, or methods under Section 105.3, the chief engineer must provide the decision within ten business days in accordance with G.S. 143-140.1.[9]

Further appeal may be taken to the Building Code Council, Residential Code Council, or to court as provided by law.[10] Procedures are in part outlined in Chapter 1 of Title 11 of the North Carolina Administrative Code.

Appeals to Applicable Council

An individual may appeal a decision of the Office of State Fire Marshal to the Building Code Council or Residential Code Council.[11] Within thirty days of the decision being appealed, the appellant must give written notice of appeal to the responsible code council through the Division of Engineering. Notice must also be provided simultaneously to the enforcement agency whose decision is being appealed.

There is no specific form required for complaints, but a complaint must be in writing, identify the parties, and provide the facts that form the basis of the complaint.[12] The 2024 N.C. Administrative Code and Policies provides that for appeals before the Building Code Council or Residential Code Council, applicants must provide Appendix E as supporting information. Supporting information must reasonably apprise the council of the matter and may be submitted in writing or made on the record during the hearing.[13]

State law empowers the applicable code council to interpret the provisions, and state courts have indicated that a code council's interpretation should be given due consideration.[14]

Hearing and Decision

The chair of the responsible council sets a reasonable time and place for the hearing (not later than the next meeting of the council) and must give reasonable notice to the parties.[15] The council must hold a hearing, and hearings before the Building

---

9. 2018 N.C.A.C.P. 203.2.2 (2024 N.C.A.C.P. 203.2.2).

10. G.S. 160D-1127.

11. G.S. 143-141(a); 160D-1127. As of this writing, the statutes address the Residential Code Council, but the administrative code does not. This discussion presumes that the prior rules for the Building Code Council will now apply to the Residential Code Council as well.

12. 2018 N.C.A.C.P. 103.1 (2024 N.C.A.C.P. 103.2.1).

13. 2024 N.C.A.C.P. 103.2.2.

14. Appeal of Medical Center, 91 N.C. App. 107, 370 S.E.2d 597 (1988).

15. G.S. 143-141(a).

Code Council or Residential Code Council are governed by the rules for administrative hearings outlined in Article 3A of G.S. 150B.[16] The council may designate a member to preside or, if there is no designation, then the chair or vice chair presides. The presiding officer rules on motions and other requests, except for motions that would decide the case, which shall be determined by a majority of the council.[17] The chair has discretion to grant requests for continuance of a hearing for good cause.[18] After the conclusion of the hearing and within a reasonable time, the council must issue a written decision with findings of fact and conclusions.[19]

Council Interpretations

In hearing appeals, the applicable code council must give interpretations pertinent to the appeal. If the council finds the enforcement agency's interpretation was wrong, the council must remand the case to the agency with instructions to take action as directed.[20]

Variation or Modification

On appeal, the Building Code Council and Residential Code Council may grant variations to the Building Code in certain circumstances. Where the council finds that the proposed materials or methods of construction are as good as those required by the code, the council "shall remand the case to the enforcement agency with instructions to permit the use of such materials or methods of construction."[21] Additionally, the council shall initiate procedures to amend the applicable code to permit such materials or methods.

The Administrative Code and Policies provides additional guidance for such variations.[22] The applicable council may grant modifications in individual cases where "there are practical difficulties involved in carrying out the provisions of the technical codes." The council must find on appeal that

> (1) special individual reasons, conditions, and/or circumstances exist that make the strict letter of the technical codes impractical,
>
> (2) the modification is in compliance with the intent and purpose of the technical codes, and
>
> (3) the modification does not lessen health, accessibility, life, fire-safety or structural requirements.

16. 2018 N.C.A.C.P. 103.2 (2024 N.C.A.C.P. 103.3).
17. 2018 N.C.A.C.P. 103.3 (2024 N.C.A.C.P. 103.4).
18. 2018 N.C.A.C.P. 103.4 (2024 N.C.A.C.P. 103.5).
19. G.S. 143-141(a).
20. G.S. 143-141(b).
21. G.S. 143-141(c).
22. 2018 N.C.A.C.P. 103.5 (2024 N.C.A.C.P. 103.6).

Posting of Council Decisions

The Office of State Fire Marshal must post to the website of the applicable code council "all appeal decisions, interpretations, and variations of the Code issued by the responsible Code Council within 10 business days of issuance."[23]

Code officials may find it beneficial to review code council decisions to inform their current practice. Similarly, when faced with an appeal, reviewing code council decisions on similar issues may provide helpful guidance.

Appeal to Court

A person may appeal a decision of the Building Code Council or Residential Code Council to court.[24] Some decisions by the Office of State Fire Marshal may also be appealed to court. Such appeals go to superior court, either in Wake County or in the county in which the building is located. "When any question arises as to any provision of the Code, judicial notice shall be taken of that provision of the Code."[25]

Appeal of Building Code Stop Work Order

An owner or builder may appeal a stop work order for an alleged violation of the North Carolina State Building Code to the State Fire Marshal or designee.[26] Notice of the appeal must be submitted in writing within five days after the order was issued to the Office of State Fire Marshal, with a copy to the local inspector. The State Fire Marshal or designee must promptly conduct an investigation. The appellant and inspector are permitted to submit evidence, and the Office of State Fire Marshal or designee must provide a written decision. The decision may be further appealed to the Building Code Council, Residential Code Council, or superior court.

Stop work orders for other development regulations (not under the North Carolina State Building Code) are appealed to the local board of adjustment pursuant to G.S. 160D-405.

---

23. G.S. 143-141(c1).
24. G.S. 143-141(d).
25. G.S. 143-138(l).
26. G.S. 160D-1114.

Part 3

Existing Structures and Unsafe Situations

Building and property safety is not merely about construction of new buildings. It is equally about existing structures and related unsafe situations. While property owners have rights to enjoy their property, they cannot use their property in a way that creates a nuisance for neighbors or a detriment to the public.[1]

The chapters in Part 3 explore the legal authority and procedures for addressing unsafe situations on private property. This list highlights the key statutory authority referenced in those chapters. (Sample documents related to property maintenance and code compliance are provided in Appendix F.)

- **Chapter 10:** Unsafe Structures (G.S. 160D-1118 to -1125—authority to declare structures unsafe, post notice closing the building, and require corrective action)
- **Chapter 11:** Commercial Maintenance Code (G.S. 160D-1129—authority to establish and enforce standards for commercial building maintenance)
- **Chapter 12:** Minimum Housing and Abandoned Structures (G.S. 160D, Art. 12—authority to establish and enforce standards for residential building maintenance and abandoned structure maintenance)
- **Chapter 13:** Nuisance Code and Abatement (G.S. 160A, §§ 174, 193; 153A §§ 121, 140—authority to adopt and enforce a nuisance code to address unsafe situations on property, for example, overgrown lots, solid waste, or imminent danger to the public)

1. Appeal of Parker, 214 N.C. 51, 197 S.E. 706, 710 (1938) ("The provisions of the Constitution are not intended to so protect the individual in the use of his property as to enable him to use it to the detriment of the public.").

- **Chapter 14:** Zoning Enforcement for Existing Structures and Uses (G.S. 160D, Art. 4 & 7—authority to adopt and enforce regulations for land use activities on existing properties)
- **Chapter 15:** Vacant Building Receivership (G.S. 160D-1130—authority to petition the court to place vacant property into receivership)

For more detailed authority and enforcement procedures, see Table P3.1.

Even beyond the topics discussed in these chapters, there are more options for local governments regulating dangerous situations on private property. While these topics are not discussed in detail here, they are worth highlighting.

- In some cases, local governments may coordinate with North Carolina Alcohol Law Enforcement if the nuisance involves alcohol, drugs, weapons, or other criminal activities. Chapter 19 of the General Statutes outlines authority to abate such nuisances.
- Local governments may take steps to address abandoned vehicles and vessels,[2] as well as regulate solid waste, pollutants, and contaminants.[3]
- Historic preservation and demolition-by-neglect ordinances can address the maintenance and redevelopment of designated historic properties.

Rules of Thumb

The following chapters outline the detailed requirements for the specific authorities. Here are some overarching rules of thumb for local governments exercising the various authorities for existing structures and unsafe situations on private property.

Know the statutory authority. As shown in Table P3.1, there are many overlapping authorities to deal with existing structures and unsafe situations on property. Each authority has its own procedural requirements and legal limits. A local government must know which authority it is acting under in order to ensure legal compliance.

Adhere to the state requirements and local procedures. Procedural requirements are not suggestions. They are legally mandated in order to exercise the authority. "Substantial compliance with these procedures is a condition precedent to the authority of the city to forbid the use of a dwelling house for human habitation."[4]

Provide the required notice. Notice must meet the minimum standards required by statute. Additional notice (beyond the statutory minimum) is permissible and in some situations may be prudent. The officer must review the public record to determine who gets notice, but there is no obligation to go beyond the public record.[5]

Provide an opportunity to be heard. An administrative hearing is an opportunity for the owner to present evidence and make arguments regarding the case. It may be necessary to provide additional hearings if the substance of the case evolves (from

---

2. Sections 205.6, 303, and 303.2 of Chapter 160A of the North Carolina General Statutes (hereinafter G.S.); G.S. 153A, §§ 132, 132.2.

3. G.S. 160A-185; 153A-136.

4. Dale v. City of Morganton, 270 N.C. 567, 576, 155 S.E.2d 136, 144 (1967).

5. Patterson v. City of Gastonia, 220 N.C. App. 233, 242, 725 S.E.2d 82, 89 (2012).

an *order to repair* to an *order to demolish*, for example).[6] For some powers (unsafe structures, commercial maintenance, minimum housing), an administrative hearing is required. For other powers (nuisance code, zoning), an administrative hearing may be appropriate or the appeal process may provide the opportunity to be heard.

Provide opportunity to correct. Except in limited situations, the government must provide the property owner an opportunity to correct the violation prior to government action to remedy the problem.[7] "To require [private property] destruction, without giving the owner a reasonable opportunity thus to remove the existing threat to the public health, safety and welfare, is arbitrary and unreasonable."[8]

Honor the timeframe of the opportunity to correct. If the property owner has been given sixty days to repair, give them sixty days (don't shorten it).[9] Once that period passes, the officer may evaluate if enforcement should proceed or if more time to correct is warranted.

Do not act beyond the authority. Local governments have limited and specific power to address unsafe conditions on private property. Any action must stay within those legal limits. If a local government goes beyond that limited power, it may have liability. "Where a municipal corporation, in the exercise of its governmental power to abate nuisances, enters upon and damages private property by the destruction of trees, buildings, etc., thereon, it is liable for the payment of just compensation unless its acts were in fact necessary to remove or abate a nuisance."[10]

Only pursue summary abatement in rare circumstances. In rare circumstances, a public safety emergency may be so dire and time-sensitive that a local government must act without giving the property owner notice and an opportunity to be heard.[11] But those circumstances are rare. In all other situations, the local government should follow the required procedures of inspection, notice, hearing, and deliberate enforcement action.

Document, document, document. If a case is appealed, the court will closely examine the record: Did the local government follow the required procedures? Did the local government have sufficient evidence to support the orders issued? Proper documentation is essential to protecting the actions of public officials and local governments.[12]

---

6. Newton v. City of Winston-Salem, 92 N.C. App. 446, 374 S.E.2d 488 (1988).

7. *Patterson*, 220 N.C. App. at 242, 725 S.E.2d at 89) (for a minimum housing demolition order, sixty days for correction was sufficient).

8. Horton v. Gulledge, 277 N.C. 353, 363, 177 S.E.2d 885, 892 (1970), *overruled on other grounds by* State v. Jones, 305 N.C. 520, 290 S.E.2d 675 (1982).

9. Wiggins v. City of Monroe, 73 N.C. App. 44, 326 S.E.2d 39 (1985).

10. Rhyne v. Town of Mount Holly, 251 N.C. 521, 528, 112 S.E.2d 40, 46 (1960).

11. Monroe v. City of New Bern, 158 N.C. App. 275, 278, 580 S.E.2d 372, 374 (2003) ("Section 160A-193 only applies to a situation where a structurally unsafe building poses an imminent danger to the safety of the public such that the owner could not be provided notice and a hearing without endangering the public. Cities may not summarily demolish dwellings pursuant to Section 160A-193 merely because it is quicker and easier than providing the owners notice and an opportunity to be heard.").

12. Carolina Holdings, Inc. v. Hous. Appeals Bd. of City of Charlotte, 149 N.C. App. 579, 561 S.E.2d 541 (2002).

Table P3.1. Key Authorities for Property Safety

Chapter in This Book	Authority *Municipal Jurisdiction*	Process Overview	Local Government Abatement and Cost Recovery
Unsafe Structures (Ch. 10) Authority to determine a structure is unsafe, post notice closing the building, and require corrective action	**G.S. 160D-1118 to -1125** *Corporate limits and extraterritorial jurisdiction (ETJ)*	Building inspector inspection, determination, and posted notice; if not corrected, then notice of condemnation and administrative hearing; inspector holds administrative hearing and issues order of corrective action; order may be appealed to governing board; owner has an opportunity to correct; enforcement may include preventing occupancy, building removal or demolition, misdemeanor, and more; local government may pursue receivership after failure to comply with an order	If owner fails to comply with order of corrective action, local government may cause the structure to be removed or demolished; local government must sell usable materials, fixtures, and personal property (credit against cost); cost of removal is a lien against the property and any other property in the jurisdiction owned by same owner
Commercial Maintenance Code (Ch. 11) Authority to establish and enforce standards for commercial building maintenance	**G.S. 160D-1129** *Corporate limits and ETJ*	Adoption of a code with minimum standards to address dangerous conditions and designated public officer; officer inspection; written complaint and notice of administrative hearing; officer holds administrative hearing; officer issues written decision or order to correct; order may be appealed to either the housing appeals board or the board of adjustment; owner has an opportunity to correct; if owner fails to comply, governing board may adopt an ordinance for enforcement; then officer may proceed with either (1) repair, alteration, or improvement, or (2) removal or demolition; additional process if owner abandons intent to repair; local government may pursue receivership after failure to comply with an order	After the governing board adopts an ordinance, officer may take action to cause compliance (repair, close, or remove); local government must sell usable materials, fixtures, and personal property (credit against cost); the cost is a lien against the property; the lien has the same priority as a special assessment; in a municipality the cost is also a lien against other property in the jurisdiction owned by the same owner (aside from owner's residence)
Minimum Housing and Abandoned Structures (Ch. 12) Authority to establish and enforce standards for residential building maintenance *and* abandoned structure maintenance	**G.S. 160D, Art. 12** *Corporate limits and ETJ*	Adoption of a code with minimum standards to address fitness of a dwelling for human habitation; code must designate an enforcement officer; inspection by officer, complaint of violation, and notice of administrative hearing; officer holds an administrative hearing; officer issues an order (to repair, alter, or improve; to close and vacate; or to remove or demolish); additional notice and waiting period prior to demolition; owner has an opportunity to correct; owner may appeal to housing appeals board; if owner fails to comply then local government may adopt ordinance for office to take action to cause compliance; additional process if owner abandons intent to repair; local government may pursue receivership after failure to comply with an order	After the governing board adopts an ordinance, officer may take action to cause compliance (to repair, close, or remove); local government must sell usable materials, fixtures, and personal property (credit against cost); the cost is a lien against the property; the lien has the same priority as a special assessment; in a municipality the cost is also a lien against other property in the jurisdiction (and within one mile of the jurisdiction) owned by the same owner (aside from owner's residence)

Chapter in This Book	**Authority** *Municipal Jurisdiction*	Process Overview	Local Government Abatement and Cost Recovery
Nuisance Code (Ch. 13) Authority to adopt and enforce a nuisance code to address unsafe situations on property (overgrown lots, solid waste)	**G.S. 160A-174; 153A-121** *Municipal corporate boundaries*	Procedures are not fully specified in statute; the following are prudent or required: adoption of a nuisance code or ordinance to define nuisance; public officer inspection and notice of violation; option for notice to chronic violators; owner has an opportunity to correct; owner may appeal to designated board; enforcement by misdemeanor, fine, civil penalty, or court order	Clear authority for abatement and cost recovery by court order; clear authority for administrative abatement and cost recovery for properly noticed chronic violators; potential authority for administrative abatement under the nuisance code; clear authority for administrative abatement and cost recovery if nuisance code is aligned with Public Health Nuisance Authority (see below)
Abatement of Public Health Nuisance (Ch. 13) Authority to address situations that are dangerous or prejudicial to the public health or public safety	**G.S. 160A-193; 153A-140** *Municipal corporate boundaries plus one mile*	Procedures are not fully specified in statute; the following are prudent or required: municipality may summarily remove, abate, or remedy unsafe situation in emergency situations, but notice and opportunity to be heard is warranted in non-emergency situations; county must provide adequate notice, hearing, and right to appeal; municipality and county must make findings before removing a pool	Summary abatement for municipalities in certain situations; abatement for counties with due process; cost of abatement must be paid by the person in default or it is a lien upon the property and collected as unpaid taxes; in a municipality the cost is also a lien against other property in the jurisdiction (and within one mile of the jurisdiction) owned by the same owner
Zoning (Ch. 14) Authority to adopt and enforce regulations for land use activities on property	**G.S. 160D, Art. 4 & 7** *Corporate limits and ETJ*	Adoption of zoning ordinance or unified development ordinance; investigation by zoning enforcement officer and notice of violation; enforcement may include revocation of development approvals, withholding of certificates of occupancy, civil penalties, and legal proceedings in court; appeals go to the board of adjustment	Abatement and cost recovery by court order
Vacant Building Receivership (Ch. 15) Authority to petition for court to put vacant property into receivership	**G.S. 160D-1130** *Corporate limits and ETJ*	After an owner fails to comply with an order to take corrective action (for unsafe structure, commercial maintenance, or minimum housing), the local government petitions court to appoint a receiver for the property; notice is provided to the owner; receiver must meet certain qualifications; receiver has the authority to rehabilitate, demolish, sell, and foreclose on a lien	Receiver has authority to rehabilitate, demolish, sell, and foreclose on a lien; local government may charge an administrative fee up to 5 percent of the sale price

Chapter 10
Unsafe Structures

Overview

North Carolina law authorizes local governments to enforce against unsafe structures, including removing such structures, on private property. Such action, however, is a significant exercise of government power and requires careful process to protect individual rights.

The North Carolina Supreme Court upheld the authority and constitutionality of condemning unsafe structures in *Walker v. City of Charlotte.*[1] In a long-running dispute about a dilapidated structure, the owner claimed that the statutes and ordinances concerning removal of unsafe structures were unconstitutional. The court found that the authority was permissible under the general regulatory powers and that the procedures adequately protected individual rights.

Local governments must adhere to the procedural requirements set forth in state law (and outlined below) in order to exercise the regulatory authority.[2] (See Appendix G for sample inspection, enforcement, and hearing forms related to unsafe structures.)

Duty to Notify

An inspector has a duty to notify the owner or occupant of a building if they find

- any defects in the building,
- the building has not been constructed in accordance with the applicable state and local laws, or
- the building's condition is dangerous or contains fire hazardous conditions.

Upon notice, "[t]he owner or occupant shall each immediately remedy the defects, hazardous conditions, or violations of law in the property."[3]

---

1. 276 N.C. 166, 171 S.E.2d 431 (1970).

2. Dale v. City of Morganton, 270 N.C. 567, 576, 155 S.E.2d 136, 144 (1967) ("Substantial compliance with these procedures is a condition precedent to the authority of the city to forbid the use of a dwelling house for human habitation.").

3. Chapter 160D, Section 1118 of the North Carolina General Statutes (hereinafter G.S.).

> **Fourth Amendment Reminder**
>
> For a detailed discussion of Fourth Amendment limits on inspections, see Chapter 4. In brief, code officials must honor constitutional privacy protections, obtain consent or a warrant when needed, and rely only on observations made lawfully.

Condemn Unsafe Buildings

General Authority for Determinations

If an inspector determines a building is "especially dangerous to life," they must post notice of the dangerous character of the structure. Notice must be affixed in a conspicuous place on the exterior wall of the building. State law lists situations that may be especially dangerous to life, including "liability to fire or because of bad condition of walls, overloaded floors, defective construction, decay, unsafe wiring or heating systems, inadequate means of egress, or other causes."[4]

If an individual removes notice of an unsafe structure, they are guilty of a Class 1 misdemeanor.[5]

The owner of a building or structure condemned as unsafe has an obligation to take prompt corrective action.

Additional Authority for Blight in Target Areas

In addition to the general authority to condemn buildings that are "especially dangerous to life," local governments have supplemental authority to declare buildings unsafe due to vacancy and blight in certain community development target areas.

In such areas, the inspector may declare a building or structure unsafe if both of the following findings are made:

> (1) It appears to the inspector to be vacant or abandoned.
> (2) It appears to the inspector to be in such dilapidated condition as to cause or contribute to blight, disease, vagrancy, or fire or safety hazard, to be a danger to children, or to tend to attract persons intent on criminal activities or other activities that would constitute a public nuisance.[6]

4. G.S. 160D-1119.
5. G.S. 160D-1120.
6. G.S. 160D-1119(b).

After making these findings, "the inspector must affix a notice of the unsafe character of the structure to a conspicuous place on the exterior wall of the building."[7]

Community development target areas include:

- an area that has characteristics of an urban progress zone under Chapter 143B, Section 437.09 of the North Carolina General Statutes (hereinafter G.S.),
- a "nonresidential redevelopment area" under G.S. 160A-503(10), or
- an area with similar characteristics designated by the governing board as being in special need of revitalization for the benefit and welfare of its citizens.[8]

The additional authority applies to nonresidential buildings and structures. A local government may expand that authority to residential structures by ordinance after a legislative hearing and published notice pursuant to G.S. 160D-601.[9]

Notice of Hearing

If the owner fails to take prompt corrective action, the inspector must give written notice of the condemnation and hold an administrative hearing.[10]

The local government must send notice by certified mail to the owner's last known address or by personal service. If, after due diligence, the inspector cannot determine the name or whereabouts of the owner, posted and published notice is sufficient. In such cases, the notice must be posted on the outside of the building or structure for at least ten days prior to the hearing and published in a local newspaper at least once and at least one week prior to the hearing.[11]

Notice must include the following information:

> (1) That the building or structure is in a condition that appears to meet one or more of the following conditions:
>
> a. Constitutes a fire or safety hazard.
>
> b. Is dangerous to life, health, or other property.
>
> c. Is likely to cause or contribute to blight, disease, vagrancy, or danger to children.
>
> d. Has a tendency to attract persons intent on criminal activities or other activities that would constitute a public nuisance.
>
> (2) That an administrative hearing will be held before the inspector at a designated place and time, not later than 10 days after the date of the notice,

7. G.S. 160D-1119(c).
8. *Id.*
9. G.S. 160D-1119(d).
10. G.S. 160D-1121.
11. *Id.*

at which time the owner will be entitled to be heard in person or by counsel and to present arguments and evidence pertaining to the matter.

(3) That following the hearing, the inspector may issue such order to repair, close, vacate, or demolish the building or structure as appears appropriate.[12]

Administrative Hearing and Order of Corrective Action

After notice, the inspector holds an administrative hearing on the matter. The hearing is held before the inspector at a time and place designated in the notice. It must occur within ten days of the date of the notice.

The hearing is a procedural step to protect the property owner and ensure due process. The owner has a right to be heard and may speak for themselves or have legal counsel. The owner or attorney may present arguments and evidence related to the condemnation.[13]

At the conclusion of the hearing, the inspector makes findings and issues an order. If, based on the evidence, the inspector finds that "the building or structure is in a condition that constitutes a fire or safety hazard or renders it dangerous to life, health, or other property," the inspector must issue an order of corrective action.[14]

The order of corrective action is a written order directed to the owner of the building or structure. It requires the owner "to remedy the defective conditions by repairing, closing, vacating, or demolishing the building or structure or taking other necessary steps."[15] The order must specify a timeline for remedy. In general, the timeline for corrective action must allow at least sixty days, but if the inspector finds there is "imminent danger to life or other property" they may order corrective action in less than sixty days "as may be feasible."[16] When there is no imminent threat, the local government must give the owner an opportunity to repair before proceeding with demolition.[17]

Notice of Lis Pendens

Lis pendens is Latin for *suit pending.* A notice of lis pendens is notice recorded with the court to give notice to successors and assigns that the property is subject to pending action.

---

12. *Id.*
13. *Id.*
14. G.S. 160D-1122.
15. *Id.*
16. *Id.*
17. Horton v. Gulledge, 277 N.C. 353, 177 S.E.2d 885 (1970) (overruled on other grounds by State v. Jones, 305 N.C. 520, 290 S.E.2d 675 (1982)).

State law governing civil procedure allows a local government to file a notice of lis pendens relating to unsafe structure actions under Article 11 of Chapter 160D and minimum housing actions under Article 12 of Chapter 160D.[18] The notice is filed with the office of the clerk of superior court. The notice must be filed with a copy of the complaint and notice of hearing or order. A copy of the notice of lis pendens is also served on the current owners and parties of interest (pursuant to G.S. 160D-1121 for unsafe structures and G.S. 160D-1206 for minimum housing).

Such notice is indexed and cross-indexed according to the rules for lis pendens at G.S. 1-117. The notice is binding upon future owners (as well as other parties of interest) of the subject building or property. The notice remains in effect until it is canceled. The ordinance may specify the circumstances that authorize cancellation.

Appeal to Governing Board

An owner may appeal an order of corrective action to the local governing board. Notice of appeal must be filed with the inspector and the local government clerk within ten days of the issuance of the order. Without an appeal, the inspector's order is final.[19]

Appeals of inspector orders of corrective action are quasi-judicial decisions.[20] The governing board reviews the decision as a court would, not as a political body. The procedures for the evidentiary hearing and quasi-judicial decision are set forth in G.S. 160D-406 and include sworn testimony, formal legal procedures, and a written decision based on the evidence in the record. The governing board may affirm, modify and affirm, or revoke the order. Its decision must be rendered within a reasonable time.[21]

A decision of the governing board may be appealed to superior court, as with other quasi-judicial development decisions.

Enforcement

Any appropriate action. If an owner fails to comply with an order of corrective action, the local government "may initiate any appropriate action or proceedings to prevent, restrain, correct, or abate the violation or to prevent the occupancy of

---

18. G.S. 1-120.2.

19. G.S. 160D-1123.

20. *Id.*; Coffey v. Town of Waynesville, 143 N.C. App 624 (2001); Hillsboro Partners, LLC v. City of Fayetteville, 226 N.C. App. 30, 738 S.E.2d 819, *review denied*, 367 N.C. 236, 748 S.E.2d 544 (2013).

21. G.S. 160D-1123.

the building or structure involved" (as is the case with any building code violation that is denominated as a misdemeanor).[22]

Building removal or demolition. In lieu of other action the local government may cause the building or structure to be removed or demolished. "If the building or structure is removed or demolished by the local government, the local government shall sell the usable materials of the building and any personal property, fixtures, or appurtenances found in or attached to the building."[23] Any proceeds from such sale are a credit against the cost of removal or demolition, and any remaining balance must be deposited with the clerk of superior court to be disbursed to the person entitled to it.[24]

Lien. The cost of removal or demolition is a lien against the property. Such lien is treated the same as a lien for a special assessment as outlined in Article 10 of Chapter 160A.[25]

The cost of removal or demolition is also a lien against any other real property owned by the same owner and located in the local government's jurisdiction, except for the owner's prior residence. For a municipality with ETJ, that includes properties within the ETJ. For a municipality without ETJ, that includes any property within a mile of the municipal limits. Such additional liens are treated the same as the primary lien, "except that this additional lien is inferior to all prior liens and shall be collected as a money judgment."[26]

Misdemeanor. It is a Class 1 misdemeanor if an owner fails to comply with an order of corrective action.[27]

Other nuisance enforcement. The authority for condemnation of unsafe structures and enforcement of orders for corrective action does not undermine authority to define, declare, and abate nuisances.[28]

Receivership. If an owner fails to comply with an order to take corrective action, the local government may pursue court-appointed receivership, as discussed in Chapter 15.[29]

22. G.S. 160D-1125(a).
23. G.S. 160D-1125(b).
24. *Id.*
25. *Id.*
26. G.S. 160D-1125(c).
27. G.S. 160D-1124.
28. G.S. 160D-1125(d).
29. G.S. 160D-1130.

Chapter 11
Commercial Maintenance Code

Overview

State law authorizes a local government to adopt regulations setting minimum standards for maintenance, sanitation, and safety of nonresidential buildings and structures. This chapter outlines the authority and procedures for such commercial maintenance codes. (See Appendix H for sample forms related to nonresidential structure code enforcement.)

Authority for Local Regulation

Commercial maintenance regulations "shall address only conditions that are dangerous and injurious to public health, safety, and welfare and identify circumstances under which a public necessity exists for the repair, closing, or demolition of such buildings or structures." The regulations may apply to the entire planning and development regulation jurisdiction, or they may be limited to "one or more designated zoning districts, municipal service districts, or defined geographical areas designated for improvement and investment in an adopted comprehensive plan."[1]

The local government must adhere to the procedural requirements set forth in state law (and outlined below) in order to exercise the regulatory authority.[2]

The local government may appropriate funds—as well as apply for grants and donations—to carry out the purposes of a nonresidential maintenance code.[3]

The authority granted for such nonresidential maintenance requirements is supplemental to other local government powers.[4] This authority does not limit, for example, the local government's power "to define and declare nuisances and to cause their removal or abatement by summary proceedings or otherwise."[5]

---

1. Chapter 160D, Section 1129(a) of the North Carolina General Statutes (hereinafter G.S.).
2. Dale v. City of Morganton, 270 N.C. 567, 576, 155 S.E.2d 136, 144 (1967) ("Substantial compliance with these procedures is a condition precedent to the authority of the city to forbid the use of a dwelling house for human habitation.").
3. G.S. 160D-1129(n).
4. G.S. 160D-1129(*l*).
5. G.S. 160D-1129(i)(3).

Standards

As with any regulation, clear guiding standards are essential for a commercial maintenance code. Commercial maintenance codes are about safe maintenance, not aesthetic preferences. The statute authorizes standards that address "only conditions that are dangerous and injurious to public health, safety, and welfare." Such standards may include, among other things, structural safety; maintenance of roofs and walls; maintenance and closure of windows and doors; maintenance of safe electrical, plumbing, drainage, and related systems; and safe maintenance of site conditions, including parking and yard space.

A commercial maintenance code may include a registration requirement. While state law limits registration for *residential* properties, there is no such limitation for nonresidential properties.

Officer

The regulation must provide for a public officer to exercise the powers.[6] The local government "may authorize the public officer to exercise any powers necessary or convenient to carry out and effectuate the purpose and provisions" of the maintenance ordinance, including the following powers:

> (1) To investigate nonresidential buildings and structures in the local government's planning and development regulation jurisdiction to determine whether they have been properly maintained in compliance with the minimum standards so that the safety or health of the occupants or members of the general public are not jeopardized.
>
> (2) To administer oaths, affirmations, examine witnesses, and receive evidence.
>
> (3) To enter upon premises pursuant to subsection (b) of this section for the purpose of making examinations in a manner that will do the least possible inconvenience to the persons in possession.
>
> (4) To appoint and fix the duties of officers, agents, and employees necessary to carry out the purposes of the ordinances adopted by the governing board.
>
> (5) To delegate any of his or her functions and powers under the ordinance to other officers and agents.[7]

Fourth Amendment Reminder

For a detailed discussion of Fourth Amendment limits on inspections, see Chapter 4. In brief, code officials must honor constitutional privacy protections, obtain consent or a warrant when needed, and rely only on observations made lawfully or in plain view.

6. G.S. 160D-1129(a).
7. G.S. 160D-1129(*l*).

Process for Enforcement

Investigation, Complaint, and Notice

If the public officer believes a property is not properly maintained such that it creates a safety concern for occupants or the public, the officer has a duty to undertake a preliminary investigation. If entry is necessary for the investigation, the public officer may request consent from the owner or responsible party or obtain an administrate search warrant.[8]

If the investigation reveals evidence of a violation of minimum standards, the officer serves a complaint upon the owner and parties in interest. The complaint must state the problem and give notice of the administrative hearing.[9] The complaint must

- state the charges;
- contain a notice that an administrative hearing will be held before the public officer, or his or her designated agent, at a place within the county scheduled not less than ten days nor more than thirty days after the serving of the complaint;
- state that the owner and parties in interest shall be given the right to answer the complaint and to appear in person, or otherwise, and give testimony at the place and time fixed in the complaint; and
- state that the rules of evidence prevailing in courts of law or equity are not controlling in hearings before the public officer.

Notice (or Service) of Complaints and Orders

Complaints and orders must be served upon persons personally or by certified mail. The means of notice must be "reasonably designed to achieve actual notice."[10]

Mailed notice deemed sufficient. For service by certified mail, a copy may also be sent by regular mail. Service is deemed sufficient if the certified mail is refused by the recipient and the regular mail is not returned within ten days after mailing. In such case, the notice must also be posted in a conspicuous place on the premises.

Service by publication. If, after reasonable diligence, the identity or whereabouts of owners cannot be ascertained, service may be provided by publication. The public officer must make an affidavit that they were not able to ascertain identity or whereabouts by reasonable diligence. The service must be published at least once in a newspaper having general circulation in the area no later than the time personal service is required. Notice must also be posted in a conspicuous place on the premises.

---

8. G.S. 160D-1129(b).
9. G.S. 160D-1129(c).
10. G.S. 160D-1129(h).

Administrative Hearing and Order

The administrative hearing is held before the officer or designated agent, in the county where the property is located, and between ten and thirty days after the complaint is served. The owner or other parties in interest have the right to answer the complaint, appear in person or otherwise, and give testimony. The hearing does not follow the formal rules of evidence applicable in court proceedings.[11]

If the officer determines that the owner has failed to maintain the property to the minimum standards set in the regulation such that safety and health are jeopardized, the officer shall state written findings of fact to support that determination and shall issue and serve an order. The order may require remedial action, within a reasonable time, subject to applicable procedures.[12]

An order may require the owner to repair, alter, or improve the building to meet minimum standards or to vacate and close the building. If the cost of repair, alteration, or improvement would exceed 50 percent of the current value, an order may require the owner to remove or demolish the nonresidential building or structure.

For recognized historic properties, the order may not require demolition but may require the building to be vacated and closed until compliance. To qualify for this protection, the property must

- be officially designated as a local historic landmark, be listed on the National Register of Historic Places, or be situated within a locally designated historic district or one listed on the National Register of Historic Places;
- have been found by the governing board to hold individual historic significance or contribute to the character of the historic district; and
- not be classified as unsafe or condemned.[13]

For vacant manufacturing facilities or vacant industrial warehouse facilities, an order may not require repairs, alterations, or improvements to preserve manufacturing or warehouse use. An order may require such a building to be vacated and closed, and an order may require repairs when necessary to maintain structural integrity or to abate a health or safety hazard that is not addressed by closing the building.[14]

Appeal

An appeal from a public officer's decision or order goes either to the housing appeals board or the board of adjustment (depending on the procedure set forth in the local nonresidential maintenance code). A person aggrieved has the same remedies as

---

11. G.S. 160D-1129(c).
12. G.S. 160D-1129(d).
13. G.S. 160D-1129(e)(2).
14. G.S. 160D-1129(e)(3).

in a minimum housing appeal as outlined at Chapter 160D, Section 1208 of the North Carolina General Statutes (hereinafter G.S.).[15]

Opportunity to Correct

The local government must provide a reasonable time for the owner to comply and must honor that time. For an order to remove or demolish, in particular, "[n]o ordinance shall be adopted to require demolition of a nonresidential building or structure until the owner has first been given a reasonable opportunity to bring it into conformity with the minimum standards established by the governing board."[16]

Notice of Lis Pendens

As discussed in Chapter 10, state law governing civil procedure allows a local government to file a notice of lis pendens relating to unsafe structure actions under Article 11 of Chapter 160D and minimum housing actions under Article 12 of Chapter 160D.[17] Such notice is plainly authorized for unsafe structures and minimum housing. Arguably, a local government may also file a notice of lis pendens for a commercial maintenance action.

General Enforcement Options

State law outlines enforcement options for development regulations generally. Since commercial maintenance codes fall under the broad umbrella of development regulations (authorized by Chapter 160D), those general enforcement options likely apply. G.S. 160D-403 and -404 specify some of the tools for enforcement: inspections, revocation of development approvals, withholding of certificates of occupancy, notices of violation, stop work orders, and "appropriate action or proceedings" to prevent work or activity in violation of development regulations. G.S. 160D-404 also cross-references enforcement tools for general police power ordinances outlined in G.S. 160A-175 and 153A-123. These include civil penalties, legal proceedings in court, and treating the violation as a misdemeanor (subject to some limitations on criminal enforcement).[18]

Additionally, the statutory section for commercial maintenance codes specifically states that the local government may impose civil penalties for any person

---

15. G.S. 160D-1129(m).

16. G.S. 160D-1129(f)(2).

17. G.S. 1-120.2.

18. Adam Lovelady, *Enforcement of Development Regulations*, Coates' Canons: NC Loc. Gov't L. (blog) (Feb. 11, 2022), https://canons.sog.unc.edu/2022/02/enforcement-of-development-regulations/; Adam Lovelady, *Limits on Criminal Enforcement of Development Regulations*, Coates' Canons: NC Loc. Gov't L. (blog) (Feb. 11, 2022), https://canons.sog.unc.edu/2022/02/limits-on-criminal-enforcement-of-development-regulations/.

who fails to comply with an order under the code.[19] Civil penalties are discussed in more detail in Chapter 14.

Ordinance and Enforcement

If an owner fails to comply with an order, the governing board may adopt an ordinance for enforcement.[20] The ordinance directs the public officer to proceed with enforcement. Any such ordinance must describe the noncompliant property or properties. It must also be recorded with the register of deeds and indexed under the owner's name in the grantor's index.

For an order to repair, alter, or improve, or to vacate and close, after adoption of the ordinance, the public officer may proceed with repair, alteration, or improvement or may cause the building to be vacated and closed. The public officer may post at the main entrance to the building a placard stating: "This building is unfit for any use; the use or occupation of this building for any purpose is prohibited and unlawful." It is a Class 3 misdemeanor to occupy or knowingly allow occupancy of a building so posted.[21]

For an order to remove or demolish, after the ordinance is adopted, the public officer may cause the building or structure to be removed or demolished.[22]

If an owner fails to comply with an order to take corrective action, the local government may pursue court-appointed receivership as discussed in Chapter 15.[23]

Abandonment of Intent to Repair

After the governing board adopts an ordinance or the public officer issues an order to repair or to vacate and close, and the building or structure has been vacated and closed for a period of two years (or five years for vacant manufacturing facilities or vacant industrial warehouse facilities), the governing board may make findings and proceed with further enforcement.[24]

The findings must include a determination that

- the owner has abandoned the intent and purpose to repair, alter, or improve the building or structure, and
- continuing to keep the building or structure in a vacated and closed status would be harmful to the health, safety, and welfare of the

---

19. G.S. 160D-1129(k).
20. G.S. 160D-1129(f).
21. G.S. 160D-1129(f)(1).
22. G.S. 160D-1129(f)(2).
23. G.S. 160D-1130.
24. G.S. 160D-1129(g).

> local government because it would likely continue to deteriorate, create fire or safety hazards, pose a threat to children and vagrants, attract persons engaged in criminal activities, or contribute to blight and declining property values in the area.

Upon making such findings, the governing board may adopt and serve on the owner an ordinance for repair and/or removal or demolition. The ordinance must set forth the following:

> (1) If the cost to repair the nonresidential building or structure to bring it into compliance with the minimum standards is less than or equal to fifty percent (50%) of its then current value, the ordinance shall require that the owner either repair or demolish and remove the building or structure within 90 days.
>
> (2) If the cost to repair the nonresidential building or structure to bring it into compliance with the minimum standards exceeds fifty percent (50%) of its then current value, the ordinance shall require the owner to demolish and remove the building or structure within 90 days.

The ordinance must be recorded with the register of deeds and indexed in the owner's name in the grantor index. If the owner fails to comply with the ordinance, the public officer may carry out its provisions.

Liens

The cost to the local government to perform the repairs, closing, or demolition is a lien against the property.[25]

The lien is filed, has the same priority, and is collected in the same manner as a lien for a special assessment, as provided in Article 10 of Chapter 160A of the General Statutes.

If the property is within an incorporated city, the amount of the costs is also a lien on other real property of the owner within the city limits (aside from the owner's residence). These additional liens are inferior to all prior liens and are collected as a money judgment.

In the case of removal or demolition, the public officer shall offer for sale any materials, fixtures, appurtenances, and personal property. Proceeds from the sale are a credit against the cost of removal. If there is any excess balance, the public officer must deposit that amount with the superior court and the court shall disburse the funds to the persons entitled to them.

---

25. G.S. 160D-1129(i).

Ejectment of Occupant Refusing to Vacate

If an occupant refuses to vacate a building as required by order, the public officer may file a civil action to remove the occupant.[26] Such civil action to vacate is filed in the name of the local government and in the nature of summary ejectment.

The steps are as follows:

- At least thirty days before filing a complaint to remove an occupant by summary ejectment, the occupant must be served with notice that the governing board has ordered the public officer to proceed and to vacate and close or remove and demolish the nonresidential building or structure.
- The public officer files a complaint naming as parties-defendant any person occupying the nonresidential building or structure.
- The clerk of superior court issues a summons requiring the defendant to appear before a magistrate at a certain time, date, and place—no more than ten days after issuance of the summons—to answer the complaint.
- The summons and complaint are served as provided in G.S. 42-29.
- The summons is returned according to its tenor. If, on its return, it appears to have been duly served, and if at the hearing the public officer produces a certified copy of an ordinance adopted by the governing board to vacate the occupied nonresidential building or structure, the magistrate enters judgment ordering that the premises be vacated and all persons removed.
- The judgment ordering that the nonresidential building or structure be vacated is enforced in the same manner as the judgment for summary ejectment under G.S. 42-30.
- An appeal from any judgment entered by the magistrate may be taken as provided in G.S. 7A-228, and execution of the judgment may be stayed as provided in G.S. 7A-227.

---

26. G.S. 160D-1129(j).

Chapter 12

Minimum Housing and Abandoned Structures

Overview

North Carolina local governments are authorized to establish minimum housing standards and enforce those rules to ensure habitability for residents. Such governmental regulation, though, demands careful legal process. This chapter outlines the authority, procedures, and enforcement of minimum housing codes in North Carolina. (See Appendix I for sample forms related to minimum housing and abandoned structures enforcement.)

Scope: Dwellings *and* Abandoned Structures

Article 12 of Chapter 160D of the North Carolina General Statutes (hereinafter G.S.) authorizes local governments to adopt local regulations to address unsafe dwellings and abandoned structures. For dwellings, local governments are authorized to exercise police powers to repair, close, or demolish dwellings unfit for human habitation. Additionally, the authority for minimum housing code standards and enforcement extends to "any abandoned structure that the governing board finds to be a health or safety hazard."

Dwellings are defined as "[a]ny building, structure, manufactured home, or mobile home, or part thereof, used and occupied for human habitation or intended to be so used. . . ."[1] However, for minimum housing purposes, "the term does not include any manufactured home, mobile home, or recreational vehicle, if used solely for a seasonal vacation purpose."[2] For dwellings, state law recognizes the important public safety rationale for ensuring they are fit for human habitation.[3] The authorization notes the following scenarios warranting government action:

- dwellings that are unfit for human habitation due to dilapidation;
- defects increasing the hazards of fire, accidents or other calamities;

1. Chapter 160D, Section 102(15) of the North Carolina General Statutes (hereinafter G.S.).
2. *Id.*
3. G.S. 160D-1201(a).

- lack of ventilation, light, or sanitary facilities; or
- other conditions rendering the dwellings unsafe or unsanitary, or dangerous or detrimental to the health, safety, morals, or otherwise inimical to the welfare of the residents of the local government.[4]

For abandoned structures, state law authorizes repair, closing, or demolition when the governing board finds

- a health or safety hazard as a result of the attraction of insects or rodents,
- conditions creating a fire hazard,
- dangerous conditions constituting a threat to children, or
- frequent use by vagrants as living quarters in the absence of sanitary facilities.[5]

The power to adopt and enforce a minimum housing code is supplemental to other powers held by courts or local governments to enforce other ordinances or regulations.[6] The adoption and enforcement of a minimum housing code, for example, does not prevent action for nuisance abatement.[7]

The authority for minimum housing codes does not diminish the protections for owners of private property to receive just compensation for the taking of property.[8]

Housing Code Standards

Generally

In conjunction with establishing a local housing code, the local governing board must adopt by ordinance findings that unsafe dwelling conditions and/or unsafe abandoned building conditions exist.[9] The code must designate an enforcement officer and comply with statutory requirements for investigation and enforcement, as outlined below.

The housing code may allow the public officer to "determine that a dwelling is unfit for human habitation" if the officer finds conditions that are "dangerous or injurious to the health, safety, or welfare of the occupants of the dwelling, the

4. *Id.*
5. G.S. 160D-1201(b).
6. G.S. 160D-1212.
7. *See* G.S. 160D-1203(7)(c) ("Nothing in this section shall be construed to impair or limit in any way the power of the local government to define and declare nuisances and to cause their removal or abatement by summary proceedings or otherwise.").
8. G.S. 160D-1209.
9. G.S. 160D, §§ 1201, 1203.

occupants of neighboring dwellings, or other residents of the jurisdiction."[10] State law lists the following conditions as "defective situations" but allows that other conditions may also render a dwelling unfit:

- defects therein increasing the hazards of fire, accident, or other calamities;
- lack of adequate ventilation, light, or sanitary facilities;
- dilapidation;
- disrepair;
- structural defects; or
- uncleanliness.[11]

State law allows the local housing code to "provide additional standards to guide the public officers in determining the fitness of a dwelling for human habitation."[12]

Heat Source Requirement in Large Cities

For cities with a population over 200,000, in addition to the general standards for human habitation, the local housing code must address adequate provision of heating. G.S. 160D-1204 requires that the local housing code ensure that every dwelling unit leased as rental property has central heating, electric heating, or a heating appliance (with sufficient chimneys, flues, or gas vents). The required level of heating is "to heat at least one habitable room, excluding the kitchen, to a minimum temperature of 68 degrees Fahrenheit measured 3 feet above the floor with an outside temperature of 20 degrees Fahrenheit."[13] The statute allows cities to impose more stringent heating requirements.

Owners are required to maintain such heating systems in good and working order or to install new heating to meet the standard.[14]

Portable kerosene heaters are not acceptable heating sources but may be used as supplemental heating in a single family home or duplex.[15]

Public Officer and Administration

The housing code must designate one or more public officers to exercise the powers of the housing code.[16] In contrast to building code inspections, state law does not require specific certification or qualifications for a housing code officer. The local ordinance or policies may set standards for professional qualification.

---

10. G.S. 160D-1205.
11. *Id.*
12. *Id.*
13. G.S. 160D-1204(a).
14. G.S. 160D-1204(b).
15. G.S. 160D-1204(c).
16. G.S. 160D-1203.

The local ordinance may authorize a public officer "to exercise any powers necessary or convenient to carry out and effectuate the purpose and provisions" of the minimum housing code law.[17] Such powers include:

> (1) To investigate the dwelling conditions in the local government's planning and development regulation jurisdiction in order to determine which dwellings therein are unfit for human habitation.
> (2) To administer oaths, affirmations, examine witnesses, and receive evidence.
> (3) To enter upon premises for the purpose of making examinations in a manner that will do the least possible inconvenience to the persons in possession.
> (4) To appoint and fix the duties of officers, agents, and employees necessary to carry out the purposes of the ordinances.[18]

The local government is authorized to make appropriations to cover the expenses of administering the minimum housing code and may accept grants and donations to assist with such expenses. Upon adoption of a minimum housing code, the local government must prepare an estimate of the expenses required to administer the code (including equipment, personnel, and supplies needed for investigations and administration).[19]

Fourth Amendment Reminder

For a detailed discussion of Fourth Amendment limits on inspections, see Chapter 4. In brief, code officials must honor constitutional privacy protections, obtain consent or a warrant when needed, and rely only on observations made lawfully.

Process for Enforcement

The local government must adhere to the procedural requirements set forth in state law (and outlined below) to exercise its regulatory authority.[20] Enforcement action may begin even if the violation has existed for years without prior citation.[21]

17. G.S. 160D-1210.
18. *Id.*
19. G.S. 160D-1211.
20. Dale v. City of Morganton, 270 N.C. 567, 576, 155 S.E.2d 136, 144 (1967) ("Substantial compliance with these procedures is a condition precedent to the authority of the city to forbid the use of a dwelling house for human habitation.").
21. Carolina Holdings, Inc. v. Hous. Appeals Bd. of City of Charlotte, 149 N.C. App. 579, 561 S.E.2d 541 (2002) (finding the city is not estopped from enforcement of the housing code due to the fact that the violations had existed for years without citation).

Initiation and Preliminary Investigation

A public officer may initiate an investigation when it appears that a dwelling is unfit for human habitation. Alternatively, a public authority[22] or a group of at least five residents of the jurisdiction may file a petition charging that a dwelling is unfit. Upon initiation, the public officer shall perform a preliminary investigation.

Complaint and Notice

If the violation is confirmed by preliminary investigation, the public officer must serve a complaint stating the charges and provide notice of an administrative hearing, including the time and place.

The complaint and notice must be served upon the owner and any parties in interest.[23] "Owner" is defined as "[t]he holder of the title in fee simple and every mortgagee of record." "Parties in interest" is defined as "[a]ll individuals, associations, and corporations that have interests of record in a dwelling and any that are in possession of a dwelling."[24]

The officer must make reasonable efforts to identify the owner and parties in interest from the public record but does not have to go beyond the public record.[25] In *Patterson v. City of Gastonia*, the court ruled that neither the statutes nor caselaw impose a duty on the local government to go "beyond a public record search and conduct an investigation to uncover whether there might have been owners other than those appearing of record."[26]

As outlined in G.S. 160D-1206, in a housing code enforcement matter, any complaint or order must be served personally or by certified mail. When serving by certified mail, notice may also be sent by regular mail, and service is deemed sufficient if the certified mail is refused but the regular mail is not returned within ten days. In such cases, notice must also be posted in a conspicuous place on the premises.

Service by publication is acceptable in certain circumstances: (1) if the identity or whereabouts of persons are unknown and cannot be determined after reasonable due diligence, or (2) if the owners have refused to accept service by certified mail. Service by publication must be in a newspaper having general circulation

---

22. "Public authority" is defined as "[a]ny housing authority or any officer that is in charge of any department or branch of the government of the city, county, or State relating to health, fire, building regulations, or other activities concerning dwellings in the local government." G.S. 160D-1202.

23. For a more detailed discussion of the obligations involved in identifying who must be served with notice, see Tyler Mulligan, "Who Is an Owner 'of Record' to Be Served with Complaints and Orders Under NC Minimum Housing Codes?" Coates' Canons: NC Loc. Gov't L. (blog) (June 19, 2012), https://canons.sog.unc.edu/2012/06/who-is-an-owner-of-record-to-be-served-with-complaints-and-orders-under-nc-minimum-housing-codes/.

24. G.S. 160D-1202.

25. Lawyer v. City of Elizabeth City, 199 N.C. App. 304, 681 S.E.2d 415 (2009) (remanded for further consideration of the standard of care for determining the owners for notice).

26. 220 N.C. App. 233, 242, 725 S.E.2d 82, 89 (2012).

in the jurisdiction "at least once no later than the time at which personal service would be required." Along with notice by publication, notice must also be posted in a conspicuous place on the property.

Administrative Hearing

The administrative hearing is held by the public officer or a designated agent within the county where the property is located. The hearing must be held between ten and thirty days after the complaint is served. The owner and parties in interest have the right to file an answer to the complaint, to appear in person (or otherwise), and to give testimony. The formal judicial rules of evidence do not control administrative hearings before the public officer.

Findings and Order

After notice and administrative hearing, if the public officer determines that the dwelling is unfit for human habitation, the officer shall issue written findings of fact to support the determination and an order as appropriate. The order may be for repair, alteration, or improvement, or alternatively, the order may be for removal or demolition.

Order to repair, alter, or improve. If repair can be done at a reasonable cost in relation to the value of the dwelling, the order shall require the owner to repair, alter, or improve the dwelling within a time specified.[27] The housing code may specify a certain percentage of value as reasonable. Notably, setting the percentage is a policy choice by the local government. Setting the percentage higher will lead to more orders to repair. Setting the percentage lower will lead to more orders to demolish. The order must state that failure to comply shall make the dwelling subject to issuance of an unfit order.

Order to close and vacate. Under some circumstances, an order to repair may also require that the property be vacated during repair. "The order may require that the property be vacated and closed only if continued occupancy during the time allowed for repair will present a significant threat of bodily harm, taking into account the nature of the necessary repairs, alterations, or improvements; the current state of the property; and any additional risks due to the presence and capacity of minors under the age of 18 or occupants with physical or mental disabilities."[28]

Order to remove or demolish. If a dwelling cannot be repaired for a reasonable cost relative to the value of the dwelling, the order shall require the owner to remove or demolish the dwelling within the specified time.[29] Caselaw warns against a direct order to demolish without some opportunity to correct. In the case of *Horton v. Gulledge*, the city ordered an owner to demolish a dwelling. On appeal,

---

27. G.S. 160D-1203(3)(a).

28. *Id.*

29. G.S. 160D-1203(3)(b). In *Patterson*, 220 N.C. App. at 233, 725 S.E.2d at 82, the court held that sixty days was a sufficient time for an opportunity to correct a demolition order.

the central question for the court was: May the city require demolition (without compensation) without affording the owner an opportunity to bring the property into compliance? For the case at hand, the court said no. When there is not an imminent threat to safety, the city must give an opportunity to repair. "Where an unsafe structure could be remedied by private action, "[t]o require its destruction, without giving the owner a reasonable opportunity thus to remove the existing threat to the public health, safety and welfare, is arbitrary and unreasonable."[30]

Additional notice prior to demolition. When the public officer issues an order that a dwelling must be vacated and closed, or removed or demolished, additional notice and waiting is required. The public officer must provide notice of the order by first-class mail "to any organization involved in providing or restoring dwellings for affordable housing that has filed a written request for such notices." The public officer must certify the mailing for the record. From the date of the mailing, the public officer must wait at least forty-five days before removal or demolition by the public officer. The waiting period is intended "to allow the opportunity for any organization to negotiate with the owner to make repairs, lease, or purchase the property for the purpose of providing affordable housing."[31]

Delayed demolition for historic properties. If a dwelling is in a historic district and "is of particular significance or value toward maintaining the character of the district," as determined by the historic district commission, an order of demolition may be delayed. If the property was not condemned as unsafe, the order may require the dwelling to be vacated and closed for a period up to one year, consistent with the historic preservation authority at G.S. 160D-949.[32]

Additional enforcement considerations. The orders discussed above are the options authorized by state law. While at least one case affirmed civil penalties included in a housing code,[33] civil penalties are not specifically authorized by statute. Article 4 of Chapter 160D sets forth the general authorities for enforcement of development regulations and incorporates the enforcement powers of G.S. 160A-175 and G.S. 153A-123 (including civil penalties). But Article 4 also states the following: "To the extent there is a conflict between the provisions of this Article and other Articles, the more specific provision shall control. This Article does not expand, diminish, or alter the scope of authority for development regulations authorized by this Chapter."[34] That argues against authority for civil penalties for minimum housing enforcement.

---

30. Horton v. Gulledge, 277 N.C. 353, 363, 177 S.E.2d 885, 892 (1970), *overruled on other grounds by* State v. Jones, 305 N.C. 520, 290 S.E.2d 675 (1982).

31. G.S. 160D-1203(9).

32. G.S. 160D-1208.

33. City of Charlotte v. King, 158 N.C. App. 304, 580 S.E.2d 380 (2003) (decided on ordinance interpretation, not statutory authority).

34. G.S. 160D-401.

Appeal

An interested party may appeal a decision or order from the public officer to the housing appeals board, as discussed below. Such appeals must be filed within ten days from the decision or service of the order.[35]

Opportunity to Correct

The local government must provide a reasonable time for the owner to comply and must respect the stated time. For an order to remove or demolish, in particular, the owner must be "given a reasonable opportunity to bring it into conformity with the housing code" before any ordinance may be adopted.[36]

In *Patterson v. City of Gastonia*, the court ruled that sixty days was a sufficient amount of time for an opportunity to correct.[37] In contrast, in *Wiggins v. City of Monroe*,[38] the building inspector gave the owner ten days to commence repairs and sixty days to complete them. Within ten days, the owner obtained what they believed to be building permits to begin repairs. On day thirteen, the building inspector proceeded with demolition even though the owner had commenced repairs and the sixty-day window for cure had not run. The court found that the evidence tended to show that the building official's behavior was "corrupt or malicious or that he acted outside of and beyond the scope of his duties."

Notice of Lis Pendens

As discussed in Chapter 10, state law governing civil procedure allows a local government to file a notice of lis pendens relating to unsafe structure actions under Article 11 of Chapter 160D and minimum housing actions under Article 12 of Chapter 160D.[39] The notice is filed with the office of the clerk of superior court. The notice must be filed with a copy of the complaint and notice of hearing or order. A copy of the notice of lis pendens also must be served on the current owners and parties of interest.

Such notice is indexed and cross-indexed according to the rules for lis pendens at G.S. 1-117. The notice is binding upon future owners (as well as other parties of interest) of the subject building or property. The notice remains in effect until it is canceled. The ordinance may specify the circumstances that authorize cancellation.

General Enforcement Options

State law outlines enforcement options for development regulations generally. Since minimum housing codes fall under the broad umbrella of development regulations (authorized by Chapter 160D), those general enforcement options likely are available. G.S. 160D-403 and -404 specify some of the tools for enforcement:

35. G.S. 160D-1203(3)(b).
36. G.S. 160D-1203(5).
37. Patterson v. City of Gastonia, 220 N.C. App. 233, 242, 725 S.E.2d 82, 89 (2012).
38. Wiggins v. City of Monroe, 73 N.C. App. 44, 326 S.E.2d 39 (1985).
39. G.S. 1-120.2.

inspections, revocation of development approvals, withholding of certificates of occupancy, notices of violation, stop work orders, and "appropriate action or proceedings" to prevent work or activity in violation of development regulations. G.S. 160D-404 provides a cross-reference to the enforcement tools for general police power ordinances outlined at G.S. 160A-175 and 153A-123. That includes civil penalties, legal proceedings in court, and treating the violation as a misdemeanor (subject to some limitations on criminal enforcement).[40]

Ordinance After Failure to Comply

If an owner fails to comply with an order to repair, alter, or improve, or if an owner fails to comply with an order to remove or demolish, the governing board[41] may, by ordinance, order the public officer to proceed with enforcement ("to effectuate the purpose of this Article"). The ordinance must describe the property or properties that have been found to be unfit for human habitation.[42] "This ordinance shall be recorded in the office of the register of deeds in the county where the property or properties are located and shall be indexed in the name of the property owner in the grantor index."[43]

If an owner fails to comply with an order to take corrective action the local government may pursue court-appointed receivership as discussed in Chapter 15.[44]

Officer Action to Cause Compliance

After an owner fails to comply with an order, and the local governing board properly adopts an ordinance to that effect, the public officer may take action to cause compliance with the order as appropriate.

For repair orders, "the public officer may cause the dwelling to be repaired, altered, or improved or to be vacated and closed." The public officer may post a placard on the main entrance stating the following: "This building is unfit for human habitation; the use or occupation of this building for human habitation is prohibited and unlawful."[45] It is a Class 1 misdemeanor to occupy a building so posted.

---

40. Adam Lovelady, *Enforcement of Development Regulations*, Coates' Canons: NC Loc. Gov't L. (blog) (Feb. 11, 2022), https://canons.sog.unc.edu/2022/02/enforcement-of-development-regulations/; Adam Lovelady, *Limits on Criminal Enforcement of Development Regulations*, Coates' Canons: NC Loc. Gov't L. (blog) (Feb. 11, 2022), https://canons.sog.unc.edu/2022/02/limits-on-criminal-enforcement-of-development-regulations/.

41. State law refers to the "governing board," the legislative body such as a town council or county commission with the authority to adopt ordinances. One case, though, allowed a local ordinance to assign the duty of adopting ordinances to the local housing commission. Moores v. Greensboro Minimum Hous. Standards Comm'n, 198 N.C. App. 384, 679 S.E.2d 480 (2009).

42. G.S. 160D-1203(4), (5).

43. *Id.*

44. G.S. 160D-1130.

45. G.S. 160D-1203(4).

Table 12.1. Repair Cost and Ordinance Requirements (per G.S. 160D-1203(6))

Cost of Repair	Ordinance Requirement
Less than 50% of dwelling value	*Owner must repair or demolish and remove the dwelling within 90 days*
Greater than 50% of dwelling value	*Owner must demolish and remove the dwelling within 90 days*

For an order to remove or demolish, after failure to comply and adoption of an ordinance, "the public officer may cause such dwelling to be removed or demolished."[46]

Ejectment

If an occupant refuses to vacate a dwelling pursuant to an order, the public officer may bring a civil action to remove the occupant.[47] Such action is in the nature of summary ejectment under Chapter 42 of the General Statutes. The action is commenced by filing a complaint naming as defendant any person occupying the dwelling. The occupant must be served at least thirty days before filing the summary ejectment proceeding, with notice of the governing board ordinance authorizing the public officer to enforce the order to vacate.

Abandonment of Intent to Repair

The governing board may adopt an ordinance finding that an owner has abandoned intent to repair if the dwelling has been vacated and closed for a period of one year. The calculation of the one-year time period begins with adoption of an ordinance to repair or vacate and close, or after a public officer issues an order or commences proceedings under the minimum housing code.[48]

The ordinance must specify one of the following requirements, depending on whether the cost of repair is greater or less than 50 percent of the dwelling's value (see Table 12.1).

"This ordinance shall be recorded in the office of the register of deeds in the county wherein the property or properties are located and shall be indexed in the name of the property owner in the grantor index." If the owner fails to comply, "the public officer shall effectuate the purpose of the ordinance."[49]

---

46. G.S. 160D-1203(5).
47. G.S. 160D-1203(8).
48. G.S. 160D-1203(6).
49. *Id.*

Liens

The costs incurred by the local government to complete the repair, or to vacate and close, or to remove or demolish, is a lien against the property. This lien has the same priority as a lien for special assessments (specified in Article 10 of Chapter 160A). Additionally, if the property is in a municipality, the cost is also a lien against any other real property of the owner within the municipality or within one mile of the municipality (excluding the owner's primary residence). Such additional lien is subordinate to prior liens and is collected as a money judgment.[50]

For removal or demolition, the local government must sell any materials, personal property, fixtures, and appurtenances, and apply the proceeds toward the cost of removal or demolition. Any proceeds are to be deposited with the superior court for disbursement.[51]

Housing Appeals Board

The local government may establish a housing appeals board or assign its duties to the board of adjustment.[52]

An appeal from a decision or order issued by the public officer may be taken by any person aggrieved or by any officer, board, or commission of the local government. Such appeal is a quasi-judicial matter and must follow the formal procedures for quasi-judicial decision-making outlined in G.S. 160D-406.[53]

Filing an appeal. An appeal must be filed within ten days of the decision or service of the order. The appealing party must file with the public officer and the housing appeals board a notice of appeal specifying the grounds for appeal. Upon filing the notice, the public officer must transmit to the board "all the papers constituting the record upon which the decision appealed from was made."[54]

Tolling. If the appeal concerns a decision *preventing* a party from taking action, the decision remains in effect until modified or reversed on appeal. If the appeal concerns a decision *requiring* a party to take action, the decision is suspended until the hearing by the board (unless the public officer certifies to the board that it is a matter of imminent peril to life or property).[55]

Appeal hearing. The housing appeals board must set a reasonable time for hearing appeals and provide due notice to the parties. Parties may appear in person or be represented by an agent or attorney.

---

50. G.S. 160D-1203(7)(a)–(b).

51. G.S. 160D-1203(7)(c); *see also* Town of Hertford v. Harris, 169 N.C. App. 838, 611 S.E.2d 194 (2005) (the municipality must sell personal property and fixtures and credit that against the cost of the demolition).

52. G.S. 160D, §§ 305, 1208(a).

53. G.S. 160D-1208(b).

54. *Id.*

55. G.S. 160D-1208(a).

Decision. The board must issue a decision within a reasonable time. It has all of the powers of the public officer, so it may reverse or affirm, in whole or in part, or modify the decision or order to take the action the board determines is appropriate. Notably, a vote of four members (out of five) is necessary to reverse or modify a decision or order of the public officer.[56]

Unnecessary hardship. In cases of unnecessary hardship, the board may adapt the standards of the ordinance. If the board determines that "unnecessary hardships would result from carrying out the strict letter of the ordinance," it may "adapt the application of the ordinance to the necessities of the case to the end that the spirit of the ordinance is observed, public safety and welfare secured, and substantial justice done."[57]

Appeal from the housing appeals board. An appeal of a decision of the housing appeals board must be filed within fifteen days of the decision of the board. It is subject to review in the nature of certiorari.[58]

Alternatively, state law provides a separate appeal option to restrain enforcement of an order or decision. A person aggrieved by either an order of a public officer or a decision by a housing appeals board may petition the superior court for an injunction restraining enforcement of the order or decision, including a temporary injunction while final disposition is pending. Such petition must be filed within thirty days of the issuance of the order or decision. The hearing shall be held within twenty days of the petition and shall have priority over other matters on the court calendar.[59]

Caselaw affirms that the state law delegating authority for minimum housing sets forth the process for individuals to appeal and seek administrative remedies. If an individual fails to exhaust administrative remedies, they cannot circumvent the established procedure by bringing an untimely lawsuit.[60] In limited circumstances, though, an individual may still bring a constitutional challenge if the administrative process did not provide adequate remedy to the alleged constitutional violation.[61]

Enforcement, Generally

If a dwelling is in violation of the minimum housing code, "the public officer or board may institute any appropriate action or proceedings to prevent the unlawful erection, construction, reconstruction, alteration, or use; to restrain, correct, or

---

56. G.S. 160D-1208(b).

57. *Id.*

58. G.S. 160D-1208(c).

59. G.S. 160D-1208(d).

60. Harrell v. City of Winston-Salem, 22 N.C. App. 386, 206 S.E.2d 802 (1974); Axler v. City of Wilmington, 25 N.C. App. 110, 212 S.E.2d 510 (1975); Cheatham v. Town of Taylortown, 254 N.C. App. 613, 803 S.E.2d 658, 659 (2017).

61. Askew v. City of Kinston, 386 N.C. 286, 902 S.E.2d 722 (2024).

abate the violation; to prevent the occupancy of the dwelling; or to prevent any illegal act, conduct, or use in or about the premises of the dwelling."[62]

Periodic Inspections

Limited Authority for Residential Buildings

In general, the inspection department may only make periodic inspections of residential buildings or structures "when there is reasonable cause to believe that unsafe, unsanitary, or otherwise hazardous or unlawful conditions may exist."

In this context, reasonable cause means one of the following:

> (i) the landlord or owner has a history of more than two verified violations of the housing ordinances or codes within a 12-month period,
> (ii) there has been a complaint that substandard conditions exist within the building or there has been a request that the building be inspected,
> (iii) the inspection department has actual knowledge of an unsafe condition within the building, or
> (iv) violations of the local ordinances or codes are visible from the outside of the property.[63]

For multifamily buildings, if the inspections department determines that a unit has a safety hazard posing an immediate threat to the occupant, the department may inspect other units in the multifamily building even without a specific complaint or actual knowledge of an unsafe condition.[64]

For periodic inspections, the inspections department must treat all residential buildings equally—the department must not discriminate between single-family and multifamily buildings, nor between owner-occupied and renter-occupied dwellings.[65]

Acting under state authority and limitations, inspectors are authorized to enter premises at reasonable hours and upon presentation of credentials for inspection or other enforcement action. The limitations on periodic inspections do not prohibit periodic inspections conducted pursuant to the state fire code or other state rules.[66]

Periodic Inspections in Targeted Areas

A local government may require periodic inspections within a designated target area to respond to blighted or potentially blighted conditions.

---

62. G.S. 160D-1208(e).
63. G.S. 160D-1207(a).
64. *Id.*
65. *Id.*
66. *Id.*

The target area must be designated by the local government and must "reflect the local government's stated neighborhood revitalization strategy and shall consist of property that meets the definition of a *blighted area* or *blighted parcel*.[67] Procedurally, the local government must do the following to designate a target area for periodic inspections:

> (i) provide notice to all owners and residents of properties in the affected area about the periodic inspections plan and information regarding a legislative hearing regarding the plan,
> (ii) hold a legislative hearing regarding the plan, and
> (iii) establish a plan to address the ability of low-income residential property owners to comply with minimum housing code standards.[68]

The local government must not discriminate in the selection of areas or in the selection of housing types. The aggregate area of designated targeted areas may be no more than the greater of one square mile or five percent of the area within the local government jurisdiction.[69]

Limits on Residential Rental Permits, Registration, and Fees

General Limits

G.S. 160D-1207(c) sets forth notable limits on a local government's authority to regulate the rental of residential property. The statute also provides specific exceptions for particular properties, as discussed below.

In general, a local government may not

- require a permit under the building code or housing code to lease or rent residential property (except for properties with verified violations or those in the top ten percent for crime or disorder, as discussed below);
- require registration of rental property (except for properties with verified violations or those in the top ten percent for crime or disorder, as discussed below);
- require participation in a governmental program as a condition for obtaining a certificate of occupancy;
- levy a special fee or tax on residential rental property that is not also levied against other commercial and residential properties (subject to an exception discussed below);

---

67. As defined in G.S. 160A-503(2) ("blighted area") and -503(2a) ("blighted parcel"). Notably, the planning board does not have to make a determination under this provision.
68. G.S. 160D-1207(b).
69. *Id.*

- make a rental registration ordinance punishable as a criminal offense; or
- require an inspection of rental property before receiving utility service provided by the local government.

Properties with Verified Violations

While a local government generally may not require a permit or registration for residential rental property, there is an exception allowing permits or registration for properties with a certain number of verified violations: "those individual properties that have more than four verified violations in a rolling 12-month period or two or more verified violations in a rolling 30-day period."[70]

A "verified violation" is defined as either of the following:

> (1) The aggregate of all violations of housing ordinances or codes found in an individual rental unit of residential real property during a 72-hour period.
> (2) Any violations that have not been corrected by the owner or manager within 21 days of receipt of written notice from the local government of the violations.

Regarding failure to correct, if the same violation occurs twice within a twelve-month period, the local code may provide that the owner or manager no longer has the option to correct the violation. Additionally, for tenant behavior that constitutes a violation, it is deemed a correction if the owner or manager brings a summary ejectment action within thirty days of written notice of the violation.

Property in the Top 10 Percent for Crime or Disorder

Similarly, while a local government generally may not require a permit or registration for residential rental property, there is an allowance to require permits or registration for properties with high levels of crime or disorder: "property being identified within the top ten percent (10%) of properties with crime or disorder problems as set forth in a local ordinance."[71]

The process for such designation is as follows:

- Identify the property "as being in the top ten percent (10%) of properties with crime or disorder problems."
- "[N]otify the landlord of any crimes, disorders, or other violations that will be counted against the property to allow the landlord an opportunity to attempt to correct the problems."
- The local government and county or municipal law enforcement "shall assist the landlord in addressing any criminal activity, which may include testifying in court in a summary ejectment action or

70. G.S. 160D-1207(c).
71. *Id.*

other matter to aid in evicting a tenant who has been charged with a crime."[72]

Special Tax or Fee

In general, a local government may not levy a special fee or tax on residential rental property. However, there is an allowance to levy such a fee or tax if it is:

- "expressly authorized by general law" or
- "applicable only to an individual rental unit or property [qualifying with verified violations or top ten percent crime and disorder] and the fee does not exceed five hundred dollars ($500.00) in any 12-month period in which the unit or property is found to have verified violations."[73]

Appeals of Residential Rental Permits, Registration, and Fees

If a local government takes action against an individual rental unit pursuant to the limited allowances for residential rental permits, registration, or fees, the owner of the rental unit may appeal. Such appeals go to the housing appeals board, board of adjustment, planning board, or governing board, depending on which boards are established and operating.[74]

The board must handle the procedures by fixing a reasonable time for appeals, providing due notice to the owner of the unit, and rendering a decision within a reasonable time. The owner has the right to be heard, either in person or by agent or attorney. "The board may reverse or affirm the action, wholly or partly, or may modify the action appealed from, and may make any decision and order that in the opinion of the board ought to be made in the matter."

72. G.S. 160D-1207(d).
73. G.S. 160D-1207(c).
74. G.S. 160D-1207(e).

Chapter 13
Nuisance Code and Abatement

Overview

Public nuisance is a broad term encompassing many different situations that threaten public health, safety, and welfare. An overgrown lot on a quiet suburban street may be a public nuisance, and a major, ongoing chemical spill at a manufacturing facility may be a public nuisance. An illegal gambling hall, a commercial building crumbling onto a downtown sidewalk, or a motel with frequent criminal activity—all may be public nuisances.

State and local governments may pursue public nuisance enforcement in several different ways. They can file lawsuits in court claiming a common law public nuisance.[1] Local governments, among others, may bring legal action to abate a public nuisance as defined in Chapter 19 of the North Carolina General Statutes (hereinafter G.S.) (which outlines Offenses Against Public Morals).[2] In addition, local governments can use their general police powers to declare an activity a nuisance and enforce that designation through ordinances and court proceedings.[3]

This chapter focuses on local government authority to address public nuisances under their local government police powers: (1) the authority to adopt ordinances to regulate nuisances as outlined in G.S. 160A-147 and G.S. 153A-121 (the Nuisance Code Authority), and (2) the separate authority to abate public health nuisances as outlined in G.S. 160A-193 and G.S. 153A-140 (the Public Health Nuisance Abatement Authority). Under the Nuisance Code Authority, local governments in North Carolina commonly address issues such as overgrown vegetation, discarded appliances, solid waste and yard debris, and similar situations. Under the Public Health Nuisance Abatement Authority, local governments in North Carolina may address situations that present an imminent danger. (See Appendix J for sample forms related to nuisance code violations, notices, and abatement.)

---

1. *See* State *ex rel.* Howes v. W.R. Peele, Sr. Tr., 876 F. Supp. 733 (E.D.N.C. 1995) (bringing common law public nuisance claim along with CERCLA liability for environmental cleanup).

2. *See* State on Rel. of City of Albemarle v. Nance, 266 N.C. App. 353, 831 S.E.2d 605 (2019) (relating enforcement against a hotel operator where criminal activity occurred); State v. Arellano, 165 N.C. App. 609, 599 S.E.2d 415, 416 (2004) (bringing criminal enforcement against a massage parlor as a public nuisance).

3. *See* City of Fayetteville v. Spur Distrib. Co., 216 N.C. 596, 5 S.E.2d 838 (1939) (city seeking injunction to prevent construction of a gasoline storage facility in the city fire district).

Deciphering the Authority

The North Carolina statutes offer two distinct but overlapping authorities for local governments to address public nuisances: the Nuisance Code Authority and the Public Health Nuisance Abatement Authority. Because of the overlap, there is some ambiguity regarding the scope and requirements of these separate authorities.

School of Government faculty have highlighted this lack of clarity in the past. Rich Ducker explored how this area of law is a mess in not one but two blogs titled, "Nuisance Abatement and Local Governments: What a Mess" (Parts I and II).[4] Trey Allen asked, "May a City Mow an Overgrown Lot Without a Court Order?"[5] This chapter builds on that tradition: walking through the authorities, investigating the ambiguities, and suggesting potential approaches to manage the unknowns.

An overarching question in nuisance enforcement by local governments in North Carolina is this: what process is due? This question is especially critical when local officials enter private property to abate a nuisance. While the statutes provide some guidance, they also muddy the waters. This chapter outlines essential issues and guiding principles to help navigate the ambiguities in this context:

- **Limited statutory guidance.** State statutes provide little guidance on the scope of authority or necessary process for enforcement of a nuisance code or abatement of a public health nuisance.
- **Constitutional caution.** Because constitutionally protected property and individual rights are implicated, a cautious and procedural approach to enforcement is advisable.
- **Other enforcement tools may guide the process.** Since the nuisance statutes do not fully specify procedures, local governments may consider looking to similar authorities (such as those for unsafe structures, minimum housing, and zoning) for procedural guidance on due process.
- **Ambiguity about the process for abatement.** The statutes offer some guidance but leave considerable ambiguity about when and how local governments may enter private property to abate a public nuisance. Court-ordered abatement is clearly authorized and provides the most protection for local governments. Administrative abatement (without a court order but with some level of notice and

---

4. Richard Ducker, "Nuisance Abatement and Local Governments: What a Mess," Coates' Canons: NC Loc. Gov't L. (blog) (June 16, 2011), https://canons.sog.unc.edu/2011/06/nuisance-abatement-and-local-governments-what-a-mess/; Richard Ducker, "Nuisance Abatement and Local Governments: What a Mess – Part II," Coates' Canons: NC Loc. Gov't L. (blog) (July 31, 2013), https://canons.sog.unc.edu/2013/07/nuisance-abatement-and-local-governments-what-a-mess-part-ii/.

5. Trey Allen, *May a City Mow an Overgrown Lot Without a Court Order?*, Coates' Canons: NC Loc. Gov't L. (blog) (Apr. 10, 2017), https://canons.sog.unc.edu/2017/04/may-a-city-mow-an-overgrown-lot-without-a-court-order/.

process) is authorized in certain situations, but not all. Summary abatement (without pre-abatement process) is discussed next. The final section of this chapter explores the authority for different types of abatement.

- **Caution regarding summary abatement.** Summary abatement (without a court order, notice, or opportunity to be heard) is available to municipalities. Caselaw suggests that such authority is limited to situations of imminent danger. If there is no imminent danger, it is prudent for local governments to follow standard procedures, including notice and an opportunity to be heard.

As described elsewhere in Part 3, local governments have specific authorities for dealing with unsafe structures (Chapter 10), maintenance of commercial buildings (Chapter 11), maintenance of residential buildings and abandoned structures (Chapter 12), unauthorized activities and land uses (Chapter 15), and vacant building receivership (Chapter 15). The statutes allowing for nuisance codes and public health nuisance abatement offer additional authority to address unsafe situations on property not covered by those specific authorities.

Nuisance Code Authority

North Carolina counties and municipalities "may by ordinance define, regulate, prohibit, or abate acts, omissions, or conditions detrimental to the health, safety, or welfare of its citizens and the peace and dignity of the city [or county], and *may define and abate nuisances*."[6] Some local governments use this authority to adopt a nuisance code that defines particular nuisances and sets forth procedures for enforcement.

With regard to geographic jurisdiction, a municipal nuisance code is a police power ordinance that may be enforced within the municipal corporate limits. A nuisance code is not a development regulation under Chapter 160D of the General Statutes, so the nuisance code is not part of the extraterritorial jurisdiction (ETJ) regulations. The Nuisance Code Authority, at G.S. 160A-174, does not mention enforcement beyond the municipal corporate limit, but the Public Health Nuisance Abatement Authority, at G.S. 160A-193, allows enforcement within one mile of the municipal corporate limit. A county nuisance code applies to any part of the county outside of a municipality. A municipality may permit a county ordinance to be applicable within the municipality.[7]

Given the overlap and distinctions between the Nuisance Code Authority and the Public Health Nuisance Abatement Authority, when drafting a nuisance code,

---

6. Chapter 160A, Section 174 of the North Carolina General Statutes (hereinafter G.S.); G.S. 153A-121 (italics added).

7. G.S. 153A-122.

a local government may consider referencing both authorities. Drafters and public officers, though, must take care that the ordinance and enforcement adhere to the required procedures and limits of each authority.

Following litigation over condemned cottages on the beach at Nags Head,[8] state law was clarified to confirm that local governments may adopt and enforce ordinances, including a nuisance code, on the state's ocean beaches. This includes the authority to regulate "equipment, personal property, or debris upon the State's ocean beaches."[9] Municipal authority adds language to specifically allow regulation of "structures that are uninhabitable and without water and sewer services for more than 120 days."[10] For uninhabitable structures, state law requires that such action include a determination by the city and notice to the owner of record by certified mail.[11]

A nuisance ordinance may be used in conjunction with a broader solid waste program. In one case, the North Carolina Court of Appeals confirmed that a county program operated to remove junk and waste from private property at the owners' request was a governmental function.[12]

Nuisance Code Adopted as Ordinance

The authority from state law requires that the regulations be adopted into an ordinance but does not give much guidance on necessary standards or procedures. The state and federal constitutions, though, demand due process when regulating and limiting the property rights of individuals. The procedures from other property codes, outlined in Chapters 10, 11, and 12, provide instructive guidance for procedures appropriate for a nuisance ordinance, including clear standards for what constitutes a violation; procedures for inspection; notice and opportunity to correct; clear enforcement authority; and the right to appeal.

Like other property codes, it is appropriate for the nuisance code to assign responsibility for enforcement. Depending on the size and organization of the jurisdiction, nuisance code enforcement might be handled by the inspections department, planning, community development, solid waste, or another related department.

---

8. Town of Nags Head v. Cherry, Inc., 219 N.C. App. 66, 723 S.E.2d 156, *review denied*, 366 N.C. 386, 733 S.E.2d 85 (2012); Sansotta v. Town of Nags Head, 724 F.3d 533 (4th Cir. 2013).

9. G.S. 160A-205; 153A-145.3.

10. *Id.*

11. *Id.*

12. Est. of Hewett v. Cnty. of Brunswick, 199 N.C. App. 564, 681 S.E.2d 531 (2009).

Clear Standards for Violation

While public nuisances may arise in many varied ways, it is appropriate for the nuisance code to clearly identify the common situations that constitute a public nuisance subject to local government enforcement. Common examples include uncontrolled grass and weeds above a certain height, accumulation of waste that may attract pests or otherwise be dangerous to public health, accumulation of bulky and/or combustible waste, accumulation of unusable construction or demolition debris, stagnant water, and other conditions that pose a risk to public health or safety.

Nuisance Code Inspections

Inspections for potential nuisance violations must comply with constitutional limits, as noted in the sidebar.

Fourth Amendment Reminder

For a detailed discussion of Fourth Amendment limits on inspections, see Chapter 4. In brief, code officials must honor constitutional privacy protections, obtain consent or a warrant when needed, and rely only on observations made lawfully.

Notice and Process for a Nuisance Code

Notice of Violation and Order to Correct

If an officer identifies a violation, they should generally issue a notice of violation and an order to correct. Except for chronic violators, discussed below, the statutes do not specify the notice needed for nuisance code violations. Local governments may reasonably draw from other property codes, such as zoning or housing codes, as guides for notice requirements and include those in the nuisance code.

The notice requirements for a notice of violation related to development regulations (such as zoning), as outlined in G.S. 160D-404, are instructive. The following forms of comparable notice may be used to initiate nuisance code enforcement:

- notice to the owner of the property and the holder of the development approval (if different);
- notice by personal delivery, electronic delivery, or first-class mail;
- notice may also be provided to the occupant or person undertaking the activity; and
- notice may also be posted on the property.

An officer must certify to the local government (for the record) what notice was provided.

If a nuisance enforcement action moves to abatement by the local government, heightened notice is prudent. In the minimum housing context, notice must be served upon the owner and any parties in interest, and an administrative hearing is required to establish findings.

When the owner and parties of interest cannot be located, service by publication may be appropriate in situations similar to those acceptable for housing code violations.

Notice to Chronic Violators

For chronic violators, the local government may give annual notice and then take action without further notice. A chronic violator is the owner of property for which the local government has issued at least three notices of violation of the public nuisance ordinance in the prior calendar year. A local government may notify a chronic violator that "if the violator's property is found to be in violation of the ordinance, the [local government] shall, without further notice in the calendar year in which notice is given, take action to remedy the violation, and the expense of the action shall become a lien upon the property and shall be collected as unpaid taxes."[13]

The municipal statutes give specific procedures for this notice; notice must be sent by registered or certified mail. In addition, the local government may send notice by regular mail. "Service shall be deemed sufficient if the registered or certified mail is unclaimed or refused, but the regular mail is not returned by the post office within 10 days after the mailing." It is prudent to post a copy of the notice in a conspicuous place on the property (and it is required to post notice if the regular mail option is used).[14] While the municipal statutes call for notice to the owner of the property, it is prudent to provide notice to other parties in interest. The county version of the statute provides less guidance on procedures. For counties "notice shall be sent by certified mail."[15] Beyond that, a county may use the municipal statutes as a guide.

Opportunity to Correct

Generally, a property owner is given an opportunity to correct the violation. The appropriate amount of time for correction may depend upon the nature of the nuisance code violation. Ten days may be reasonable for overgrown grass, but a longer time may be necessary for more extensive clean-up of trash or overgrowth. For properties that have been identified as chronic violators, state law allows the

13. G.S. 160A-200.1; 153A-140.2.
14. G.S. 160A-200.1.
15. G.S. 153A-140.2.

local government to take action to remedy the violation without additional notice or opportunity to be heard.

Appeals

While it is not directly required by state law, due process typically includes an opportunity to be heard. Moreover, other related codes—housing codes, commercial maintenance, and zoning codes—include an opportunity for an administrative or quasi-judicial evidentiary hearing. Similarly, a nuisance code ordinance could outline a process for an owner to provide evidence and challenge an officer's determination. The local code may use the other appeal procedures as instructive models. In the housing code context, there is an administrative hearing before the officer, and appeals are taken to the housing appeals board. In the unsafe structures context, appeals go to the governing board. For zoning, appeals of administrative decisions go to the board of adjustment.

Enforcement of a Nuisance Code

A local nuisance code may be enforced with a variety of enforcement tools. The ordinance should specify which tools are available for enforcement. Here are the options.

Misdemeanor and Fine

Violation of a local government ordinance may be defined as a misdemeanor or infraction, but it must be specified in the ordinance. (State law prohibits imposition of criminal penalties in ordinances regulating certain activities like zoning, but nuisance codes are not included on that list.)[16] With regard to misdemeanor violations of local ordinances, G.S. 14-4 sets a presumption that fines are $50 or less, but allows fines up to $500 if expressly stated in the ordinance.

Civil Penalty

A civil penalty is a monetary penalty for a violation of a local ordinance. Civil penalties are generally authorized for enforcing local ordinances. The local ordinance may establish that each day's continuing violation is a separate and distinct offense, so civil penalties may accrue over time, with a separate charge for each day of noncompliance.[17] The statutes do not set a maximum or minimum amount for civil penalties. The range of fines for criminal penalties may be a useful guide for setting civil penalties. A civil penalty is treated as a debt owed to the local

16. G.S. 160A-175(b1).
17. G.S. 160A-175(g); 153A-123(g).

government. While the civil penalty is not an automatic lien against the property, the local government may bring a civil action in court to recover the penalty as a debt.[18]

Court Order

A local government may seek court-ordered compliance through an injunction or abatement order. G.S. 160A-175 and G.S. 153A-123 authorize a local government to bring a civil action against a violator to address violations. In such actions, the court may issue remedial orders, such as "mandatory or prohibitory injunction and order of abatement commanding the defendant to correct the unlawful condition upon or cease the unlawful use of the property."

Local Government Abatement

In some situations, a local government may abate a nuisance code violation, as discussed in more detail below.

Public Health Nuisance Abatement

Beyond the general authority to adopt and enforce a nuisance code, North Carolina local governments have authority to abate public health nuisances: A local government may "remove, abate, or remedy everything . . . that is dangerous or prejudicial to the public health or public safety."[19] This authority presents flexibility, but it also carries a risk for the local government. It allows a local government to address immediate safety situations that are unanticipated or do not fit neatly into an ordinance, but it grants broad power without procedural guardrails. If not exercised properly, the Public Health Nuisance Abatement Authority may leave a local government open to constitutional challenge and litigation. This authority could be incorporated into and made part of a local nuisance code which, in turn, could provide due process.

Municipal Authority

The municipal authority for public health nuisance abatement is especially broad—it allows for summary abatement. A municipality may "summarily remove, abate, or remedy everything . . . that is dangerous or prejudicial to the public health or public safety." This authority applies within the municipal limits and, notably, to any area within one mile of the municipal limits.[20] As discussed in more detail below in the Abatement section, there are open questions about the scope of this authority for summary abatement.

---

18. G.S. 160A-175(c); 153A-123(c).
19. G.S. 160A-193; *see also* G.S. 153A-140 (containing comparable language).
20. G.S. 160A-193(a).

The statute also authorizes a municipal governing board to "order the removal of a swimming pool and its appurtenances upon a finding that the swimming pool or its appurtenances is dangerous or prejudicial to public health or safety."

The person in default (generally the property owner) is obligated to pay the expense of the abatement action. If they do not pay the expense, it becomes a lien against the property with the same priority as unpaid ad valorem taxes. Unpaid expenses are also a lien against any other real property owned by the person within the municipality or within one mile of the municipal limit. Those liens, though, are inferior to any prior liens and must be collected as a money judgment. If the person can show the nuisance was created solely by the actions of another, they may avoid such liens.[21]

There is a specific limit in the statute on applying municipal bans on burning to residents outside of the municipal corporate limits. A municipality may not impose an ordinance banning outdoor burning on residents living within one mile of the municipality unless the municipality provides those residents with solid waste collection or drop-off sites on the same basis as municipal residents.[22]

County Authority

County authority to abate public health nuisances is more limited than municipal authority. A county does not have authority to *summarily* abate nuisances; additional process is required. In order to exercise the authority, the county must provide "adequate notice, the right to a hearing, and the right to appeal."[23]

Similar to a municipality, a county board of commissioners may order the removal of a pool upon finding it is dangerous or prejudicial to public health or safety.

The expense of abatement must be paid by the person in default. If not, it becomes a lien upon the property and may be collected as unpaid taxes.

County authority over agriculture and forestry operations is limited, but public health nuisance abatement may still apply to "any use of farm property for nonfarm purposes."[24]

Abatement by the Local Government

Can a local government go onto private property to abate a nuisance? The short answer is it depends. It depends upon the nature of the nuisance, the legal process provided to the individual, and the authority under which the local government is acting. In the case of a true public health nuisance that is creating imminent

21. G.S. 160A-193(b).
22. G.S. 160A-193(c).
23. G.S. 153A-140.
24. G.S. 106-701; 153A-140.

danger, a municipality may act to abate the nuisance even without a court order or even prior notice. In many situations, however, a court order or notice and process is necessary prior to abatement by the local government. Determining what situations justify summary abatement is challenging, as noted by the United States Supreme Court back in the late 1800s: "It is not easy to draw the line between cases where property illegally used may be destroyed summarily and where judicial proceedings are necessary for its condemnation."[25]

This discussion considers different types of abatement: court-ordered abatement (authorized by civil court proceedings), administrative abatement (without a court order, but with notice and process), and summary abatement (without a court order or administrative notice and process). The following sections consider each in turn.

Abatement by Court Order

A local government may go to court to seek court-ordered compliance with the nuisance code, and, if the owner fails to comply, the local government may then abate the violation. "An order of abatement may direct that buildings or other structures on the property be closed, demolished, or removed; that fixtures, furniture, or other movable property be removed from buildings on the property; that grass and weeds be cut; that improvements or repairs be made; or that any other action be taken that is necessary to bring the property into compliance with the ordinance."[26]

If the violator fails to comply within the time allowed by the court, they may be cited for contempt of court, and the local government may execute the court's order of abatement. If the local government executes the order of abatement, it has a lien on the property for the costs of abatement. The lien is in the nature of a mechanic's and materialman's lien. "The defendant may secure cancellation of an order of abatement by paying all costs of the proceedings and posting a bond for compliance with the order."[27]

Court-ordered abatement provides the clearest authority for local government action.[28]

---

25. Lawton v. Steele, 152 U.S. 133, 140–41, 14 S. Ct. 499, 502, 38 L. Ed. 385 (1894) (holding that fishing nets used illegally may be determined to be a public nuisance and destroyed prior to judicial review).

26. G.S. 160A-175(e); 153A-123(e).

27. *Id.*

28. *See* 6A McQuillin Mun. Corp. § 24:79 (3d ed.) (*Abatement by Municipality—Limitations and Considerations*) ("Although a prior judicial determination of nuisance is not required before destruction, ordinarily it is a better course for a municipal corporation to secure an adjudication from the courts before proceeding to abate a nuisance, particularly where there is some doubt as to whether or not a nuisance does in fact exist, this is true because otherwise a municipal corporation may be held liable for destruction or impairment of property if it is determined that no nuisance existed in fact.").

Administrative Abatement

The authority for administrative abatement (with notice and opportunity to be heard, but without a court order) is mixed. It is not clearly authorized under the Nuisance Code Authority, but it is authorized under the Chronic Violators statutes and the Public Health Nuisance Abatement Authority.

First, consider the Nuisance Code Authority. On the one hand, state law plainly authorizes local governments to "define *and abate* nuisances."[29] But the following section of the state law outlines enforcement options, and abatement is only mentioned in relation to court-ordered abatement. This leaves an open question: Under the Nuisance Code Authority, can a local government go onto private property to remedy a nuisance code violation without a court order?

As noted by former School of Government faculty member Trey Allen, "[t]he more cautious approach is to assume that the law grants no such authority, but reasonable arguments can be made in favor of interpreting [the Nuisance Code Authority] to permit cities to mow overgrown lots without first going to court."[30] The statute itself says local governments may "abate nuisances;"[31] police power statutes, such as those for nuisance codes, are to be broadly construed when there is ambiguity;[32] a North Carolina court case accepted administrative abatement in a nuisance code by implication;[33] and, the chronic violator statute seems to relieve the local government of notice requirements for administrative abatement, implying that even for non-chronic violators there may be administrative abatement with proper notice.[34] Within this context, one may argue that a local government can pursue administrative abatement under the Nuisance Code Authority, but it is not clear.

Next, administrative abatement is authorized under the Chronic Violators statutes. With proper notice and procedure, state law allows local governments to remedy violations by chronic violators of the local nuisance code or overgrown vegetation ordinance. A local government may notify a chronic violator that "if the violator's property is found to be in violation of the ordinance, the [local government] shall, without further notice in the calendar year in which notice is given, take action to remedy the violation, and the expense of the action shall become a lien upon the property and shall be collected as unpaid taxes."[35]

---

29. G.S. 160A-174; 153A-121.

30. Trey Allen, *May a City Mow an Overgrown Lot Without a Court Order?*, Coates' Canons: NC Loc. Gov't L. (blog) (Apr. 10, 2017), https://canons.sog.unc.edu/2017/04/may-a-city-mow-an-overgrown-lot-without-a-court-order/.

31. G.S. 160A-174; 153A-121.

32. King v. Town of Chapel Hill, 367 N.C. 400 (2014).

33. Rhyne v. Town of Mount Holly, 251 N.C. 251 (1960) (while the case did not directly address the authority for administrative abatement, the court accepted the town employee's entry on the property for abatement under the ordinance).

34. G.S. 160A-200.1; 153A-140.2.

35. *Id.*

Finally, consider the Public Health Nuisance Abatement Authority. The municipal and county statutes each authorize administrative abatement. A local government may "remove, abate, or remedy everything . . . that is dangerous or prejudicial to the public health or public safety."[36] Under the statutes, municipalities may act "summarily."[37] The full extent of that authority is explored below, but it would seem to include administrative abatement when due process is provided. The county statute does not grant authority for summary abatement, but it does allow for administrative abatement "upon adequate notice, the right to a hearing, and the right to appeal to the General Court of Justice."[38] Under the Public Health Nuisance Abatement Authority, the expense of administrative abatement shall be paid by the person in default and is a lien against the property if it is not paid.

The municipal and county versions of Public Health Nuisance Abatement Authority have specific provisions for administrative abatement of unsafe pools. After the governing board finds that a swimming pool is dangerous or prejudicial to public health or safety, the governing board may order the removal of the pool, and the expense is charged against the property owner or becomes a lien against the property.[39]

With this combination of authorities, while court-ordered abatement may be the safest route for abatement, administrative abatement arguably is allowed under the Nuisance Code Authority, the Chronic Violators statutes, and the Public Health Nuisance Authority. To cover all bases, it is prudent for a local nuisance code to reference these authorities for enforcement authority. That said, the statutes provide little, if any, procedural guidance. If a local government pursues administrative abatement of nuisance code violations without a court order, it should take steps to ensure due process.

Limited Authority for Summary Abatement

The precise scope of authority for summary abatement is not clear. The Nuisance Code Authority does not expressly authorize summary abatement. The Public Health Nuisance Abatement Authority allows summary abatement by municipalities, but not by counties.

The Public Health Nuisance Abatement Authority for municipalities states that "[a] city shall have authority to *summarily* remove, abate, or remedy everything in the city limits, or within one mile thereof, that is dangerous or prejudicial to the public health or public safety."

In North Carolina, we have guidance from *Monroe v. City of New Bern*. In *Monroe*, the North Carolina Court of Appeals interpreted the authority in G.S. 160A-193. Although that case involved a major use of summary abatement—the demolition

36. G.S. 160A-193; *see also* G.S. 153A-140 (containing comparable language).

37. G.S. 160A-193.

38. G.S. 153A-140.

39. G.S. 160A-193; 153A-140.

of a residence—its analysis and interpretation provides guidance on the general scope of the municipal Public Health Nuisance Abatement Authority for summary abatement.

The court "construe[d] Section 160A–193 narrowly in accordance with legislative intent."[40] It considered the broader statutory context of authority and noted that a city has authority to demolish an individual's residence in non-emergency situations under the minimum housing code authority,[41] which sets forth notice and hearing requirements. The court determined that "Section 160A–193 only applies to a situation where a structurally unsafe building poses an imminent danger to the safety of the public such that the owner could not be provided notice and a hearing without endangering the public."[42]

A limited reading of *Monroe* might confine the case to demolitions in the minimum housing context, but its reasoning can be instructive beyond residential demolitions. Just as minimum housing statutes provide a process for demolition when there is no imminent danger, other statutes provide processes for other nuisance situations absent imminent danger. Local governments have distinct authority for remedying unsafe commercial structures, dealing with junked automobiles, mowing overgrown lots, and clearing unsafe piles of rubbish. Interpreting *Monroe* broadly, municipalities should follow the applicable procedures (unsafe structure procedures, junked vehicle procedures, nuisance code procedures, etc.) for notice and abatement unless there is an imminent danger that justifies summary action. Indeed, even when no separate authorities and procedures exist for a particular nuisance, if there is no imminent danger, it is prudent for the municipality to proceed with administrative abatement under the Public Health Nuisance Abatement Authority (with notice and opportunity to be heard) as discussed above.

Applying *Monroe* generally, the court's guidance could be read like this:

> [W]e interpret Section 160A–193 as providing a city with the authority to summarily [abate a nuisance] only if the [nuisance] constitutes an imminent danger to the public health or safety, creating an emergency necessitating the [nuisance]'s immediate [abatement]. . . . Cities may not summarily [abate a nuisance] pursuant to Section 160A–193 merely because it is quicker and easier than providing the owners notice and an opportunity to be heard.[43]

Limits on Abatement, Generally

Even when a local government is authorized to enter private property to abate a nuisance, it cannot take or damage private property "unless its acts were in fact

---

40. Monroe v. City of New Bern, 158 N.C. App. 275, 278, 580 S.E.2d 372, 374 (2003).
41. Currently codified at G.S. 160D, Article 12; previously codified at G.S. 160A-441 *et seq.*
42. *Monroe*, 158 N.C. App. at 278.
43. *Id.*

necessary to remove or abate a nuisance."[44] In cases of housing code enforcement involving removal or demolition, local governments must sell any materials, personal property, fixtures, and appurtenances, and credit the proceeds toward the cost of removal or demolition. Similar procedures may be appropriate for local government abatement of nuisance code violations.

44. Rhyne v. Town of Mount Holly, 251 N.C. 521, 528, 112 S.E.2d 40, 46 (1960); *see also* Yates v. City of Raleigh, 46 N.C. App. 221, 264 S.E.2d 798 (1980).

Chapter 14

Zoning Enforcement for Existing Structures and Uses

Overview

Zoning regulations commonly impact new development—the proposed shopping center, the new residential subdivision, and the industrial park associated with the new economic development project. At the same time, zoning also applies to existing structures and uses. Can a property be used as a junkyard? Can a landlord operate a boarding house in a single-family home? Can a homeowner park a fleet of commercial trucks and equipment at a residential property? Can a bar owner operate in a run-down building downtown? While these may be questions of unsafe structures, housing codes, or nuisance codes, they are also questions of zoning. Therefore, zoning enforcement is one way of addressing the existing structures and uses.

Zoning Authority

Chapter 160D of the North Carolina General Statutes (hereinafter G.S.) authorizes counties and municipalities to adopt and enforce local development regulations. Article 4 of Chapter 160D provides details on "Administration, Enforcement, and Appeals." North Carolina local governments are authorized to "appoint administrators, inspectors, enforcement officers, planners, technicians, and other staff to develop, administer, and enforce development regulations authorized by this Chapter." Among many other duties, these staff members are tasked with "conducting inspections; issuing or denying certificates of compliance or occupancy; enforcing development regulations, including issuing notices of violation, orders to correct violations, and recommending bringing judicial actions against actual or threatened violations."[1]

G.S. 160D-403 and -404 specify some of the tools for enforcement: inspections, revocation of development approvals, withholding of certificates of occupancy, notices of violation, stop work orders, and "appropriate action or proceedings" to

1. Chapter 160D, Section 402 of the North Carolina General Statutes (hereinafter G.S.).

prevent work or activity in violation of development regulations. The enforcement authority for zoning and development regulations also cross-references enforcement tools for general police power ordinances.[2] They include civil penalties, legal proceedings in court, and treating violations as misdemeanors (limitations on criminal enforcement are discussed below).

Inspections

Before there can be enforcement, there must be inspection. The enforcement office must assess the situation, gather evidence, determine if there is (or may be) a violation, and potentially have an initial conversation with the owner or occupant.

Inspections for zoning and development regulations may occur in conjunction with a permitted development project (an approved commercial site or a residential subdivision, for example) or unrelated to any permit or approval (unpermitted construction or a prohibited land use activity, for example). For inspections of permitted work, the inspection could occur at multiple steps of the development process: during development and construction (to confirm permitting and sign-off on work in progress); at the conclusion of construction (to certify compliance and completion); and after construction (related to ongoing compliance).

For permitted work, G.S. 160D-403(e) authorizes local administrative staff to inspect work done pursuant to a development approval to ensure that it is done in accordance with state law, local law, and the terms of the approval. Staff may enter the premises during reasonable hours and upon presenting credentials, but the inspector must have consent or an administrative search warrant to inspect areas that are not open to the public. While an application form may request consent to inspect areas of work, an application may not be used to require broad consent to inspections. As stated in G.S. 160D-403, "[a]dministrative staff are prohibited from requiring unrestricted written consent from a permit applicant to enter any premises or areas not open to the public as a condition to accepting an application for, or the issuance of, development approvals."

Inspections unrelated to a permit may arise in many ways. The enforcement officer may see a violation while they are out in the field, another public official may report a violation, or, commonly, a complaint is filed. For potential violations that relate to unpermitted work or unauthorized activities, the general authority for inspections applies.[3] The zoning inspector is obligated to perform an investigation when there is a valid complaint of a violation (investigation is a ministerial duty). As stated by the North Carolina Court of Appeals in *Midgette v. Pate*, "[t]hough the zoning administrator may exercise discretion in assessing the alleged violations,

2. G.S. 160D-404; 160A-175; 153A-123.

3. G.S. 160D-402(b).

this does not lessen the duty to investigate the charges of a plaintiff who has legal right to have the duty enforced."[4]

> **Fourth Amendment Reminder**
>
> For a detailed discussion of Fourth Amendment limits on inspections, see Chapter 4. In brief, code officials must honor constitutional privacy protections, obtain consent or a warrant when needed, and rely only on observations made lawfully

Building the Record

When it comes to enforcement, details and documentation matter. As noted by the North Carolina Court of Appeals in a dispute over zoning enforcement, the local government "carries the burden of proving the existence of a violation of a local zoning ordinance."[5]

So, when approaching an investigation and potential enforcement action, the enforcement officer needs to pay attention to the details and build a record of evidence.

- What ordinance is being enforced? Zoning, subdivision, minimum housing, stormwater, nuisance, something else?
- For that ordinance, what are the specific details of the language that applies? What section? What standard? Is there any need for interpretation or justification?
- For this particular scenario, what are the facts on the ground that constitute a violation? Take pictures, take notes, capture screenshots from the relevant website, and preserve all documents.

If the officer determines that a violation exists, documentation and communication are essential. Photographs, field notes, internal documents, and communications with the violator should be carefully collected and maintained. This evidence of the violation and the correspondence with the violator will be critical to a successful enforcement action.

Informal Notice

There is no state law requirement for informal notice. It is a matter of local ordinance and policy. Depending on the nature of the violation and the policies of the local government, the initial communication may be a conversation, a phone call, or

4. 94 N.C. App. 498, 503–04, 380 S.E.2d 572, 576 (1989).

5. MR Ent., LLC v. City of Asheville, 295 N.C. App. 136, 143, 905 S.E.2d 246, 251 (2024), *review denied*, 912 S.E.2d 821 (N.C. 2025), and *review dismissed*, 912 S.E.2d 823 (N.C. 2025).

a courtesy letter seeking compliance. For some violations, it may be appropriate to proceed directly to enforcement penalties. However, if informal notice is required by local ordinance or policy, the local government must adhere to that requirement.

Formal Notice

The enforcement action formally begins with formal notice. That notice could be a notice of violation, a stop work order, or some other formal written decision. The statutory details for notices of violation (NOVs) and stop work orders are discussed below, but there are overarching concepts and requirements for any formal notice.

- Identify the specific property.
- Cite and quote the relevant ordinance provision(s).
- Identify the facts that constitute the violation (document with pictures or otherwise).
- Specify the necessary action and deadline for the opportunity to correct, if any (for example, remove the vehicle within __ days; install the landscaping within __ days; cease the activity immediately).
- Identify possible next steps of enforcement if the violation is not corrected (civil penalties, court proceedings, etc.).
- Provide contact information for the relevant staff and/or department.
- Note the opportunity to appeal (including a brief description of the process and time limit).
- Deliver the notice to the property owner and, potentially, other relevant actors (tenant, operator, contractor, etc.).

Specificity in the Notice

The details of the ordinance and notice matter. The notice should be clearly tied to an applicable ordinance and clearly demonstrate the existence of the violation. *MR Entertainment, LLC v. City of Asheville* illustrates the point. In that case, the city brought an enforcement action against a local bar for a sign ordinance violation. The initial notice of violation (NOV) was for the local bar parking a truck with a sign in the bed in the parking lot (the ordinance, the notice, and the photo evidence all pertained to the parked truck). Two years later, the city issued a follow-up NOV for driving the truck around town. The city argued that this was a continuing violation and sought injunctive relief and $57,400 in civil penalties. Looking at the language of the ordinance and the initial NOV, however, the court ruled that the ordinance and notice applied only to the parked truck, not to driving around town (plus there was no evidence of the truck driving around town anyway). As such, the court limited the violation to when the truck was parked in the bar parking lot. The evidence indicated that the bar corrected that violation within the given time, so no further enforcement was allowed.[6]

Notice of Violation

A notice of violation (NOV) may be issued when it is determined that work or activity is in violation of a local development regulation, a development approval, or a state law delegated to the local government for enforcement.[7] The NOV must be delivered to the holder of the development approval and the landowner, if different. It may also be delivered to the occupant or person undertaking the work or activity. Notice must be delivered by personal delivery, electronic delivery, or first-class mail. The NOV may also be posted on the property. The administrator providing the NOV must certify for the file the timing and content of the notice, and that certification must be deemed conclusive in the absence of fraud. Aside from building permits and housing code violations, which have their own appeal processes, NOVs are appealed to the board of adjustment.[8]

Stop Work Order

A stop work order may be issued for illegal or dangerous work *or activity*. While stop work orders are commonly used for state building code violations, they are not limited to such violations. Stop work orders are a general enforcement tool used to stop illegal or dangerous development and activities on land. Under G.S. 160D-404(b), if any work or activity subject to a local development regulation or a state regulation delegated for local enforcement is undertaken in substantial violation of state or local law, or in a manner that endangers life or property, staff may issue a stop work order for the specific work or activity causing the violation or hazard. For example, if a business owner undertakes an activity that is not allowed in that zoning district, the local inspector may issue a stop work order. Upon issuance of a stop work order, no further work or activity may take place in violation of the order.

A stop work order must be in writing and directed to the person doing the work or activity. The order must state the work or activity to be stopped, the reasons for the order, and the conditions under which the work or activity may be resumed. The stop work order must be delivered by hand delivery, electronic mail, or first-class mail to the holder of the development approval and the property owner, if different. The administrator issuing the stop work order must certify for the file the timing and content of the order. This certification is deemed conclusive in the absence of fraud.

Generally, appeals of stop work orders go to the board of adjustment, but, as discussed previously, appeals of stop work orders under the building code or housing code follow the appeal provisions for those articles.

---

6. 295 N.C. App. at 136, 905 S.E.2d at 247.
7. G.S. 160D-404(a).
8. G.S. 160D-405.

Administrative Hearing

Some development regulations require an administrative hearing as part of the enforcement process. In particular, administrative hearings are mandated for unsafe structure condemnation (G.S. 160D-1121), commercial maintenance codes (G.S. 160D-1129(c)), and minimum housing codes (G.S. 160D-1203(2)).

There is not a general requirement for an administrative hearing. So, for zoning, subdivision, and other development regulations, there is no need for an administrative hearing unless mandated by a local ordinance.

Certainly, as part of the enforcement action, the local government official may communicate with the alleged violator to hear counterarguments, explore options, and discuss resolution. If the alleged violator seeks a formal forum to present evidence and make legal arguments, that will be through an appeal to the board of adjustment. In terms of due process, the appeal to the board of adjustment is a sufficient opportunity to be heard.

Opportunity to Correct

While some cases may warrant immediate correction, it is common for the local government to give the property owner a reasonable time to correct the violation. A local ordinance or policy may specify opportunities to correct.

The appropriate amount of time will depend upon the nature of the violation. Moving a vehicle could be managed in a matter of hours. Moving a building will take longer. An owner could end an illegal activity right away, but it could take weeks or months to obtain a necessary permit.

Along with the opportunity to correct, a reinspection is usually needed to confirm if the violation is indeed corrected. Again, *MR Entertainment, LLC v. City of Asheville* is illustrative. In that case about the truck with a sign, the notice of violation (NOV) gave the bar twenty-four hours to correct the violation. By email, the bar indicated that it had moved the truck and corrected the violation. There was no evidence in the record that the code enforcement officer reinspected. Per the court: "The City's own failure to re-inspect the site cannot defeat Petitioner's timely notice of cure."[9]

Continuing Violation

For enforcement actions that continue over time, the local government is wise to continue gathering evidence of the continuing violation. As noted before, "[t]he

9. 295 N.C. App. at 143, 905 S.E.2d at 251 (2024).

City carries the burden of proving the existence of a violation of a local zoning ordinance."[10]

For some violations, proof of continued violation may be relatively straightforward: the building is still sitting in the setback or the required vegetative buffering is still not planted. For more temporary or movable violations, though, documentation is critical. For a commercial vehicle improperly parked in a residential district, for a sweepstakes machine placed in the back of the gas station, or for the house that is operating as a late-night bar on the weekends, the local government will need to take steps to document continued or recurring violations.

Enforcement

Civil Penalties

A civil penalty is a monetary penalty for a violation of a local ordinance. The underlying purpose of civil penalties is to secure compliance, cover administrative costs for enforcement, and ensure equity with those who are complying with applicable rules. Civil penalties are not intended for revenue generation. They are commonly used in conjunction with a notice of violation when a violator has not complied. The local ordinance may establish that each day's continuing violation is a separate and distinct offense (G.S. 160A-175(g); 153A-123(g)), so civil penalties may accrue over time, with an additional charge for each day of noncompliance.

While the statutes do not set a maximum or minimum amount for civil penalties, a civil penalty likely should not exceed the maximum for criminal penalties. With regard to misdemeanor violations of local ordinances, G.S. 14-4 sets a presumption that fines are $50 or less but allows fines up to $500 if expressly stated in the ordinance. Using the limits on criminal fines as a gauge, civil penalties should not exceed $500 per day.

Given the accruing nature, amounts owed for civil penalties may become substantial. Importantly, the maximum amount of the penalty may not exceed an amount reasonably related to the harm of the violation and the cost to the local government to secure compliance. Courts may cap the amount to be recovered accordingly.

While civil penalties may be assessed from the time the violation began, the local government should give notice to the violator that civil penalties are accruing. Generally, civil penalties begin with the notice of violation or after allowing a specified time for compliance. The assessment of a civil penalty may be appealed to the board of adjustment. If a violator fails to appeal the determination of a violation or imposition of a civil penalty within thirty days of notice, the violator waives those claims (except in appeals challenging the constitutionality of the ordinance).

10. *MR Ent., LLC*, 295 N.C. App. at 143, 905 S.E.2d at 251.

A civil penalty is treated as a debt owed to the local government. While the penalty is not an automatic lien against the property, the local government may bring a civil action in court to recover the penalty as a debt.[11]

Withhold Permits

At the conclusion of work under a development approval, a local government may conduct final inspections to ensure that the work complies with applicable laws and the terms of the approval before issuing a certificate of compliance or occupancy (G.S. 160D-403(g)). For projects requiring a building permit, a certificate of compliance is required before the structure may be occupied. For other development approvals, local governments may choose to require a certificate of compliance at the conclusion of the work. If the work fails to comply with applicable state laws, local ordinances, or permit requirements, the final certificate of compliance or occupancy may be withheld.

Notably, a local government may not withhold permits on one property or parcel in order to compel compliance on another property or parcel.[12]

Revoke Development Approvals

In addition to other general enforcement actions, a local government may revoke a development approval. As required by G.S. 160D-403, a local government *shall* revoke a development approval for

- any substantial departure from the approved application, plans, or specifications;
- refusal or failure to comply with the requirements of any applicable local development regulation or any state law delegated to the local government for enforcement purposes in lieu of the state; or
- false statements or misrepresentations made in securing the approval.

A local government *may* revoke a mistakenly issued development approval. In exercising this discretion, the administrator should consider multiple factors:

- Was it a clear error? A clear error is more defensible than revoking a permit issued based on a judgment call or close interpretation.
- How long has the owner relied on the development approval? The longer the mistake stands, the less defensible it is to revoke the permit.
- How much has the owner relied on the development approval? The more money and effort the owner has expended on the mistakenly issued permit, the less defensible a revocation becomes.

For any revocation, the local government must follow the same notice, review, and decision-making process that applied to the issuance of the development

11. G.S. 160A-175(c); 153A-123(c).
12. G.S. 160D-1110.

approval. For example, a staff member could not unilaterally revoke a special use permit; the matter would need to go back before the board that originally approved the permit.

The local government must provide written notice to the permit holder stating the reason for revocation. A revocation by a staff person may be appealed as an administrative decision under G.S. 160D-405, including the applicable provisions on stays of enforcement.

Note that revocation is an option in addition to stop work orders and notices of violation. An enforcement official might issue a stop work order or notice of violation (NOV) as an immediate administrative action and then pursue a full revocation process if the owner fails to take corrective action.

Separate sections of the state statutes have specific provisions for the revocation of development agreements (G.S. 160D-1008) and building permits (G.S. 160D-1115).

Court Action

A local government may take a violator to court to secure compliance. Under G.S. 160D-404(c)(1), a local government "may institute any appropriate action or proceedings to prevent the unlawful erection, construction, reconstruction, alteration, repair, conversion, maintenance, use, or development; to restrain, correct or abate the violation; to prevent occupancy of the building, structure, or land; or to prevent any illegal act, conduct, business, or use in or about the premises."

G.S. 160A-175 and G.S. 153A-123 also authorize a local government to bring a civil action against a violator to address violations of land development regulations. In such actions, the court may issue remedial orders, such as "mandatory or prohibitory injunction and order of abatement commanding the defendant to correct the unlawful condition upon or cease the unlawful use of the property." With regard to judicial orders of abatement, if the violator fails to comply, they may be cited for contempt of court. The local government may then execute the court's order of abatement and place a lien on the property for the costs of abatement.

Note that civil actions in court are subject to the applicable statutes of limitation.[13]

Limited Criminal Enforcement

In 2021, the North Carolina General Assembly adopted broad criminal justice reform. Among other things, the legislation dramatically curtailed criminal enforcement of local ordinances. Under the new statutory language adopted as part of S.L. 2021-138, a local government must amend its ordinances to specifically identify any violations that may be enforced criminally. The law specifically

---

13. *See* Adam Lovelady, *Tick Tock! The Clock Is Now Running for Zoning Enforcement*, Coates' Canons: NC Loc. Gov't L. (blog) (Sept. 26, 2017), https://canons.sog.unc.edu/2017/09/tick-tock-the-clock-is-now-running-for-zoning-enforcement/.

addresses local development regulations: among the ordinances that may not be enforced criminally are "[a]ny ordinance adopted under . . . Chapter 160D of the General Statutes, except for those ordinances related to unsafe buildings." In other words, most zoning, subdivision, and general land use regulations may no longer carry criminal penalties.

However, ordinances related to unsafe buildings may still be enforced criminally. Additionally, some ordinances related to development are authorized outside of Chapter 160D. Arguably, those may still be enforced through criminal penalties. These issues are discussed in more detail in a School of Government blog post titled "Limits on Criminal Enforcement of Development Regulations."[14]

Appeals

Appeals of administrative development decisions are assigned to the local board of adjustment. State law sets forth the procedures and standards for those appeals.

No development regulation can address every possible scenario. Properties are unique, landowners are creative, and land uses evolve. Moreover, no ordinance is perfect. Inevitably, there are ambiguities, contradictions, and gaps. Public officials must apply these imperfect regulations to an array of scenarios, and the correct application is not always clear. Sometimes reasonable people may disagree about the proper interpretation of an ordinance. Sometimes the public official did not have access to complete information when determining the violation. In such cases, an appeal can help resolve the disagreement.

An appeal is not the right process for everything, however. If an owner wants a waiver of a requirement because the strict application of the rules will cause hardship, that owner should pursue a variance, not an appeal. Similarly, if a citizen is simply seeking a change to the rules, that requires an ordinance amendment, not an appeal.

Board of Adjustment

Administrative decisions for zoning, subdivision, and other development regulations are appealed to the local board of adjustment.[15] The statute allows these appeals to be assigned to other boards if authorized by statute or local ordinance. However, if the ordinance assigns any appeals of administrative decisions to another board, that board must follow quasi-judicial procedures just as the board of adjustment does.[16]

---

14. Adam Lovelady, *Limits on Criminal Enforcement of Development Regulations*, Coates' Canons: NC Loc. Gov't L. (blog) (Feb. 11, 2022), https://canons.sog.unc.edu/2022/02/limits-on-criminal-enforcement-of-development-regulations/.

15. G.S. 160D-405.

16. G.S. 160D-405(a).

The Decision

"Determination"

For an administrative decision to be appealed, the public official must have made an official determination—a written, final, and binding order, requirement, or determination.[17]

Examples of final, binding determinations include a formal notice of violation, a zoning compliance permit, a formal ordinance interpretation, and other final written decisions. A formal determination that a particular activity is permitted in a zoning district is an appealable determination.[18] Similarly, a written determination that the owner has complied with applicable height limits is also appealable.[19]

Some staff actions are not formal determinations and therefore are not subject to appeal to the board of adjustment. If a written statement affects no rights and is merely advisory in nature, it is unlikely to be appealable. For example, a letter that states the basic zoning district of a property is not a binding decision; it is merely a recitation of the current rules. A written statement about how the ordinance might be interpreted in the future is not an appealable decision.[20] A written communication that is simply a recommendation at a preliminary stage of the permit review process is not a final, binding decision.[21] Inaction by staff is not a decision that can be appealed, but a party may seek a court order to require staff action that is not discretionary.

The administrator cannot defer a question to the board before making a staff decision. When a decision is assigned to staff, the administrator must first make the decision and then allow an appeal to the board of adjustment.[22]

Notice of the Decision

Pursuant to G.S. 160D-403, the local government official who made the decision must provide written notice of the decision to the property owner and the requesting party, if different from the owner. This written notice may be delivered personally, by email, or by first-class mail. The timing of this notice is important, as it starts the clock running for the appeal period.

A property owner or developer who wants to start the clock for neighbor appeals can establish constructive notice by posting a sign on the property in question pursuant to G.S. 160D-403(b). The sign must clearly state "Zoning Decision" or "Subdivision Decision" in letters at least six inches high and provide a way to contact an official about the decision. The sign must be posted for at least

---

17. G.S. 160D, §§ 405(d), 102(10).

18. S.T. Wooten Corp. Bd. of Adjustment, 210 N.C. App. 633, 711 S.E.2d 158 (2011).

19. Meir v. City of Charlotte, 206 N.C. App. 471, 698 S.E.2d 704 (2010).

20. *In re* Appeal of the Society for the Preservation of Historic Oakwood, 153 N.C. App. 737, 571 S.E.2d 588 (2002).

21. Ashe Cnty. v. Ashe Cnty. Plan. Bd., 376 N.C. 1, 852 S.E.2d 69 (2020); Wilson v. Mebane Bd. of Adjustment, 212 N.C. App. 176, 710 S.E.2d 403 (2011).

22. Tate v. Bd. of Adjustment, 83 N.C. App. 512, 350 S.E.2d 873 (1986).

ten days, and the person posting it must provide verification of the posting to the official who made the decision. An ordinance may require such posted notice of decisions, but if not specified in the ordinance, posting the sign is optional for the property owner. Note that this sign to establish constructive notice is separate from the routine notice required in advance of any quasi-judicial hearing, including an appeal of a staff decision.

Filing an Appeal

Deadline for Appeal

Parties have thirty days from the notice of the decision to appeal.[23] For a party receiving written notice from staff, the thirty-day period begins upon receipt of the notice. Notice sent by email or hand delivery is presumed received on the date it is sent or delivered. Mailed notice is presumed received on the third business day following the deposit of the notice for mailing. For other parties, the thirty-day period begins with any notice—actual or constructive—of the decision. Such notice could be a letter from the property owner, a posted sign as discussed above, the beginning of construction on the site, or any other method of learning about the decision. If a party fails to appeal within thirty days, the board of adjustment cannot hear the appeal.

Standing to Appeal

State law allows an appeal of an administrative decision by a person with legal standing. As outlined in G.S. 160D-1402(c), this includes individuals with an ownership interest in the subject property, applicants for permits or recipients of notices of violation (if different from the owner), the local government, any person who will suffer special damages from the decision, and certain associations that have members who will suffer special damages.

For some of these parties, standing is clear. The applicant, the owner, and the local government are easily identified as parties with standing to appeal. Determining whether a neighbor will suffer special damages requires more analysis. In short, the courts consider factors such as proximity, property value impacts, and other adverse impacts (noise, pollution, traffic, etc.) to determine special damages. The application form for an appeal may request information to confirm legal standing, and at the hearing, the question of standing is a threshold matter for the board to determine. If the person filing the appeal lacks standing, the board has no authority to hear the appeal.

Notice of Appeal

A person seeking to appeal an administrative decision must file a notice of appeal with the local government clerk or other official designated by the local government

23. G.S. 160D-405(d).

ordinance. The notice of appeal must state the grounds for appeal. Local governments commonly provide a form or application for appeals of administrative decisions. Once a complete application is properly filed, staff is obligated to put the request on the agenda for the board; staff cannot make decisions on legal questions, such as standing.[24]

Stays of Enforcement and Permitting

For an appeal of an enforcement action, the appeal stays enforcement. Civil penalties and other enforcement actions are paused during the appeal. However, if the enforcement official certifies that "a stay would cause imminent peril to life or property or, because the violation is transitory in nature, a stay would seriously interfere with enforcement of the development regulation," enforcement is stayed only by a restraining order.[25]

For an appeal of an approved development permit, the appeal "does not stay the further review of an application for development approvals to use the property." However, either the person appealing the permit or the local government may request that the board of adjustment stay any final decision on the development approval applications, including building permits.[26]

Quasi-Judicial Procedures

An appeal of an administrative development decision must follow quasi-judicial procedures, as outlined in G.S. 160D-406. Among other requirements, notice must be mailed and posted on the property; witnesses must provide sworn testimony and factual evidence; and the board must base its decision on competent, substantial, and relevant evidence in the record. Politics and personal preference are not legitimate bases for the decision.

Administrator Compiles the Record

Before the hearing, the official who made the decision being appealed must compile the record on which the decision was based, including all applicable documents and exhibits. The administrator must provide that record to the board and also give a copy to the individual appealing the decision and the property owner, if different.

Administrator Appears as a Witness

As required by G.S. 160D-406(e), the public official who made the decision being appealed "shall be present at the evidentiary hearing as a witness." If that individual is no longer employed by the local government, the individual currently occupying that position must appear as a witness.

---

24. Morningstar Marinas/Eaton Ferry, LLC v. Warren Cnty., 368 N.C. 360, 360, 777 S.E.2d 733, 734 (2015).

25. G.S. 160D-405(f).

26. *Id.*

This role of appearing as a witness is different from the staff role in other types of quasi-judicial decisions. In a variance or special use permit case, a staff person may serve as a clerk and/or witness providing support and analysis for the board, but in appeals of staff decisions, the staff person acts as a party defending the interpretation of the ordinance. This creates heightened concerns about *ex parte* communications between the board and the staff person. Local government staff often interact with board members outside of meetings, but when a staff person is a party to the appeal, they should be careful not to discuss the substance of the appeal with board members outside of the hearing.

This dynamic of *staff-person-as-party* also may complicate the role of the local government attorney, who is called in to advise the board and the staff member appearing before it. For this reason, some local governments assign separate attorneys, one for staff and one for the board, for appeals of staff decisions.

Additional Evidence

In some cases, the party making the appeal, or that party's attorney, may submit in advance a written analysis (essentially a legal brief) for the board's consideration. If so, copies should be provided to the board and the other parties just as the rest of the record is shared.

The extent to which new evidence is needed or appropriate depends on the case. In some cases, the parties may agree on the basic facts (such as the proposed building and the applicable section of the ordinance) but disagree on the legal question of how to interpret the ordinance correctly (for example, does the proposed building qualify as a single-family home?).

In other cases, the board may need to supplement the record with additional facts to make its decision. In an appeal of a notice of violation, for example, the parties may dispute whether and when a certain land use occurred on the property. The property owner may have documents or testimony that challenge the record provided by staff. The evidentiary hearing may produce additional evidence for the record, and the board must resolve any contested facts in its decision.

The chair of the board of adjustment is authorized to issue subpoenas to compel the production of evidence. A party may submit a written request to the chairperson explaining why a subpoena is necessary to compel certain witnesses or evidence, and the chairperson shall issue the subpoena if they determine it to be relevant, reasonable in nature and scope, and not oppressive.[27]

Decision and Appeal

The board of adjustment must decide an appeal within a reasonable time. As with any quasi-judicial decision, the board's decision must be based on competent, material, and substantial evidence in the record. The board must resolve any contested facts and apply the relevant legal standards. The board has all of the powers of

27. G.S. 160D-406(g).

the official who made the original decision—it essentially steps into the shoes of the administrative staff. The board may affirm the staff decision, reverse the staff decision, or modify the staff decision, and it may "make any order, requirement, decision, or determination that ought to be made."

Appeals of administrative decisions are decided by a simple majority vote. The decision "shall be reduced to writing, reflect the board's determination of contested facts and their application to the applicable standards, and be approved by the board and signed by the chair or other duly authorized member of the board." The decision of the board of adjustment may be appealed to the superior court in the nature of certiorari pursuant to G.S. 160D-1402.

Alternatives to the Board of Adjustment

Instead of taking an appeal to the board of adjustment, the parties may agree to mediation or another form of alternative dispute resolution. The ordinance may set standards and procedures to facilitate this process.

When the basis of the appeal is a challenge to the enforceability or validity of the regulation itself—or a claim that the regulation is unconstitutional, beyond the statutory authority of the local government, or constitutes an unconstitutional regulatory taking—a person with standing may opt to bypass the board of adjustment and take those legal challenges straight to superior court.

Chapter 15
Vacant Building Receivership

Overview

In certain circumstances, North Carolina local governments are authorized to seek a court order for a vacant building to be taken into receivership. This chapter outlines that authority and required procedures.

Prior to Petition for Appointment

The governing board or a delegated commission may petition the superior court "for the appointment of a receiver to rehabilitate, demolish, or sell a vacant building, structure, or dwelling. . . ."[1] Such a petition may only be filed after one of the following conditions, each deemed a nuisance per se, is met:

- The owner fails to comply with
  - an order to take corrective action under Chapter 160D, Section 1122 of the North Carolina General Statutes (hereinafter G.S.);
  - an order from the governing board following an appeal of an order to take corrective action under G.S. 160D-1122;
  - an ordinance order under a nonresidential maintenance code, as authorized by G.S. 160D-1129(f)(1). In this case, the appointment of a receiver is deemed compliance with the ordinance; or
  - an order for action under a minimum housing code pursuant to G.S. 160D-1203, related to dwellings that are unfit for human habitation.
- Or an owner or partial owner of the vacant building, structure, or dwelling requests the appointment of a receiver.

1. Chapter 160D, Section 1130(a) of the North Carolina General Statutes (hereinafter G.S.).

Petition for Appointment

The petition must include the following information:

> (i) a copy of the original violation notice or order issued by the city or, in the case of an owner request to the governing board for a petition for appointment of a receiver, a verified pleading that avers that at least one owner consents to the petition;
>
> (ii) a verified pleading that avers that the required rehabilitation or demolition has not been completed; and
>
> (iii) the names of the respondents, which shall include the owner of the property, as recorded with the register of deeds, any mortgagee with a recorded interest in the property, and all other parties in interest, as defined in G.S. 160D-1202(2).[2]

Notice

State law sets forth the notice requirements for a petition for the appointment of a receiver. The local government must provide notice to owners and certain other parties of interest within ten days of filing the petition. Those parties then have thirty days to apply to intervene and be appointed as the receiver. If the local government fails to provide notice to a party of interest, the proceeding may continue, but the receiver's lien does not have priority over that party's lien.[3]

Qualified Receiver

After a local government petitions for the appointment of a receiver and provides proper notice, "[t]he court shall appoint a qualified receiver."

To be considered *qualified*, a receiver must demonstrate the following to the court:

> (i) the financial ability to complete the purchase or rehabilitation of the property,
>
> (ii) the knowledge of, or experience in, the rehabilitation of vacant real property,
>
> (iii) the ability to obtain any necessary insurance, and
>
> (iv) the absence of any building code violations issued by the city on other real property owned by the person or any member, principal, officer, major stockholder, parent, subsidiary, predecessor, or others affiliated with the person or the person's business.[4]

---

2. G.S. 160D-1130(b) ("If the petition fails to name a respondent as required by this subsection, the proceeding may continue, but the receiver's lien for expenses incurred . . . does not have priority over the lien of that respondent.").

3. G.S. 160D-1130(c).

4. G.S. 160D-1130(d).

Members of the local government governing board and public officers of the local government may not be appointed as a qualified receiver of an action by that local government.

The court may appoint another qualified receiver if a current receiver becomes disqualified.

Party Instead of Receiver

Instead of appointing a receiver, the court may appoint "an owner or other party in interest in the property, as defined in G.S. 160D-1202, to rehabilitate or demolish the property."[5] Such party must meet certain criteria:

> (i) demonstrates the ability to complete the rehabilitation or demolition within a reasonable time,
>
> (ii) agrees to comply with a specified schedule for rehabilitation or demolition, and
>
> (iii) posts a bond in an amount determined by the court as security for the performance of the required work in compliance with the specified schedule.

The court must determine a schedule for rehabilitation or demolition, and the appointed party must report progress to the court. If the local government determines that the appointed party is not proceeding with due diligence or according to the court's schedule, it may apply to the court for immediate revocation of the appointment of the appointed party and for appointment of a qualified receiver. If the court revokes the appointed party and appoints a qualified receiver, the bond posted by the appointed party is applied to the receiver's expenses.

Receiver Authority

Authority to Rehabilitate or Demolish

After appointment, the receiver records notice identifying the property in receivership. Upon such notice, the receiver has exclusive authority to collect rents and income from the property or to rehabilitate, demolish, or sell the property. Any individual other than the receiver who attempts these actions may be held in contempt of court.[6]

Costs and fees incurred by the receiver are a lien against the property and have priority over all other liens and encumbrances except taxes and government assessments.[7]

---

5. G.S. 160D-1130(e).
6. G.S. 160D-1130(f).
7. *Id.*

The receiver has "all necessary and customary powers" to rehabilitate or demolish the vacant building, structure, or dwelling.[8] Additionally, the receiver has the right of possession with authority to do the following:

(1) Contract for necessary labor and supplies for rehabilitation or demolition.
(2) Borrow money for rehabilitation or demolition from an approved lending institution or through a governmental agency or program, using the receiver's lien against the property as security.
(3) Manage the property prior to rehabilitation or demolition and pay operational expenses of the property, including taxes, insurance, utilities, general maintenance, and debt secured by an interest in the property.
(4) Collect all rents and income from the property, which shall be used to pay for current operating expenses and repayment of outstanding rehabilitation or demolition expenses.
(5) Manage the property after rehabilitation, with all the powers of a landlord, for a period of up to two years and apply the rent received to current operating expenses and repayment of outstanding rehabilitation or demolition expenses.
(6) Foreclose on the receiver's lien or accept a deed in lieu of foreclosure.[9]

Authority to Sell

State law sets forth the authority and process for a receiver to sell property in receivership.[10] A receiver appointed to sell a vacant building, structure, or dwelling is granted all necessary and customary powers and is authorized to do the following:

(i) sell the property to the highest bidder at public sale, following the same presale notice provisions that apply to a mortgage foreclosure under Article 2A of Chapter 45 of the North Carolina General Statutes, and
(ii) sell the property privately for fair market value if no party to the receivership objects to the amount and procedure.

The notice of private sale may describe the property by street address and reference to the deed book and page or other location where the property deed is registered. Prior to any sale, the prospective buyer (applicants to bid in a public sale or the proposed buyer in a private sale) must demonstrate the ability and experience to rehabilitate the property in a reasonable time.

Proceeds of the sale are distributed in the following order of priority:

- Expenses of the sale.
- Outstanding taxes and other government assessments.

---

8. Article 38 of G.S. Chapter 1 outlines the general receivership laws and the powers of a receiver. Those statutes and related caselaw may be instructive in determining the "necessary and customary powers" of a receiver.

9. G.S. 160D-1130(f).

10. G.S. 160D-1130(h).

- Receiver's lien.
- Local government's costs and expenses (including reasonable attorneys' fees).
- Other liens against the property in order of priority.
- Any remaining proceeds remitted to the property owner.

Authority to Foreclose on Lien

Costs and fees incurred by the receiver are a lien against the property and have priority over all other liens and encumbrances except taxes and government assessments.[11]

A receiver may foreclose on the lien by selling the property at public sale in the same manner as a mortgage foreclosure.

If the receiver has rehabilitated the property, in lieu of foreclosure, the property owner may pay the receiver's costs, fees, and expenses, or transfer the property to the receiver or an agreed-upon third party at fair market value.

After Sale

The court ratifies a sale of property in receivership. After ratification, the receiver must sign a deed "conveying title to the property to the buyer, free and clear of all encumbrances, other than restrictions that run with the land."[12] At the same time as the sale of the property, the receiver must file with the court a final accounting and a motion to dismiss the action.

Duration of Receivership

After rehabilitation, demolition, or sale of the property, a party to the receivership may file a motion to dismiss the receiver upon paying the receiver's costs, fees, and expenses. In any event, a receiver's appointment must not extend longer than two years after the rehabilitation, demolition, or sale of the property. Upon expiration of the receiver's tenure, the receiver must file with the court a final accounting.[13]

Administrative Fee for the Local Government

The local government may charge the property owner an administrative fee. This fee "is equal to five percent (5%) of the profits from the sale of the building, structure, or dwelling or one hundred dollars ($100.00), whichever is less."[14]

---

11. G.S. 160D-1130(f).
12. G.S. 160D-1130(j).
13. G.S. 160D-1130(k).
14. G.S. 160D-1130(l).

Appendixes

Appendix A
Selected North Carolina Cases

This appendix provides brief summaries of selected North Carolina cases relevant to building and property code administration. Cases are presented in chronological order, with decisions by the North Carolina Supreme Court listed first, followed by those from the North Carolina Court of Appeals. Each summary includes one or more topic headings that highlight the key legal issues addressed. Cases decided through 2025 are included.

North Carolina Supreme Court

State v. Tenant, 110 N.C. 609 (1892)

Uniformity of regulations; constitutionality

Asheville adopted an ordinance requiring that before any new construction a property owner must obtain permission from the city council. The ordinance, however, lacked any clear standards for granting that permission. The property owner, a local hotel, sought permission to build a new hospital building. Citizens opposed the request, and the city council denied it. The hospital proceeded with construction anyway, and the city initiated enforcement. On appeal, the hospital challenged the constitutionality of the ordinance. The court ruled that regulations such as building regulations must be for the general benefit, based on clear standards, applied evenly, and enforced equally against all persons and classes. Otherwise, "it is unconstitutional and void, because it fails to furnish a uniform rule of action, and leaves the right of property subject to the despotic will of aldermen, who may exercise it so as to give exclusive profits or privileges to particular persons." *Tenant*, 110 N.C. at 612.

State v. Eubanks, 154 N.C. 628 (1911)

Building permit; building official

This case arose before North Carolina had a statewide building code. State law authorized the building inspector or fire chief to issue permits for work done within the city. The property owner obtained a permit. A separate local ordinance established city fire limits and required owners to seek approval from city council prior to construction. The city brought an enforcement action against the owner for failure to obtain city council approval. The court ruled in favor of the owner—that the owner complied with state law and obtained the necessary permit and that a local ordinance could not make a lawful act illegal.

Clinard v. City of Winston Salem, 173 N.C. 356 (1917)

Building permit; mandamus

The property owner obtained a permit to add on to a building, but subsequently there was a dispute about whether the addition encroached into an alley, and the permit was withdrawn. The property owner brought legal action against the city for mandamus (to require issuance of permits) and damages. The court confirmed that building permitting is a governmental function: "The exercise of the power to grant or refuse the license to erect a building was a governmental function." *Clinard*, 173 N.C. at 358. As such, if a permit was improperly withheld, then the city is obligated to issue it, and mandamus is appropriate. As to damages, the court ruled that when a city is exercising a governmental function (like issuing building permits), the city is not liable for damages even if the city made an erroneous or arbitrary determination about a permit.

Mitchell v. Barfield, 232 N.C. 325, 59 S.E.2d 810 (1950)

Building permit; improper denial; mandamus

An applicant applied for and met the requirements for a building permit. The proposed use (hotel) was permitted in the district, so the applicant met zoning requirements as well. The city refused to issue the permit on claims that the applicant intended to use the building for an impermissible use (a nursing home, infirmary, or hospital). The court ruled that when an applicant meets the objective standards for a permit, they have "a clear legal right to the building permit sought by them, and the [local government] ha[s] no discretionary power to withhold it." *Mitchell*, 232 N.C. at 326, 59 S.E.2d at 811. Moreover, the question of an alleged illegal use must await determination after the owner attempts the use.

Rhyne v. Town of Mount Holly, 251 N.C. 521, 112 S.E.2d 40 (1960)

Public nuisance; abatement; liability

The court ruled that even when a local government is authorized to be on private property to abate a nuisance, the government cannot take or harm private property unless its actions are in fact necessary to do so.

The town determined that the petitioner's property was so overgrown as to be a nuisance. The town went onto the private property and cleared the site (cutting down trees, shrubs, and vines and leaving them in a pile on the property). The petitioner claimed, among other things, that the town owed the petitioner compensation for wrongfully cutting down over 100 oak trees on the property.

Municipal action to abate nuisances is governmental in nature, so some liability is shielded by governmental immunity for actions directly related to abating the nuisance. However, where the action negligently damages private property beyond the scope of the abatement authority, the municipality may be liable.

As the court noted: "Where a municipal corporation, in the exercise of its governmental power to abate nuisances, enters upon and damages private property by the destruction of trees, buildings, etc., thereon, it is liable for the payment of just compensation unless its acts were in fact necessary to remove or abate a nuisance." *Rhyne*, 251 N.C. at 528, 112 S.E.2d at 46.

Warner v. W&O Inc., 263 N.C. 37, 138 S.E.2d 782 (1964)

Building permits; vested rights

The owner obtained a building permit, and the zoning ordinance was subsequently amended to prohibit the proposed land use. The court ruled that the permit did not create vested rights but merely authorized the permittee to act. If there was action, the permittee might claim vested rights, but the record does not indicate any action in good-faith reliance on the permit to establish vested rights. Note that subsequent caselaw and statutory provisions control vested rights determinations.

Walker v. City of Charlotte, 262 N.C. 697, 138 S.E.2d 501 (1964)

Unsafe structure; enforcement; injunction; constitutionality

The property owner sought to enjoin enforcement of a demolition order, claiming it was unconstitutional. The court stated that the general rule is that an injunction will not issue to restrain enforcement of a criminal law based on claims of unconstitutionality. There is an exception, however, if enforcement would cause irreparable injury. Here, the property owner failed to allege the necessary facts to support a claim of irreparable injury.

State v. Walker, 265 N.C. 482, 144 S.E.2d 419 (1965)

Unsafe structure; criminal prosecution; work without permits

In a long-running dispute over a dilapidated structure, a property owner began renovation without applying for and obtaining building permits. The city, claiming the act was unlawful, malicious, and willful, brought criminal prosecution. The property owner challenged the constitutionality of the ordinance and its enforcement. The court ruled for the state. "It is within the police power of the General Assembly and of a city, when authorized, to establish minimum standards, materials, designs, and construction of buildings for the safety of the occupants, their neighbors, and the public at large." *Walker*, 265 N.C. at 484, 144 S.E.2d at 421.

Dale v. City of Morganton, 270 N.C. 567, 155 S.E.2d 136 (1967)

Housing code; due process; electric utility connection

The property owner challenged the city's actions to find the residence to be unsafe, to prohibit occupancy, and to refuse to connect electricity to the residence. The court distinguished the minimum housing action (a governmental function) and the refusal to connect electricity (an enterprise function). With regard to the electricity, a city as an electric utility must treat all customers equally and may not unfairly deny service to individuals. But, just like other electric utilities, a city may deny service due to faulty wiring.

With regard to the minimum housing action, the court found that the city had not afforded the owner due process. The city must follow procedures in the applicable statutes and ordinances. Among the procedural requirements, the city must provide the required notice, and the city must provide the property owner with an opportunity to be heard (a hearing) on the fitness of the house for human habitation.

"Substantial compliance with these procedures is a condition precedent to the authority of the city to forbid the use of a dwelling house for human habitation." *Dale*, 270 N.C. at 576, 155 S.E.2d at 144.

Walker v. City of Charlotte, 276 N.C. 166, 171 S.E.2d 431 (1970)

Unsafe structure; condemnation and order of demolition; constitutionality

In a long-running dispute about a dilapidated structure, the owner claimed that the statutes and ordinances concerning the removal of unsafe structures were unconstitutional. The court found that the authority was permissible under the general regulatory powers and that the procedures adequately protected individual rights.

Horton v. Gulledge, 277 N.C. 353, 177 S.E.2d 885 (1970), *overruled as to aesthetic regulations by* State v. Jones, 305 N.C. 520, 290 S.E.2d 675 (1982)

Housing code; opportunity to repair

The city condemned an owner's residential structure and ordered demolition as part of a broader redevelopment plan. The central question for the court was: May the city require demolition (without compensation) without affording the owner an opportunity to bring the property into compliance? For the case at hand, the court said no. When there is not an imminent threat to safety, the city must give an opportunity to repair. Quoting section 368 of volume 16 of *American Jurisprudence 2d*, Constitutional Law, the court stated: "(P)ublic necessity is the limit of the right to destroy property which is a menace to public safety or health and the property cannot be destroyed if the conditions which make it a menace can be abated in any other recognized way." Where an unsafe structure could be remedied by private action, "[t]o require its destruction, without giving the owner a reasonable opportunity thus to remove the existing threat to the public health, safety and welfare, is arbitrary and unreasonable." *Horton*, 277 N.C. at 363, 177 S.E.2d at 892.

This case was overruled by *State v. Jones*, specifically regarding the question of aesthetic-only regulations.

Greene v. City of Winston-Salem, 287 N.C. 66, 213 S.E.2d 231 (1975)

Building code; local modification

Builders challenged a local ordinance requiring sprinklers in high-rise buildings. The city argued that the sprinkler ordinance was allowed under its general police powers to protect public health and safety. The court ruled that the building code statutes establish a "complete and integrated regulatory scheme" for building safety, including sprinklers. *Greene*, 287 N.C. at 75, 213 S.E.2d at 237. As such, the state has preempted the field. Statutory provisions allowed limited local modification, but only with approval by the Building Code Council.

Lynn v. Overlook Development, 328 N.C. 689, 403 S.E.2d 469 (1991)
Building permit; liability; certificate of compliance
In August 1985, the plaintiffs moved into a newly constructed townhome. After moving in, a building inspector conducted an inspection but did not issue a certificate of compliance, inform the plaintiffs of any issues, or inform them that their occupancy was a violation of statute. The plaintiffs discovered numerous defects. These defects were the basis of a condemnation proceeding brought by the city in December 1988. The plaintiffs then brought legal action against the city for damages, alleging that the inspector's actions were willful, wanton, unlawful, culpable, and/or reckless conduct outside the scope of his duties as a city employee.

Reviewing the statutory duties of the inspections department and the facts of the case, the court ruled that the inspector's acts or omissions did not cause the damages (i.e., the purchase of a house unfit for habitation). Even if permits were issued improperly, they were issued to the builder months before the plaintiffs purchased and took title to the home. The plaintiffs occupied the building before final inspections, in violation of state law. "[P]laintiffs elected to take title and assume occupancy of the townhouse in violation of the law before the building inspector had opportunity to make final inspection and issue a certificate of compliance. This act was an intervening, independent cause of plaintiffs' damages. Therefore, the acts or omissions by the city building inspector did not proximately cause the plaintiffs' damages." *Lynn*, 328 N.C. at 697, 403 S.E.2d at 473.

City of New Bern v. New Bern-Craven County Board of Education, 338 N.C. 430, 450 S.E.2d 735 (1994)
Building code; local legislation; purpose
Legislation shifting building code enforcement was ruled unconstitutional. The General Assembly passed legislation reassigning building code responsibility from the City of New Bern to Craven County for properties of the board of education, community college, and medical center. The court found that the legislation was local legislation, not generally applicable. Under the North Carolina Constitution, local legislation cannot address subjects "[r]elating to health, sanitation, and the abatement of nuisances." The court ruled that building code enforcement affects health and sanitation, so it cannot be altered by local legislation.

Thompson v. Waters, 351 N.C. 462, 526 S.E.2d 650 (2000)

Building code; liability; public duty doctrine

Within two weeks of the completion of a home, the homeowners experienced substantial structural defects. They brought action against the county claiming that the building inspectors were grossly negligent in performing their inspections. The county argued protection under the public duty doctrine.

As adopted in *Braswell v. Braswell*, 330 N.C. 363, 370, 410 S.E.2d 897, 901 (1991), the public duty doctrine provides "that a municipality and its agents act for the benefit of the public, and therefore, there is no liability for the failure to furnish police protection to specific individuals." In *Braswell*, the North Carolina Supreme Court applied the public duty doctrine to law enforcement. In *Thompson*, the court declined to extend the public duty doctrine to building inspections.

Morris Communications Corp. v. City of Bessemer City Zoning Board of Adjustment, 365 N.C. 152, 712 S.E.2d 868 (2011)

Building permit; interpretation; nonconformities; vested rights

In July 2005, the state condemned for a road-widening project a portion of the property on which the plaintiff had a lawful billboard. In August 2005, the plaintiff secured a sign permit from the city for a relocated billboard and, in November 2005, secured a building permit from the county for that work. Each permit required "work" to commence within six months. In June 2006, the county renewed the building permit. Later in June 2006, the city amended its ordinance to ban billboards. In December 2006, the plaintiff relocated the billboard, which was apparently the initial physical construction on site. The city contended that the plaintiff's sign permit had expired after six months (in February 2006) because there was no work on site, so the county's renewal of the building permit was in error, and the city's June 2006 billboard ban precluded issuance of a permit for the relocation. On appeal of the city's notice of a violation of the city ordinance, the board of adjustment, trial court, and court of appeals upheld the city's interpretation of the law.

The court reversed, noting that interpretation of the ordinance is a de novo question of law. The term *work* was not defined by the ordinance or the permit. The court held that the zoning administrator and board of adjustment's conclusion that some physical work of the nature authorized by the permit on site was required to constitute *work* under the terms of the ordinance was unreasonable. Governmental restrictions on the use of land are to be strictly construed in favor of free use of real property. Thus, this "narrow and unduly restrictive interpretation" of an undefined and ambiguous term was inappropriate. *Morris Communications*, 365 N.C. at 158, 712 S.E.2d at 872. The court relied on several factors to conclude that *work* had commenced within the permit period. The dictionary definition of *work* includes mental efforts to achieve an objective, and the record established that the plaintiff had engaged in active negotiations with the N.C. Department of Transportation and the landowner during this period. The state's common law has also long included work beyond physical alterations on site to be considered in vested rights analysis. Further, the board of adjustment should act to prevent errors or abuse by zoning administrators and to achieve just results. Given the fact that this was an involuntary relocation of a sign to accommodate road widening, plus the town's acknowledged hostility toward billboards, the "overly restrictive" interpretation of a vague ordinance should have been reversed.

Askew v. City of Kinston, 386 N.C. 286, 902 S.E.2d 722 (2024)

Unsafe buildings; demolition; administrative remedy; Corum *suit*

Some constitutional challenges may proceed even if the challenger did not exhaust administrative remedies. In this case, the city established and pursued a general blight removal program under the unsafe structures authority. The plaintiffs' properties were condemned. The plaintiffs argued that the program targeted African-American neighborhoods and brought a constitutional challenge (a *Corum* suit, named for *Corum v. University of North Carolina*, 330 N.C. 761 (1992)), arguing that the program violated equal protection and due process rights under the North Carolina Constitution.

Lower courts dismissed the constitutional claims, finding that the plaintiffs failed to exhaust their administrative remedies (i.e., failed to timely appeal city decisions condemning the particular properties).

The North Carolina Supreme Court explored the scope and substance of *Corum* suits, and explained the need for additional review at the court of appeals. In determining if a *Corum* suit may proceed despite failure to exhaust administrative remedies, the court must consider whether the administrative remedies are adequate to address the constitutional claims. On remand, the court of appeals ruled that administrative remedies were sufficient. Askew v. City of Kinston, 295 N.C. App. 295, 906 S.E.2d 500.

North Carolina Court of Appeals

State v. Martin, 7 N.C. App. 18, 171 S.E.2d 115 (1969)

Building permit; enforcement

The local ordinance limited manufactured homes to manufactured home parks. The city enforced the ordinance against a defendant who set up a manufactured home despite being warned of its illegality. The court ruled in favor of the city. It found the ordinance sufficient: the nonconforming provision was comparable to others, and the enforcement procedures of the building inspector were adequate. The defendant claimed that other properties with trailers were not being enforced against, but "[i]t is no defense to a criminal charge nor to one of this type that others have not been penalized or the law enforced as to them." *Martin*, 7 N.C. App. at 21, 171 S.E.2d at 117.

Harrell v. City of Winston-Salem, 22 N.C. App. 386, 206 S.E.2d 802 (1974)

Housing code; appeals

The city followed the required procedures to order the repair or demolition of the owner's dwellings. The owner filed complaints in superior court to halt the action and claim damages. The court ruled, among other things, that the statutory authority for minimum housing sets forth the process for individuals to appeal and seek administrative remedies. In this case, the owner failed to exhaust those remedies and could not circumvent the established procedure by filing a court action.

Axler v. City of Wilmington, 25 N.C. App. 110, 212 S.E.2d 510 (1975)

Housing code; appeals

The property owner failed to exhaust administrative remedies and could not use a collateral attack (via injunctive relief) to avoid the procedural requirements.

Mecklenburg County v. Westbery, 32 N.C. App. 630, 233 S.E.2d 658 (1977)

Building code; definition of structure; vested rights; injunctive relief

The building permit statute at the time, Chapter 153A, Section 357 of the North Carolina General Statutes (hereinafter G.S.) required that "No person may commence or proceed with: (1) The construction . . . of any building . . . without first securing from the inspection department with jurisdiction over the site of the work each permit required by . . . local ordinance. . . ." The county issued a permit but then revoked it as mistakenly issued. The defendants claimed that they did not need permits because the structure was for storage, not dwelling. The court ruled that regardless of whether it is a mobile home dwelling or a mobile storage structure, it is a structure that requires a building permit under state law. The defendants argued vested rights based on the mistakenly issued permit, but the court ruled that vested rights require a valid governmental permit. In this case, "the planned usage was illegal from its inception." *Mecklenburg*, 32 N.C. App. at 635, 233 S.E.2d at 661. Even if the specific use was not denominated in the local ordinance, injunctive relief was available to the county under the applicable statute for building code enforcement authority.

Carolinas-Virginias Association of Building Owners and Managers v. Ingram, 39 N.C. App. 688, 251 S.E.2d 910 (1979)

Building Code Council; statutory authority; existing buildings

The Building Code Council adopted building code requirements applicable to existing high-rise buildings. Building owners challenged the regulations as beyond the council's delegated authority. Analyzing the text of the statutory grant of power authorizing the council to adopt the State Building Code, the court found that the express grant permitted rules for the construction of new buildings and structures (as well as reconstruction and altered uses), but not for existing buildings. Separately, the General Assembly had passed legislation requiring sprinkler systems in existing buildings, but that law was a specific grant of authority. The court found no such grant of authority for broader building code requirements for existing buildings.

Yates v. City of Raleigh, 46 N.C. App. 221, 264 S.E.2d 798 (1980)

Nuisance abatement

The city, in an effort to abate a nuisance, removed and disposed of tools and equipment used by the plaintiff for concrete contracting. The plaintiff argued that the concrete finishing tools did not amount to a nuisance and that such action went beyond the municipal authority. The lower court dismissed the plaintiff's claims, but the court of appeals remanded the case for further proceedings to determine whether removal of the concrete finishing tools was "in fact necessary to remove or abate a nuisance." *Yates*, 264 S.E.2d at 802 (citing *Rhyne*).

Pigott v. City of Wilmington, 50 N.C. App. 401, 273 S.E.2d 752, *writ denied*, 303 N.C. 181, 280 S.E.2d 453 (1981)

Building code; liability; public official immunity

The building inspector cited plaintiffs for two unpermitted small greenhouses and required that they be brought up to code or demolished. After the greenhouses were demolished, the inspector informed the plaintiffs that greenhouses smaller than 400 square feet were allowed without a permit. One of the demolished greenhouses was smaller than 400 square feet. The plaintiffs sued for damages based on the inspector's negligence.

The court, citing *Smith v. State*, 289 N.C. 303, 222 S.E.2d 412 (1976), and the *C.J.S.* treatise on municipal corporations, ruled that the chief building inspector is a public official protected by public official immunity. The position is created by legislation; requires taking an oath of office; performs functions delegated as part of the sovereign power of the state; and is vested with a certain measure of discretion.

A public official is protected from certain liability claims arising from the performance of their public official duties. When "a public official . . . [is] engaged in the performance of governmental duties involving the exercise of judgment and discretion," then plaintiffs must allege and point toward evidence that the act "was corrupt or malicious . . . or that he acted outside of and beyond the scope of his duties." *Pigott*, 50 N.C. App. at 405–06, 273 S.E.2d at 755 (citing *Smith v. Hefner*, 235 N.C. 1, 68 S.E.2d 783 (1952)).

Wiggins v. City of Monroe, 73 N.C. App. 44, 326 S.E.2d 39 (1985) (Wiggins I)

Housing code; opportunity to correct; liability

In this dispute over a demolition under the housing code, the lower court granted summary judgment for the building inspector and city. The court of appeals analyzed the record and reversed. A chief building inspector ordering the repair or demolition of a structure in compliance with the local housing code is a "public official" immune from liability for mere negligence in the performance of official governmental duties. The evidence tended to show, however, that the building official's behavior was "corrupt or malicious or that he acted outside of and beyond the scope of his duties," so he would not be immune. In the enforcement proceedings, the building inspector gave the owner ten days to commence repairs and sixty days to complete them. Within ten days, the owner obtained what they believed to be building permits to begin repairs. On day thirteen, the building inspector proceeded with demolition despite the owner having commenced repairs and the sixty-day window for cure not having run. With regard to city liability, the city's purchase of insurance waived its immunity in this matter. As such, the court reversed the lower court's decision of summary judgment. See *Wiggins II*, below, for a subsequent decision in the same dispute.

First American Federal Savings & Loan Association v. Royall, 77 N.C. App. 131, 334 S.E.2d 792 (1985)

Building permit; enforcement; certificate of occupancy/compliance

The developer obtained subdivision plat approval from the city with a requirement to install water infrastructure for the development. A builder constructed a building (and connected it to an existing adjacent water line), but the city refused to issue the certificate of occupancy until the required water infrastructure was installed for the overall subdivision. The case arose as a contract dispute between the builder and the developer, but it implicated authority for certificates of occupancy/compliance.

The court found authority in the statutes and the local ordinance to withhold a certificate of compliance until the required infrastructure was installed. Statutory authority states that a new building may not be occupied until a final inspection is completed and a certificate of compliance is issued, confirming that the structure complies with all applicable state and local laws. In this case, the local ordinance, the subdivision approval, and evidence in the record all showed a requirement for water infrastructure. The failure to provide that water connection was a failure to comply with applicable local law, so the certificate of compliance was properly withheld.

Wiggins v. City of Monroe, 85 N.C. App. 237, 354 S.E.2d 365 (1987) (Wiggins II)

Unsafe structure; liability; public official immunity

The building inspector issued notice to the property owner that they had ten days to commence repairs to a residence or the city would demolish the structure. After the trial court ordered a directed verdict for the city, the property owner appealed, arguing that the directed verdict was inappropriate. The court ruled that the property owner had evidence sufficient to go to a jury for decision. Notably, the evidence indicated that the inspector ordered the owners "to repair the house and then demolished the house after they had begun timely repairs." The evidence tends to show that the inspector's "behavior was malicious or outside of and beyond the scope of his duties." *Wiggins II*, 85 N.C. App. at 242, 354 S.E.2d at 366. (The court reached a similar conclusion in *Wiggins I*, above, where the court overturned the trial court's ruling of summary judgment in favor of the city).

Appeal of Medical Center, 91 N.C. App. 107, 370 S.E.2d 597 (1988)
Building code; interpretation; Building Code Council
A hospital proposed to build a hospital tower. The Department of Insurance (DOI) required that the tower be built to Type I standards, but the hospital argued that the less stringent Type II standards were applicable. The hospital appealed to the Building Code Council and then to the court. The court of appeals upheld the DOI and Building Code Council's interpretation. The court noted that state law calls for the code to be interpreted liberally in favor of health and safety, that the council is empowered to interpret the provisions, and that the council's interpretation should be given due consideration. (Subsequently, G.S. 143-138(c) was amended to guide that the code should be interpreted "reasonably," not "liberally.")

Newton v. City of Winston-Salem, 92 N.C. App. 446, 374 S.E.2d 488 (1988)
Housing code; notice
After a complaint, investigation, and hearing, the city determined that a residence was unfit for habitation and notified the owner by mail with an order to take corrective action. Return receipts on two separate letters confirmed receipt. Two years later, the city continued the enforcement action with attempts over several months to notify the owner (1) to secure the building, (2) to repair or demolish the building, and finally (3) that the city would demolish it. These notices were sent by certified mail and returned unclaimed. After demolition, the owner filed suit for trespass and damages.

On appeal, the court of appeals found that the city failed to follow required statutory procedures for notice and hearing related to the demolition order. The unclaimed certified mail notices were insufficient; the statutes outlined options for personal service and service by publication. The statutes require a hearing for an order to repair *or* an order to demolish. Here, the city held a hearing early in the process for an order to repair, but that hearing occurred three years before the order to demolish and did not address demolition. The property owner had no opportunity to be heard regarding the demolition, and the city should have provided an additional hearing. Additionally, when it came to demolition, the city failed to sell salvageable materials to recoup expenses.

Midgette v. Pate, 94 N.C. App. 498, 380 S.E.2d 572 (1989)
Enforcement; investigation; mandamus
A property owner obtained a building permit and special use permit for a swimming pool and bathhouse. A neighbor alleged that the pool was used as a commercial pool in violation of the zoning ordinance. The neighbor challenged the issuance of the permits and sought a writ of mandamus and injunction to compel town officials to enforce the zoning ordinance. As to the permits, the statute of

limitations had run, and the neighbor failed to exhaust administrative remedies, so the neighbor could not now attack the permits. As to mandamus, "[m]andamus will lie to compel the performance of a purely ministerial duty imposed by law." *Midgette*, 94 N.C. App. at 503, 380 S.E.2d at 575–76. The court found that investigating alleged violations is a ministerial duty required by statute for the zoning inspector. Notably, the court viewed the act of investigation as the ministerial duty; enforcement decisions require judgment and discretion and thus are not ministerial in nature ("Though the zoning administrator may exercise discretion in assessing the alleged violations, this does not lessen the duty to investigate the charges of a plaintiff who has legal right to have the duty enforced." *Midgette*, 94 N.C. App. at 503–04, 380 S.E.2d at 576. The neighbor alleged that as an adjacent property owner subject to the same rules, they suffered special damages. As such, the court determined that the neighbor asserted a legal right to enforce the ministerial duties of the zoning administrator.

Law Building of Asheboro, Inc. v. City of Asheboro, 108 N.C. App. 182, 423 S.E.2d 93 (1992)

Building permits; damages; unsafe structure; demolition

As part of a back-and-forth dispute over an unsafe structure, the owner claimed that the city refused to issue a building permit for repairs and sought damages for such. The court dismissed the claim, stating there is "no authority or precedent for recognizing or allowing a civil action in damages for alleged unlawful denial of a building permit by a municipality." *Law Building of Asheboro*, 108 N.C. App. at 184, 423 S.E.2d at 95. Moreover, the record indicated that the owner's application had not run its administrative course.

Simpson v. City of Charlotte, 115 N.C. App. 51, 443 S.E.2d 772 (1994)

Building permit; vested rights

A landowner who lived across the street from a quarry challenged a permit issued for a 112-acre expansion of the quarry. At the time of the permit decision, quarries were allowed in all zoning districts subject to specified findings, but the ordinance was amended shortly after the permit was issued to limit quarries to certain zoning districts. The trial court ruled that this was contrary to the requirement of G.S. 160A-381 that zoning should promote the public health, safety, and welfare. The court reversed, holding that only the validity of the permit, not the validity of the ordinance, had been properly before the trial court. The court held that there was insufficient information before the board to determine whether a vested right had been established prior to the ordinance amendment. The court ruled that a zoning permit for the quarry is not a "building permit" that creates a statutory vested right under G.S. 160A-385(b) but remanded to determine whether the $20,000 spent after receipt of the quarry permit was substantial and made in good faith. The court affirmed the conclusion that noise and vibration requirements in the ordinance apply to operation of the use, not its initial approval.

Petty v. Owen, 140 N.C. App. 494, 537 S.E.2d 216 (2000)

Building code; modular construction; Building Code Council

In a dispute over whether an individual who erects modular homes must be a licensed contractor, the court interpreted the applicable statutory provisions and reviewed the authority of the Building Code Council and Department of Insurance. In particular, the court noted the role of administrative interpretation for deciphering statutory provisions: "An administrative interpretation of a statute, acquiesced in over a long period of time, is properly considered in the construction of the statute by the courts. But an administrative interpretation can never be considered when in direct conflict with the intent and purpose of the act, or when in conflict with the interpretation of the courts." *Petty*, 140 N.C. App. at 500, 537 S.E.2d at 220 (citations and quotations omitted). In this case, the court used the Department of Insurance's interpretation as a factor.

Coffey v. Town of Waynesville, 143 N.C. App. 624, 547 S.E.2d 132 (2001)

Unsafe structure; quasi-judicial; demolition

After inspection, the code-enforcement officer posted and reposted a notice of unsafe structure. The office then mailed notice of a hearing. At the hearing, the officer ordered the building to be demolished. On appeal, the town board affirmed the demolition order. The property owner appealed to superior court, alleging that the town failed to follow procedures to order demolition and refused to give reasonable time for repairs.

The court of appeals confirmed that when a governing board decides on a demolition order, the board acts as a quasi-judicial body. As such, the superior court's review on appeal is in the nature of certiorari, similar to an appeal of other quasi-judicial decisions. While the property owner claimed the decisions were arbitrary and capricious (calling for whole record review), the court of appeals determined that the claims were actually errors of law and subject to de novo review. The court found that the town followed statutory procedures to order demolition and that the time given to show progress toward repair was reasonable.

Carolina Holdings, Inc. v. Housing Appeals Board of City of Charlotte, 149 N.C. App. 579, 561 S.E.2d 541 (2002)

Housing code; appeals; enforcement

The city investigated and determined that all units in an apartment complex had housing code violations. The owner challenged the determination and appealed to the housing appeals board. On appeal, the court of appeals ruled that the city followed the necessary procedures and had evidence to support its determinations (it had ordered repair of some units and demolition of some units). The city is not estopped from enforcement of the housing code simply because the violations had existed for years without citation.

Among other rulings, the court allowed that the housing appeals board had authority to go into closed session specifically to preserve attorney-client privilege:

"While there is a public policy against closed sessions, discussions between a board and its attorney regarding matters traditionally falling within the attorney-client privilege must be allowed to be conducted in closed sessions to preserve the attorney-client privilege, including consulting on constitutional and legal challenges which might result from actions being taken or considered by a board." *Carolina Holdings*, 149 N.C. App. at 585, 561 S.E.2d at 545.

Eastern Outdoor, Inc. v. Board of Adjustment of Johnston County, 150 N.C. App. 516, 564 S.E.2d 78 (2002), *aff'd*, 357 N.C. 501, 586 S.E.2d 90 (2003)

Building permit; revoking permits

A sign company obtained building permits for a sign. Subsequently, the county determined that the sign was not permitted under the zoning ordinance, and revoked the building permits. The court of appeals affirmed the county's authority to revoke a mistakenly issued permit.

Monroe v. City of New Bern, 158 N.C. App. 275, 580 S.E.2d 372 (2003)

Nuisance; demolition; summary abatement; due process

The city demolished the property owner's building without notice or an opportunity to be heard. The city argued it had authority for such action under G.S. 160A-193, which allows for a city to summarily abate a public health nuisance.

The court interpreted the statutory authority to be limited to emergency situations involving imminent danger: "Section 160A-193 only applies to a situation where a structurally unsafe building poses an imminent danger to the safety of the public such that the owner could not be provided notice and a hearing without endangering the public. Cities may not summarily demolish dwellings pursuant to Section 160A–193 merely because it is quicker and easier than providing the owners notice and an opportunity to be heard." *Monroe*, 158 N.C. App. at 278, 580 S.E.2d at 374.

On the question of what counts as an imminent danger, the court stated that "a city would have the authority to summarily demolish a building pursuant to Section 160A–193 if the building were in such a ruinous state that it was on the verge of falling onto a sidewalk frequented by pedestrians or in a situation where the destruction of the building is necessary to stop or control a large destructive fire." *Id.* at 279, 580 S.E.2d at 375.

The court pointed to the statutory authority for minimum housing enforcement, including the procedural requirements for demolition performed by the local government. That authority is available in non-emergency situations, and the procedural guardrails are necessary. If there is not an emergency situation, the local government may use one of the other authorities for demolition (e.g., unsafe structures, minimum housing, etc.) and must follow the required procedures "including providing the owner with notice, a hearing, and a reasonable opportunity to bring his or her dwelling into conformity with the housing code." *Id.*

In the instant case, the court determined that the building did not pose an imminent danger, so summary abatement was not authorized. The city had a minimum housing ordinance but did not follow the procedures set forth in the housing statutes, so it lacked authority for the demolition.

City of Charlotte v. King, 158 N.C. App. 304, 580 S.E.2d 380 (2003)
Housing code; enforcement
The city imposed civil penalties in relation to a minimum housing enforcement action. The property owner argued, based on the language of the ordinance, that the penalty could only be imposed if the property was occupied. The court disagreed. The plain language of the ordinance provided an exemption from civil penalties for owner-occupied dwellings, but not for unoccupied dwellings.

Town of Hertford v. Harris, 169 N.C. App. 838, 611 S.E.2d 194 (2005)
Housing code; demolition; enforcement
The town brought suit seeking to sell the owner's property to satisfy a lien for the cost of demolishing two manufactured homes on the property. The property owner filed a countersuit, claiming the town wrongfully took the property. The court ruled for the property owner. State law requires that when a municipality demolishes a dwelling under the minimum housing statutes, the municipality must sell personal property and fixtures and credit that against the cost of the demolition. In this case, there was a dispute between the town and property owner as to whether there was any personal property or fixtures of value. As such, summary judgment was not appropriate, and the court remanded to the trial court for further proceedings.

Sandy Mush Properties v. Rutherford County, 181 N.C. App. 224, 638 S.E.2d 557, *remanded by* 361 N.C. 569, 651 S.E.2d 566, *aff'd by* 187 N.C. App. 809, 654 S.E.2d 253 (2007), *review dismissed*, 363 N.C. 577, 681 S.E.2d 339 (2009)
Building permits; tolling permits; vested rights
The case involved a long-running dispute over a 180-acre tract for a crushed rock quarry.

In 2001, the plaintiff applied for three building permits at the site of the proposed quarry. The defendant county denied the permits based on a county-adopted moratorium on locating heavy industries near schools. The plaintiff challenged the validity of the moratorium based on procedural deficiencies in its adoption. In September 2001, the trial court enjoined enforcement of the moratorium and ordered the building permits issued. The defendant appealed the trial court's determination that the moratorium was invalid but nonetheless issued the building permits. Pursuant to the permits, the plaintiff in October 2001 began construction on one of the buildings, the proposed office building. In October 2001, the contested moratorium expired, and the defendant enacted an ordinance that made quarries a prohibited use at the site. Construction on the office building ceased in December 2001, prior to its completion. In 2002, the trial court upheld the moratorium. In 2004, the court of appeals declared the moratorium invalid, and in July 2004, the plaintiff sought to resume construction of the office building. The defendant contended that the building permit had expired. The plaintiff contended that the statute providing for expiration of a building permit if construction ceased for twelve months was tolled by the appeal regarding the validity of the moratorium. The plaintiff also argued that the building permit for the office building constituted a statutory or common law vesting for the use of the property as a quarry.

Since the acknowledged use of the building was as an office for the quarry, the appellate court held that the trial court's order upholding a moratorium on the quarry operation effectively prohibited continuing construction of the office building under the building permit. The court thus held that the trial court's order and the subsequent appeal tolled the statutory period in which the plaintiff could resume construction and that there had not therefore been a twelve-month lapse in construction so as to cause the building permit to expire. However, the court held that the particular building permit only authorized the construction of an office building (which by the terms of the permit could be used as offices for various uses) and did not purport to authorize any other use of the larger site. Thus, the office building permit itself constituted neither a statutory vesting nor a basis for common law vesting for the use of the site as a quarry.

On appeal, the state supreme court remanded this decision for reconsideration in light of its ruling in *Robins v. Town of Hillsborough*, 361 N.C. 193, 639 S.E.2d 421 (2007). On remand, the court of appeals affirmed its prior holding, noting that the *Robins* decision expressly stated that it was not a vested rights case but, rather, a question of town compliance with procedures mandated by its ordinance. Thus, the court held that *Robins* did not affect its prior decision.

Lawyer v. City of Elizabeth City, 199 N.C. App. 304, 681 S.E.2d 415 (2009)

Housing code; demolition; notice

Pursuant to a minimum housing code enforcement, the city demolished a dwelling owned by multiple individuals as tenants in common. They had purchased the property from a sheriff's auction. Notice of the housing code violation and the pending demolition was provided to the owner of record listed with the register of deeds and the tax department (the prior owners), but notice was not sent to all of the tenants in common.

The court held that reasonable minds could disagree about the proper standard of care for determining the owners to be notified. So the court reversed the summary judgment from below.

Moores v. Greensboro Minimum Housing Standards Commission, 198 N.C. App. 384, 679 S.E.2d 480 (2009)

Housing code; housing commission

Challenging an order to repair or demolish, the property owner argued that the housing commission was not authorized to make the order because it was not a "governing body" as required by statute. The superior court agreed and ruled for the property owner, holding that the commission was not a governing body. The court of appeals, however, deferred to the local ordinance language authorizing the housing commission as the body to make decisions on such orders.

Estate of Hewett v. County of Brunswick, 199 N.C. App. 564, 681 S.E.2d 531 (2009)

Nuisance; liability

The county operated a program to remove junk and waste from private property at the owner's request. The county mistakenly demolished a barn (they were at the wrong property). The barn owner sued for damages, and the county claimed sovereign immunity barred the claim. The court of appeals ruled that the program was "primarily a trash and junk collection service" and that it was a governmental function entitled to governmental immunity. *Estate of Hewett*, 199 N.C. at 571, 681 S.E.2d at 535.

Boor v. Spectrum Homes, 196 N.C. App. 699, 675 S.E.2d 712 (2009)

Building code; certificate of occupancy/compliance; substantial completion; statute of limitations

In this dispute between an owner and a builder, the running of the statute of limitations depended on the "substantial completion" of the home. In determining substantial completion, the court looked to the issuance of the certificate of compliance as allowing use of the property for its intended purpose. The court used the terms *certificate of compliance* and *certificate of occupancy* interchangeably.

Worthy v. Ivy Community Center, 198 N.C. App. 513, 679 S.E.2d 885 (2009)

Building code; liability; negligent inspection

After residents of an apartment were injured in a fire caused by faulty wiring, they brought a negligence complaint against the apartment owner, the City of Durham, and others. In addition to broad evidentiary disputes, the City argued that it should not be liable because the decision not to inspect was a non-justiciable political question, and that the public duty doctrine precluded liability. The court was unpersuaded and cited multiple cases to conclude that "our courts regularly adjudicate disputes regarding a governmental entity's duty to inspect." *Worthy*, 198 N.C. App. at 523, 679 S.E.2d at 891. The court also applied *Thompson*'s rule (discussed above) that the public duty doctrine does not preclude a claim of negligent inspection of a building.

Town of Nags Head v. Cherry, Inc., 219 N.C. App. 66, 723 S.E.2d 156, *review denied*, 366 N.C. 386, 733 S.E.2d 85 (2012)

Nuisance; public trust doctrine

As a result of storm damage, the defendant's beach cottage was disconnected from utilities and left on the ocean beach. The town sought to compel removal of the damaged structure as a public nuisance. The court held that the state government is the only body that can bring an action to enforce public-trust rights to freely use and enjoy the state's beaches. Because a principal aspect of the town's public-nuisance claim was that the damaged structure was blocking public access along the beach, only the state had standing to enforce these rights. The court also held that there were material questions of fact as to whether there was a reasonable likelihood of personal or property injury resulting from the damaged structure, so summary judgment on that issue was inappropriate.

(Note: The General Assembly responded with the enactment of G.S. 160A-203 and G.S. 153A-145.3. These statutes authorize cities and counties to enforce local ordinances to protect the public's rights to use state ocean beaches and to regulate placement of personal property on state ocean beaches. Cities may enforce such ordinances on state ocean beaches within or adjacent to their municipal boundaries. Also, G.S. 160A-205 was amended in 2015 to provide that if a structure is on the ocean beach, is uninhabitable, and is without water and sewer services for more than 120 days, a city can prohibit, regulate, or abate the situation.)

Patterson v. City of Gastonia, 220 N.C. App. 233, 725 S.E.2d 82 (2012)

Housing code; notice; opportunity to correct

The plaintiffs (a married couple and their adult son) owned manufactured homes located on leased real property. The city brought a housing code enforcement action and proceeded to demolish some of the manufactured homes. The plaintiffs challenged the action as violating their due process rights on several grounds.

As to proper notice, the court ruled that neither the statutes nor caselaw impose a duty on the local government to go "beyond a public record search and conduct an investigation to uncover whether there might have been owners other than those appearing of record." *Patterson*, 220 N.C. App. at 242, 725 S.E.2d at 89. Notice was provided to the married couple but not to the adult son. The court of appeals reviewed the facts and holdings from *Lawyer v. City of Elizabeth City N.C.*, 199 N.C. App. 304, 308, 681 S.E.2d 415, 418 (2009), and *Farmers Bank of Sunbury v. City of Elizabeth City*, 54 N.C. App. 110, 282 S.E.2d 580 (1981). In *Lawyer*, the court found a material issue as to whether the city had met its duty of care to determine who was a party in interest to receive notice. While the tax office and register of deeds did not reveal the litigant, a title search would have revealed them as a party in interest. In *Farmers Bank*, although a deed of trust was a matter of public record, it was unclear if the city could, with reasonable due diligence, locate the trustee and bank based on the deed of trust. "Neither case suggests that a city has a duty to investigate interests not identifiable through a search of the public record."

Patterson, 220 N.C. App. at 242, 725 S.E.2d at 89. In the present case, there was no evidence that the adult son's interest in the mobile homes would have appeared in the public record.

With regard to the opportunity to correct, the court distinguished this case from *Wiggins I*. In *Wiggins I*, the building inspector gave the owner sixty days for repair but then demolished the building on day thirteen. In *Patterson*, the code-enforcement office gave sixty days for repair, but the owners did not complete the repairs. Once the sixty days elapsed, the code-enforcement officer enforced the order. The owners could have pursued an extension but did not.

The plaintiffs claimed additional due process violations, arguing that the city council had to hold an evidentiary hearing prior to passing the ordinance ordering demolition. The court ruled that the governing board meeting to adopt an ordinance to order demolition does not require a finding by the governing board that the owner was given an opportunity to repair. The evidence and factual determinations are handled in the administrative hearing before the public officer. The court ruled that the plaintiffs had ample notice of the enforcement procedures and opportunity to appeal determinations or seek injunctive relief throughout the process.

Additionally, the court ruled that the plaintiffs had not established that the city waived sovereign immunity and that the plaintiffs could not bring a claim of inverse condemnation.

Hillsboro Partners, LLC v. City of Fayetteville, 226 N.C. App. 30, 738 S.E.2d 819, *review denied*, 367 N.C. 236, 748 S.E.2d 544 (2013)

Unsafe structure; enforcement; estoppel; takings

The plaintiff purchased property that included a building that had been damaged by a fire. The city notified the plaintiff that the building was unsafe. After a hearing, which the plaintiff did not attend, the city ordered the structure repaired or demolished. The city subsequently adopted an ordinance ordering demolition. The plaintiff then sought a permit for demolition. Approximately four months after the adoption of the demolition ordinance, the plaintiff contended that new inspections showed the building to be safe. The city nonetheless demolished the structure.

The court held that the demolition notice, hearing, and ordinance-adoption process mandated by state law and followed by the city was quasi-judicial in nature rather than administrative. That process had resulted in a substantive decision that the structure was unsafe, and that determination had not been appealed. That determination was therefore the identical issue raised in the current appeal and had been litigated in the quasi-judicial process. The plaintiff had a full and fair opportunity to contest it at that time, and a final order that could have been appealed was made. As the underlying facts were unchanged, the plaintiff could not use its own failure to adequately inspect the property as a means to avoid the prior determination. Because the determination that the building was unsafe was binding, the building was a nuisance threatening public health and safety. Its removal was a proper exercise of the police power, and no compensation under the Takings Clause was required.

Six at 109 v. Town of Holden Beach, 238 N.C. App. 469, 767 S.E.2d 400 (2014)

Unsafe structure; condemnation; public trust doctrine

The plaintiff owned a dilapidated four-unit oceanfront motel. The town inspector condemned the building as an unsafe structure under G.S. 160A-426. After a hearing at which the plaintiff presented evidence and testimony, the inspector issued an order finding that the structure had attracted criminal activity constituting a nuisance and was unsafe, a hazard to surrounding properties, a threat of disease, and a danger to children. The structure was ordered demolished pursuant to G.S. 160A-429. That order was appealed to the town council, which after notice and a hearing issued an order making similar findings and upholding the order to demolish if sufficient repairs were not made.

The plaintiff contended that the town lacked subject-matter jurisdiction because the structure was in the public-trust area. The court noted that the property was condemned as unsafe under G.S. 160A-426, an action not based on interference with public-trust rights. The court also concluded that the town council conducted a de novo review, including its own two-day hearing and site visit. The court found that there was ample evidence in the record to support the town council's conclusion that the structure was unsafe and met the statutory standards for mandated demolition.

Cheatham v. Town of Taylortown, 254 N.C. App. 613, 803 S.E.2d 658 (2017)

Housing code; demolition; administrative remedies

In a housing code enforcement action, the owner failed to exhaust his administrative remedies, so the superior court lacked jurisdiction for the appeal.

MR Entertainment, LLC v. City of Asheville, 295 N.C. App. 136, 905 S.E.2d 246 (2024), *review denied*, 912 S.E.2d 821 (N.C. 2025), and *review dismissed*, 912 S.E.2d 823 (N.C. 2025)

Housing codes; appeals; enforcement

This case involved a long-running enforcement dispute over a vehicle sign at a local bar. In 2014, the code-enforcement office issued a sign violation notice for the bar parking a truck with a sign in the bed of the truck. Two and a half years later, a different code-enforcement officer issued another citation alleging a continued violation for the bar driving the truck with the sign around the city. The city followed up with legal action seeking injunctive relief and $57,400 in civil penalties.

The parties disputed the nature of the violation: was it merely about the parked truck, or did it extend to driving the truck around? The court looked at the language of the ordinance and the original notice to rule that it was merely about the parked vehicle. The ordinance provision stated that "[s]igns or advertisements placed on vehicles or trailers that are *parked or located* for the primary purpose of displaying said sign are prohibited" (emphasis added). The notice stated that "[t]he nature of the violation is the use of a vehicle for the primary purpose of displaying off-premise signage. . . ." The court determined that the ordinance language did not extend to driving the truck in the streets. Additionally, the court looked at the evidence supporting the notice of violation. The code-enforcement officer included with the initial notice a picture of the truck parked at the bar. No other evidence was included, and the language of the notice called for site inspection to abate and cure. Under the notice, the bar had twenty-four hours to correct the violation. The court determined that the email from the bar—asking about the appeal process and asserting that the violation was corrected—sufficed as notice of cure. There was no evidence in the record that the code-enforcement officer reinspected. Per the court: "The City's own failure to re-inspect the site cannot defeat Petitioner's timely notice of cure." *MR Ent., LLC*, 295 N.C. App. at 143, 905 S.E.2d at 251, *review denied*, 912 S.E.2d 821 (N.C. 2025), and *review dismissed*, 912 S.E.2d 823 (N.C. 2025). The city claimed a continuing violation, but there was no evidence in the record to show a continuing violation—only the photos of the initial violation. "The City carries the burden of proving the existence of a violation of a local zoning ordinance." *Id.* As such, the court ruled for the bar, which, based on the evidence in the record, timely cured the initial violation.

Appendix B

Sample Fee Schedules

B1. Iredell Building Standards Fee Schedule

Iredell County Building Standards

349 North Center Street P.O. Box 788 Statesville, NC 28687

Online Permitting, Plan Review and Inspection Requests

Email Us Your Questions

IREDELL COUNTY BUILDING STANDARDS FEE SCHEDULE

Permit fees associated with all projects that include a Building Permit will be based on the latest edition of the International Code Council's Building Valuation Data; which is adjusted by a regional modifier in order to provide an 'average' construction cost per square foot. This modification is intended to reflect construction cost for this region. The Permit Fees are established using the modified **Building Valuation Data Table A** along with a Permit Fee Multiplier (0.0068). The product of the estimated Building Value from Table A multiplied by the permit fee multiplier is the permit fee for the project. The Permit Fee for these Building Projects covers the issuance of the initial permit for each sub-permit type (trade) and all inspections (with the exception of 'Temporary Power' and 'Temporary Certificate of Occupancy').

The calculated construction costs for 'Upfit', 'Renovation' and 'Shell/Dry-In' type projects are reduced to 50% of the 'average' construction cost from the Building Valuation Data Table A. The Permit Fee Multiplier for these projects is 0.0068. Specific permit fees can be found in the following list of Individual Permits / Inspections.

Permit Fees for items not listed are calculated at a rate of $7.00 per Thousand Dollars of Project Cost.

All Permit Categories have a non-refundable minimum permit fee of $75.00.

Building:

Recovery Fee (Homeowner's Recovery Fund – NCGS 87.15.6)	$10.00
Manufactured Home – Single Wide – (includes Plumbing, Mechanical & Electrical)	$375.00
Manufactured Home – Double Wide – (includes Plumbing, Mechanical & Electrical)	$475.00
Manufactured Home – Triple Wide – (includes Plumbing, Mechanical & Electrical)	$600.00
Modular Classroom – Single or Double Wide – (includes Plumbing, Mechanical & Electrical)	$500.00
Modular Classroom – Quad/ Mega Unit – (includes Plumbing, Mechanical & Electrical)	$750.00
Day Care – (includes completion of building inspector form for NC licensure)	$150.00
Change of Use – (includes new Certificate of Occupancy) – see NCGS 160D-1116	$200.00
Temporary Certificate of Occupancy (posted for 30 Days) – see NCSAP 204.8.3	$150.00
Demolition (60 days)	$200.00
Swimming Pool (includes Electrical for equipment/ luminaires & equipotential bonding)	$250.00
Construction Trailer (includes Electrical)	$200.00
Cell Tower – New - (includes Electrical)	$1500.00
Cell Tower – Co-Locate - (includes Electrical)	$1000.00
Sign (illuminated wall mount or free standing – includes Electrical)	$200.00
Commercial *Re*-Roof (no Structural Work)	$250.00
Retaining Wall (per Segment)	$200.00
Fencing (when required by the commercial building code)	$75.00
Shell Buildings	Fee Template

Electrical:	
Residential Service Change/ New Service	$125.00
Commercial Service Change/ New Service	$150.00
Construction Saw Pole	$75.00 each
Temporary Power (60 Days)	$75.00
Fire Alarm/ Security Systems	$200.00
Low Voltage (Data/ Phone)	$150.00
Install Electrical Equipment	$100.00
Plumbing:	
Gas Piping System	$100.00 each
Residential Fire Sprinkler System (NFPA 13-D)	$200.00
Combo Appliance Replacement (includes Electrical and/or Gas)	$100.00 each
Install Plumbing Equipment	$100.00
Mechanical:	
Refrigeration System	$300.00 each
Ventilation System	$300.00 each
Combo Appliance Replacement (includes Electrical and/or Gas)	$100.00 each
Install Mechanical Equipment	$100.00
Plan Review:	
Project Review (includes staff commentary and re-submittal)	$.06 per sq. ft.
Project Re-review (includes second staff commentary and resubmittals)	$200.00
Revisions to Approved Plans (RTAP) – plans require revision following permit issuance	$.06 per sq. ft.
Re-Stamp Copies of Approved Plans (lost or missing sheets/ entire plan set replacement)	$10 per sheet
Miscellaneous:	
Re-Inspection – 1st wasted trip to site	$100.00
Re-Inspection – 2nd wasted trip to site	$125.00
Re-Inspection – 3rd/ subsequent wasted trips to site	$150.00
Change of Contractor	$75.00
Safety Inspections – Electric for service re-Connect *or* ABC Permit Compliance Form	$75.00
Permits/ Certificate of Inspection for Other Agencies/ AHJs	$75.00

Due to the increase in processing and administrative costs associated with resolving NCGS 160D-1110 building violations, per the NC Administrative Code & Policies 204.6.2:

- Work Started Without Permits (1st Violation) Permit Fees will be *Doubled*
- Work Started Without Permits (2nd and Subsequent Violations) Permit Fees will be *Tripled*

Re-Inspection Fees and other Fees or Penalties will result in suspension of further inspection of the project, until
outstanding fees have been paid.
Misrepresentations on a permit application shall result in the revocation of a permit.
No refunds will be made for revoked permits.

A Non-Refundable $77.25 Application Fee is included in the charge for all permits. Refunds may only be made
on permits that have not had *any* inspections performed. All Refunds are subject to subtraction of the Application Fee in order to address administrative costs.

All permits are subject to a 3% Technology / Administrative Fee.

Projects on which permits expire will be treated as such (*expired*), and will require new applications, AHJ clearances and fees. Contractors who do not request required inspections or, obtain the required approvals, leading to permit expiration, may be subject to Building Standards withholding the issuance of permits for *all* work by that contractor (unless or, until expired projects have been re-permitted, approved, or otherwise satisfactorily resolved).

Typically, there are other permit fees for other departments or governmental units and are collected by these other authorities having jurisdiction. These other permit fees are *not* reflected in or addressed by this fee schedule.

Following are links to some of these other departments:
City of Statesville Fire Marshal
City of Statesville Planning Department
City of Statesville Utilities

Iredell County Building Standards
Iredell County Environmental Health
Iredell County Fire Marshal
Iredell County Planning and Erosion Control

Town of Troutman Planning Department
Town of Troutman Utilities

Each Building, Tenant Space, Project Phase, or Structure requires an individual permit.

296
Dec-24

TABLE A IREDELL COUNTY BUILDING VALUATION DATA

Occupancy Classification		Average Cost per Square Foot with Regional Modifiers								
		Non-Combustible Construction						Combustible Construction		
Construction Type	**Regional**	IA	IB	IIA	IIB	IIIA	IIIB	IV	VA	VB
Cost per Sq. Ft.	**Modifier**	LOCAL	LOCAL	LOCAL	LOCAL	LOCAL	LOCAL	LOCAL	LOCAL	LOCAL
A-1 Assembly, theaters, with stage	→	181.41	175.45	171.17	164.01	154.20	149.76	158.50	140.95	135.61
A-1 Assembly, theaters, without stage		166.23	160.28	155.99	148.83	139.11	134.66	143.32	125.86	120.52
A-2 Assembly, nightclubs		140.90	136.91	133.13	127.92	120.38	117.06	123.41	109.06	105.34
A-2 Assembly, restaurants, bars, banquet halls	0.80	140.10	136.11	131.53	127.12	118.78	116.26	122.61	107.46	104.54
A-3 Assembly, churches		167.87	161.92	157.63	150.47	140.94	136.50	144.96	127.69	122.36
A-3 Assembly, general, community halls, libraries, museums		140.10	134.14	129.06	122.70	112.25	108.61	117.18	99.00	94.46
A-4 Assembly, arenas		165.43	159.48	154.39	148.03	137.51	133.86	142.52	124.26	119.72
B Business	0.80	144.87	139.55	134.91	128.23	116.87	112.48	123.17	102.57	98.03
E Educational	0.80	155.18	149.84	145.44	138.86	129.32	122.48	134.07	113.01	109.34
F-1 Factory and industrial, moderate hazard		86.32	82.37	77.48	74.59	66.82	63.81	71.41	55.04	51.84
F-2 Factory and industrial, low hazard	0.80	85.52	81.57	77.48	73.79	66.82	63.01	70.61	55.04	51.04
H-1 High Hazard, explosives		80.81	76.86	72.77	69.08	62.27	58.46	65.90	50.49	N/P
H234 High Hazard	0.80	80.81	76.86	72.77	69.08	62.27	58.46	65.90	50.49	46.48
H-5 HPM		144.87	139.55	134.91	128.23	116.87	112.48	123.17	102.57	98.03
I-1 Institutional, supervised environment		143.58	138.53	134.50	128.79	118.18	115.06	128.54	106.04	102.35
I-2 Institutional, hospitals		244.38	239.06	234.42	227.74	215.58	0.00	222.67	201.27	N/P
I-2 Institutional, nursing homes	0.80	169.18	163.86	159.22	152.54	141.98	0.00	147.47	127.67	N/P
I-3 Institutional, restrained		165.06	159.74	155.10	148.42	138.26	133.06	143.35	123.95	117.82
I-4 Institutional, day care facilities		143.58	138.53	134.50	128.79	118.18	115.06	128.54	106.04	102.35
M Mercantile	0.80	105.04	101.04	96.46	92.05	84.23	81.70	87.54	72.90	69.99
R-1 Residential, hotels		144.71	139.66	135.63	129.92	119.51	116.40	129.67	107.38	103.68
R-2 Residential, multiple family	0.80	121.36	116.31	112.28	106.57	96.74	93.62	106.31	84.60	80.91
R-4 Residential, care/assisted living facilities		143.58	138.53	134.50	128.79	118.18	115.06	128.54	106.04	102.35
S-1 Storage, moderate hazard		80.01	76.06	71.17	68.28	60.67	57.66	65.10	48.89	45.68
S-2 Storage, low hazard	0.80	79.21	75.26	71.17	67.48	60.67	56.86	64.30	48.89	44.88
U Utility, miscellaneous		61.08	57.55	53.96	51.20	46.05	43.00	48.81	36.04	34.32
R-3 Residential, one- and two-family	0.85	121.70	118.35	115.40	112.43	108.03	105.32	110.10	101.02	94.66

B2. New Bern Fees and Charges

SCHEDULE OF FEES AND CHARGES*
CITY OF NEW BERN
EFFECTIVE JANUARY 15, 2025
(Revised 01/14/2025)

Wedding Permit	$100 resident/$200 nonresident
Mobile Recreation Unit (2 hour minimum)	$125/hour
Canoe/Kayak Rentals (2 hours)	$15/$10 each additional hour
Pedal boat	$10/hour
Specialty Day Camp (One Week)	$50 resident/$100 nonresident
Mobile Stage (20'x24') Daily Rental	$2,000.00
Mobile Stage Pieces (4'x8') Daily Rental	$10 per piece
Mobile Stage Deposit (Refundable)	$500.00
Staff Supervision Rate (2 staff minimum)	$35.00/hour per staff
NOTE: Indoor facility rentals are limited to 10 hours per day, and outdoor facility rentals are limited to 12 hours per day. Rentals exceeding these hours will require director's approval.	
6. Development Services:	**FEES**
Planning Fees:	
Certificate of zoning compliance letter	$30
Historic Preservation - Minor works	$50
Historic Preservation - After the fact minor fee	$150
Historic Preservation - Major works requiring design review	$150
Historic Preservation - After the fact major fee	$300
Family Care facility approval	$50
Modification of land use ordinance zoning map	$500
Modification of land use ordinance text amendment	$300
Site Plan review	$375
Special use permit	$375
P&Z General Subdivision Plan Review Application	$250 + $25/acre
Subdivision application - final review	$400
Subdivision application - minor plats & recombination	$50
Telecommunication - New wireless support structure	$1,500
Telecommunication - other	$500
Zoning compliance permit	$50
Administrative Fees:	
Starting work without a permit	Double the permit fee
Inspection Fees:	
Residential: Building Permit new/addition	$550 first 1,000 sf + .25/sf over
Residential Renovations	$75 + .20/sf
Commercial: Building Permit new/addition	$800 first 1,000 sf + .25/sf over
Commercial Renovation/upfit	$125 + .20/sf
Demolition	Residential $175; Commercial $225
Residential singlewide manufactured home	$200
Residential multiwide manufactured home or modular	$300
Temporary Certificate of Occupancy	$125, 30 days
Inspections - Reinspection (building, electrical, plumbing, HVAC, insulation)	$75/each
Inspections - Plan Review Residential	$75
Inspections - Plan Review Commercial	$150
Residential Electrical new/addition/renovation	$75 + .10/sf
Commercial Electrical new/addition/renovation	$125 + .10/sf
Shell up to 20,000 sf	$800
Shell more than 20,000 sf	$2,000
Residential Gas Piping new/addition/renovation	$75 + $20/appliance
Commercial Gas Piping new/addition/renovation	$125 + $20/appliance
House Moving Permit	$300
Residential Insulation	$75
Commercial Insulation	$125
Residential Mechanical new/addition/renovation	$125/unit
Residential Mechanical Ductwork	$75
Commercial Mechanical new/addition/renovation	$125/unit
Commercial Mechanical Ductwork	$125
Residential Plumbing new/addition/renovation	$75 + $10/fixture
Commercial Plumbing new/addition/renovation	$125 + $10/fixture
Sign Building Permit	$125
Residential Roofing	$125
Residential Deck/carport/pool/pre-built shed (up to 400 sf)	$125
Residential Dock/pier	$125
Residential Bulkhead/retaining wall	$125
Residential Rooftop Solar array	$125
Commercial Roofing	$250

SCHEDULE OF FEES AND CHARGES*
CITY OF NEW BERN
EFFECTIVE JANUARY 15, 2025
(Revised 01/14/2025)

Commercial Modular/job trailer	$125
Commercial Cell tower alteration	$200
Commercial Dock/pier	$125 + .10/sf
Commercial Bulkhead/retaining wall	$125 + .10/lf
Commercial Fuel Tanks	$125 per tank
Commercial Solar Farm	$5/panel first + 200 $1/panel each additional
Single trade-minimum fee permits:	
Mechanical, Fuel Piping, Plumbing, Electrical Residential	$75
Mechanical, Fuel Piping, Plumbing, Electrical Commercial	$125
Miscellaneous Fees:	
Floodplain Development Permit	$100
Homeowners Recovery Fee	$10
ABC Compliance Inspection	$75
Permit Modification	$25
Sign Return	$10 per sign
Permit - Tree Removal	$25
7. POLICE: (Code Section 42-32)	**FEES**
Accident report	No charge
Citizens Academy fee	$25
False Alarm	$50 on and after 3rd offense
Alarm Registration Fee	$25
Alarm Reinstatement Fee	$50
Non-Permitted Alarm System	$250
Alarm Appeal Fee	$25
Illegal Use of Automatic Voice Dialer	$100
Fingerprinting	$10
Funeral escorts	$50 per escort with 48 hours notice; $100 per escort without 48 hours notice
Off Duty Fee	$45/hr - 3 hours minimum paid to officer
Off Duty Fee for Federal/City Holiday	$45/hr - 3 hours minimum paid to officer
Pawnbroker - initial license application fee	$50
Pawnbroker - renewal license fee	$25
Permit - Alarm Registration (first permit/annual renewal)	$25
Permit - Alarm failure to register	No charge
Permit - Outdoor amplified sound	No charge
Vicious, Dangerous, or potentially Dangerous Dog Registration fee (annual)	$100
Vicious Dog Permit Fee (annual)	$500
Vicious, Dangerous, or potentially Dangerous Dog Appeal	$50
Precious Metal Permits:	
Dealer permits (annual)	$180
Special occasion permit	$180
Employee certificate of compliance	$10
Employee certificate of compliance (annual renewal fee)	$10
Fingerprints (processed for dealer permits - SBI fee)	$38
Wrecker - (includes inspection)	$250 to be on rotation list
Parking Penalties *(Code Section 70-235)*	$25, see code for further details
8. PUBLIC ASSEMBLY (PARADES AND FESTIVALS): (Code Section 66-86)	**FEES**
City Sponsored Event Fees:	
Vendor Permit Fee	$25
Food Vendor Service Fee	$35
NonCity Sponsored Event Fees:	
Vendor Permit Fee	$35
Food Vendor Service Fee	$45
Barricade (A-Frame)	$5
Barricade (concrete/water filled) + labor rates for minimum of 3 staff required for setup	$60
Safety cones	$2
City Labor: (Hourly Rates)	
Fire	$50
Police	$45
Public Works	$45
Recreation	$45
9. PUBLIC WORKS: (Code Section 66-12)	**FEES**
Repair Fees:	
Labor	Hourly rate with benefits*
Material	Actual cost
Equipment trucks	Hourly rate per FEMA schedule*

B3. Raleigh Development Fee Guide

COMPREHENSIVE GUIDE FOR RALEIGH DEVELOPMENT FEES

Development Fee Guide

July 1, 2024 - June 30, 2025

Raleigh

IV. Planning and Development

Email: planning@raleighnc.gov

Phone: 919-996-2682

The Planning and Development Department performs full project reviews and inspections for all private developments within Raleigh to promote and ensure quality, safety, usability, sustainability, and compliance in the built environment. Planning provides three main services: comprehensive planning, design and implementation, and regulation.

Fee recommendations for FY25 include the addition of a Streetscape Plan Amendment Fee and a Custom Signage Plan Fee. Both new fees are being set at the minimum permit fee.

Development fees are reviewed annually, and no fee will increase or decrease by more than 10% annually to achieve 100% cost recovery for development fees. No building permit fee will be charged below the minimum which allows us to have a base fee and simplify the fee schedule for our consumers. Each year, the fee model will be updated with personnel and benefit costs, and work time will be reviewed every three years unless there is a significant change that requires modification.

BUILDING SAFETY				
Permit Fees for New Commercial Construction				
	Fee Description	**FY24**	**FY25**	**Unit of Measure**
New Commercial Electrical Permit	New Construction Electrical Permit Fee	100%	100%	% Of Calculated Building Permit
New Commercial Mechanical Permit	New Construction Mechanical Permit Fee	76%	76%	% Of Calculated Building Permit
New Commercial Plan Review Fee	New Construction Plans Review Fee	56%	61%	% Of Calculated Building Permit
New Commercial Plumbing Permit	New Construction Plumbing Permit Fee	56%	56%	% Of Calculated Building Permit
Special Projects Fee	Additional percentage added to designated special projects. These projects are managed and inspected by our Special Projects Team of Senior Inspectors.	0.25%	0.25%	% of Calculated Construction Value, Per Trade
New Commercial Building Permit $0 - $500,000	Tier 1	0.20%	0.20%	% of Calculated Construction Value
New Commercial Building Permit $500,001-$10,000,000	Tier 2	$1,000.00	$1,000.00	Base Fee
New Commercial Building Permit $10,000,001 and up	Tier 3	$6,900.00	$6,900.00	Base Fee
Building Permit $500,001-$10,000,000	Tier 2	0.06%	0.06%	% Of Calculated Construction Value
Building Permit $10,000,001 and up	Tier 3	0.01%	0.01%	% Of Calculated Construction Value

Permit Fees for New Residential Construction				
New Residential Building Permit*	New Residential Construction Building Permit Fee	0.32%	0.35%	% Of Calculated Construction Value
New Residential Electrical Permit	New Residential Construction Electrical Permit Fee	54%	54%	% Of Calculated Building Permit
New Residential Mechanical Permit	New Residential Construction Mechanical Permit Fee	28%	28%	% Of Calculated Building Permit
New Residential Plan Review Fee	New Residential Construction Plans Review Fee	57%	57%	% Of Calculated Building Permit
New Residential Plumbing Permit	New Residential Construction Plumbing Permit Fee	34%	34%	% Of Calculated Building Permit
Permit Fees for Alterations and Repairs				
Alterations and Repairs Plan Review Fee	Alteration and Repairs Plans Review Fee	50%	50%	% Of Calculated Building Permit
Level 1 Alteration	Level 1 Alterations include the removal and replacement of the covering of existing materials, elements, equipment, or fixtures using new materials, elements, equipment, or fixtures that serve the same purpose. Minimum Permit fees per trade do apply. Fee is calculated by (Building Permit Fee x rate %)	25%	25%	% Of Calculated Building Permit
Level 2 Alteration	Level 2 Alterations include the reconfiguration of space, the addition or elimination of any door or window, the reconfiguration or extension of any system, or the installation of any additional equipment. Minimum Permit fees per trade do apply. Fee is calculated by (Building Permit Fee x rate %)	50%	50%	% Of Calculated Building Permit
Level 3 Alteration	Level 3 Alterations apply where the work area exceeds 50% of the aggregate areas of the building. Minimum Permit fees per trade do apply. Fee is calculated by (Building Permit Fee x rate %)	75%	75%	% Of Calculated Building Permit
Commercial and Residential Re-review Fee	Commercial and Residential re-review fee is set at minimum permit fee	$117.00	$117.00	Per Trade Per Hour
Specific Fees Enumerated				
Demolition of a building or structure	Demolition Permit Fee	$112.00	$112.00	Per Permit
Conditional Service Fee - Commercial	Commercial Construction Conditional Service Fee	$161.00	$177.00	Per Trade Per Unit
Conditional Service Fee - Multi-Family	Multi-Family Construction Conditional Service Fee	$161.00	$177.00	Per Trade For Up To 5 Units
Manufactured Homes	Includes all permits needed for installation of Manufactured Home (all trades)	$343.00	$343.00	Per Home Installation
Moving or relocation of building	Building Relocation Permit Fee	$352.00	$387.00	Per Permit
Sub-Water Meter	Sub-Meter Permit Fee	$131.00	$119.00	Per Trade Up To 5 Units

Temporary certificate of occupancy	Temporary Certificate Of Occupancy (TCO) Fee	$1,291.00	$1,174.00	Flat Fee
Temporary CO for Single-Family/Duplex Units	Temporary Certificate of Occupancy (TCO) Fee -Single-family/Duplex	$155.00	$170.00	Per Unit
Partial Certificate of Occupancy	Partial Certificate of Occupancy (PCO) Fee	$383.00	$348.00	Per Certificate
Pre-Construction Meeting	Pre-Construction Meeting Fee	$366.00	$381.00	Per Meeting
Alternate Means of Compliance	Fee charged for research that involves building systems that are outside of the scope of building code but may meet requirements of the building code.	$1,500.00	$1,500.00	Per Review (Up To 10 Hours)
Conditional Service Fee - Residential	Conditional Service Fee - Residential	$130.00	$130.00	Per Trade Per Unit
Alternative Means of Compliance (hourly rate)	Fee charged when staff time exceeds the minimum time of 10 hours, which is covered by the flat fee.	$176.00	$176.00	Per Hour (After 10 Hours)
Stocking Permit	Fee charged for stocking of commercial space prior to issuance of Certificate of Occupancy	$240.00	$218.00	Per Permit
Pony Express	Commercial plan review to expedite small, simple, interior alterations.	$281.00	$281.00	Per Review Per Hour
Re-inspection Fee	Private development projects which are determined by the City to not be ready or have failed the inspection	$112.00	$112.00	Per Inspection Per Trade
After Hours Inspections (Commercial)	After Hours Inspections (Commercial)	$125.00	$125.00	Per Hour
After Hours Inspections (Residential)	After Hours Inspections (Residential)	$75.00	$75.00	Per Hour
* For a multi-tenant building, the fees are applied for each tenant; except a high-rise building the inspection fees are applied to the entire structure. For multiple buildings owned by the same owner(s), inspection fees are per building as defined by the N.C. Building Code, Volume 1. Inspection fees are applicable for each State mandated fire inspection.				
Stand Alone Trade Permits				
Plumbing Utility Inspection	Plumbing Utility Inspection Fee	$117.00	$117.00	Per Permit
Boiler or Compressor - Commercial	Boiler / Compressor Permit Fee	$185.00	$203.00	Per Permit
Cell Tower/Co-locate (site)	Cell Tower/Co-locate Permit Fee	$128.00	$140.00	Per Permit
Co-locate on a Building (Building only)	Co-locate Cell on a Building Permit Fee	$224.00	$246.00	Per Permit
Ductwork - Commercial	Ductwork Permit Fee	$185.00	$203.00	Per Permit
Exhaust Hood and Duct System - Commercial	Commercial Exhaust Hood and Duct System Permit Fee	$185.00	$203.00	Per Trade Per Work Type
Exhaust Systems - Commercial	Commercial Exhaust System Permit Fee	$185.00	$203.00	Per Trade Per Work Type
New or replacement HVAC/Water Heater/ other appliance - Commercial	Commercial Forced-Air Warm Furnace Permit Fee	$185.00	$203.00	Per 1-3 Co-Located Units Per Trade
Gas Outlets - Commercial	Commercial Gas Outlet Permit Fee	$185.00	$203.00	Per Permit
Generators (Electrical only) - Commercial	Commercial Electric Generator Permit Fee	$300.00	$330.00	Per Permit

Heat Pumps/ air Conditioning - Commercial	Commercial Air Conditioning Fee	$185.00	$203.00	Per 1-3 Co-Located Units Per Trade
Incinerators - Commercial	Commercial Incinerator Fee	$185.00	$203.00	Per Trade Per Work Type
Parking Lot Lighting	Parking Lot Lighting	$239.00	$263.00	Per Permit
Photovoltaic (Solar) - Commercial	Commercial Photovoltaic Fee	$460.00	$460.00	Per Permit
Refrigeration Units - Commercial	Commercial Refrigeration Fee	$185.00	$203.00	Per Trade Per Work Type
Service Repair/Replace - Commercial	Commercial Service Repair Fee	$149.00	$163.00	Per Permit
UPS System	UPS System Fee	$254.00	$279.00	Per Permit
Fixture Replacement/ Retro-fit: 26-50 Fixtures - Commercial	Fixture Replacement/Retro-fit: 26-50 Fixtures - Commercial	$177.00	$194.00	Per Permit
Fixture Replacement/ Retro-fit: 51-100 Fixtures - Commercial	Fixture Replacement/Retro-fit: 51-100 Fixtures - Commercial	$222.00	$244.00	Per Permit
Fixture Replacement/ Retro-fit: Over 100 Fixtures - Commercial	Fixture Replacement/Retro-fit: Over 100 Fixtures - Commercial	$242.00	$266.00	Per Permit
Swimming Pool - Commercial (Building only)	Swimming Pool - Commercial (Building only)	$399.00	$439.00	Per Permit
Minimum Trade Permit Fee	Any fee not specifically listed as an individual fee will be charged at the minimum permit fee. This also applies to a minimum building plan review fee. This also applies to building field revision fees, which are assessed as per trade per review.	$112.00	$112.00	Per Trade

CONTINUOUS IMPROVEMENT AND CUSTOMER SERVICE				
Express Services - Building Services Fees				
	Fee Description	**FY24**	**FY25**	**Unit of Measure**
Express - Change of Use	Applicant wishes to change the use of the building from one type to another; Ex: Office to Restaurant	$1,403.00	$1,273.00	Per Review Per Hour
Express - Additions	Commercial building additions	$1,403.00	$1,273.00	Per Review Per Hour
Express - Alteration & Repairs	Interior project where use of the building is determined and cosmetic modifications are altering the space.	$891.00	$980.00	Per Review Per Hour
Express - Building Comments Only	Scoping review that is not for permitting but is a full review of building plans.	$842.00	$768.00	Per Review Per Hour
Express - Fit up/Interior Completion	First generation tenant upfit.	$842.00	$768.00	Per Review Per Hour
Express - Pre-submittal Conference	Opportunity for clients to have plan review by building trade reviewers only.	$685.00	$753.00	Per Review
Express - Standard Commercial	New building construction review for permitting.	$1,403.00	$1,273.00	Per Review Per Hour
Express - Field Revisions	New building construction changes after the City has issued the permit.	$842.00	$768.00	Per Trade Per Hour
Site Permit Review (Previously - Express - Concurrent)	Site plan review process	$891.00	$980.00	Per Review Per Hour

	Fee Description	FY24	FY25	Unit of Measure
Special Consultation Services	This is a conference / consultation service primarily used for Express Review and Project Advocacy.	$304.00	$304.00	Per Review
Express Services - Land Development Fees				
Express - Grading	Permit for land disturbance including change of grade on site.	$842.00	$768.00	Per Review Per Hour
Express - Preliminary Development Plan	Review to verify all UDO requirements are met.	$842.00	$842.00	Per Review Per Hour
Express - Recorded Map	Reviewed legal instrument that shows configuration of parcel plan.	$842.00	$768.00	Per Review Per Hour
Express - Sketch Plans	Scoping review that is a high-level overview of a site project.	$561.00	$510.00	Per Review
Business Support Center - Development Engineering				
Technology Fee	The tech fee was incorporated as part of the original DSD fee study which included Building and Safety, Land and Right of Way fees.	4%	4%	Per Subtotal Of All Other Fees

COMPREHENSIVE AND LONG RANGE PLANNING				
Comprehensive Planning Fees				
	Fee Description	**FY24**	**FY25**	**Unit of Measure**
Master Plan	A visual component required when a rezoning application is submitted for a Planned Development or Campus rezoning request.	$3,618.00	$3,980.00	Per Application
Master Plan Amendment	Master plan review without rezoning per UDO Sec 4.7.6	$1,184.00	$1,075.00	Per Application
Comprehensive Plan Amendment	A request to amend the Comprehensive Plan that may affect plan text/policies, Future Land Use Map, or attached area plans.	$724.00	$796.00	Per Application
Conditional Use Rezoning Case	A request to modify the City's Official Zoning Map with additional restrictive conditions offered by the applicant.	$1,448.00	$1,593.00	Per Application
General Use Rezoning Case	A request to modify the City's Official Zoning Map.	$724.00	$795.00	Per Application
Waiver petition of 24 months waiting period	A request for a waiver from the requirement prohibiting the Planning Department to accept a new rezoning petition within 24 months of a property receiving denial from City Council or withdrawal.	$218.00	$239.00	Per Application
Text Change for Zoning Conditions	A request to modify the zoning conditions that regulate development entitlement for particular parcel(s) that will not modify the City's Official Zoning Map.	$1,448.00	$1,593.00	Per Application
Annexation	A petition to annex into the City of Raleigh or a petition to defer annexation in order to connect to city services (water and sewer) for any other annexation not covered by the annexation description for a 1 or 2 family lot.	$697.00	$767.00	Per Petition

Appendix C

Permitting and Inspections Flowcharts

C1. Permitting Process for Currituck County[1]

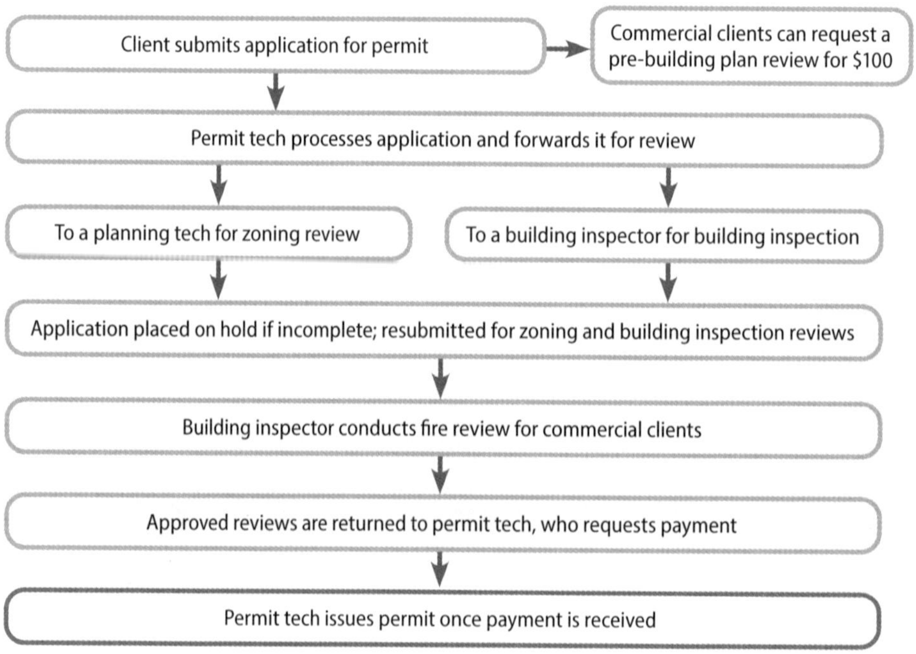

1. The flowcharts in this appendix were originally published in Obed Pasha, *Promising Practices for Timely Completion of Building Inspections in North Carolina* (UNC School of Government, Oct. 2025), https://www.sog.unc.edu/publications/reports/promising-practices-timely-completion-building-inspections-north-carolina.

Abbreviations for inspection trades and related terms: building (B), electrical (E), mechanical (M), plumbing (P), fire (F); certificate of occupancy (CO); certificate of compliance (CC); electronic plans management (EPM); information and digital technology (IDT); pre-construction minimum qualifications test (PC MQT); special inspection (SI).

C2. Inspection Process for Currituck County

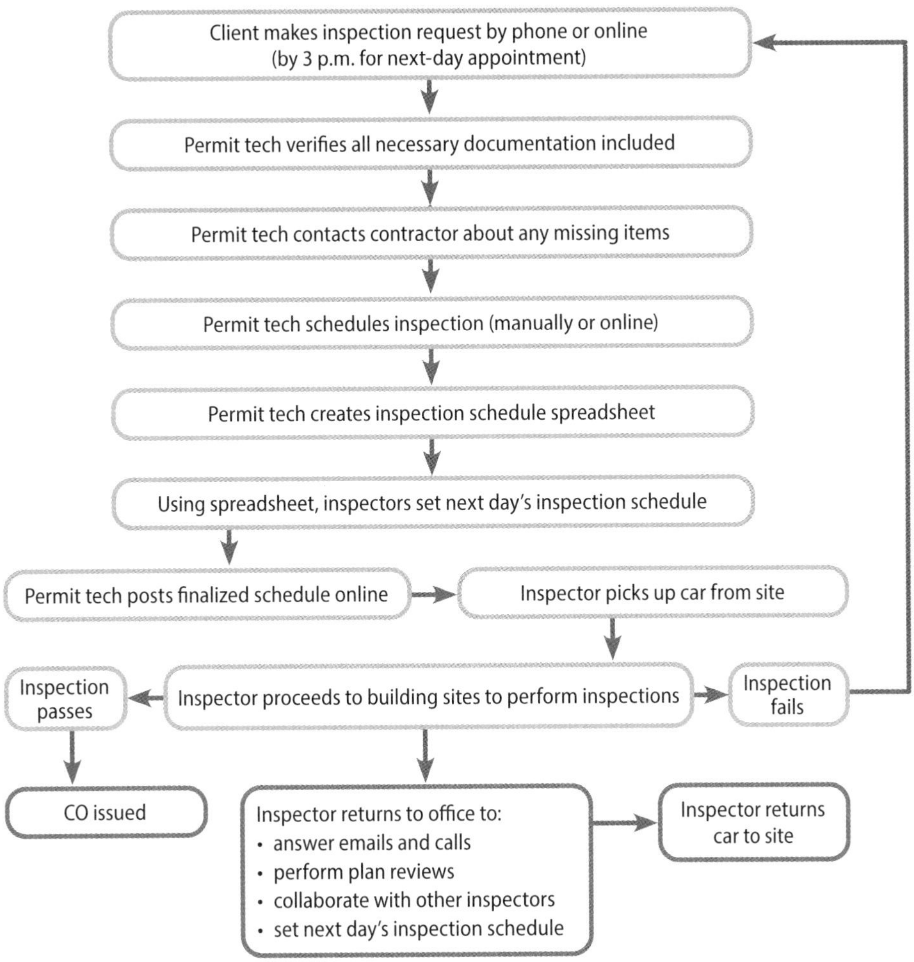

C3. Permitting and Inspection Process for the City of Fayetteville

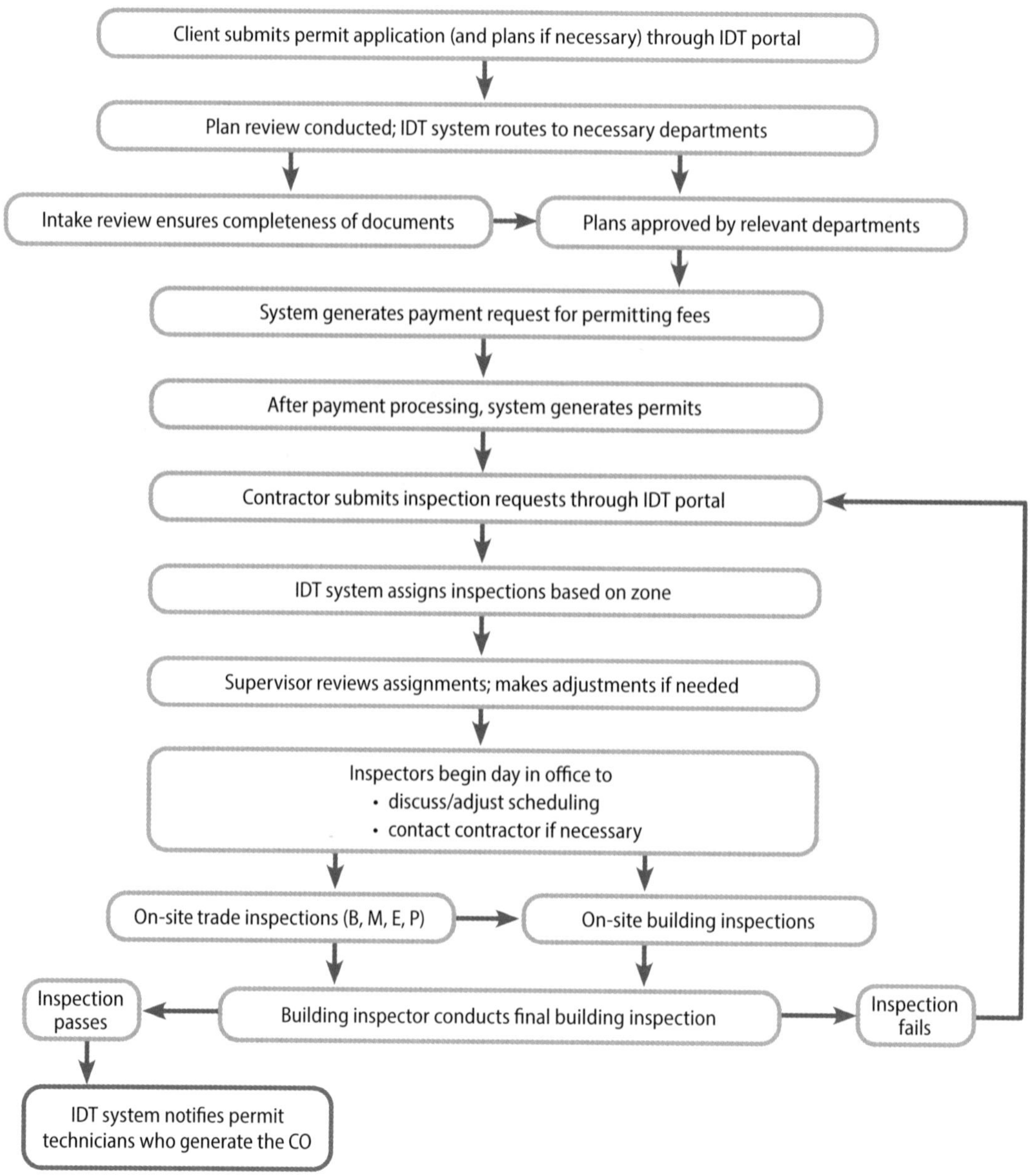

C4. Commercial Permitting and Inspections Process for Mecklenburg County

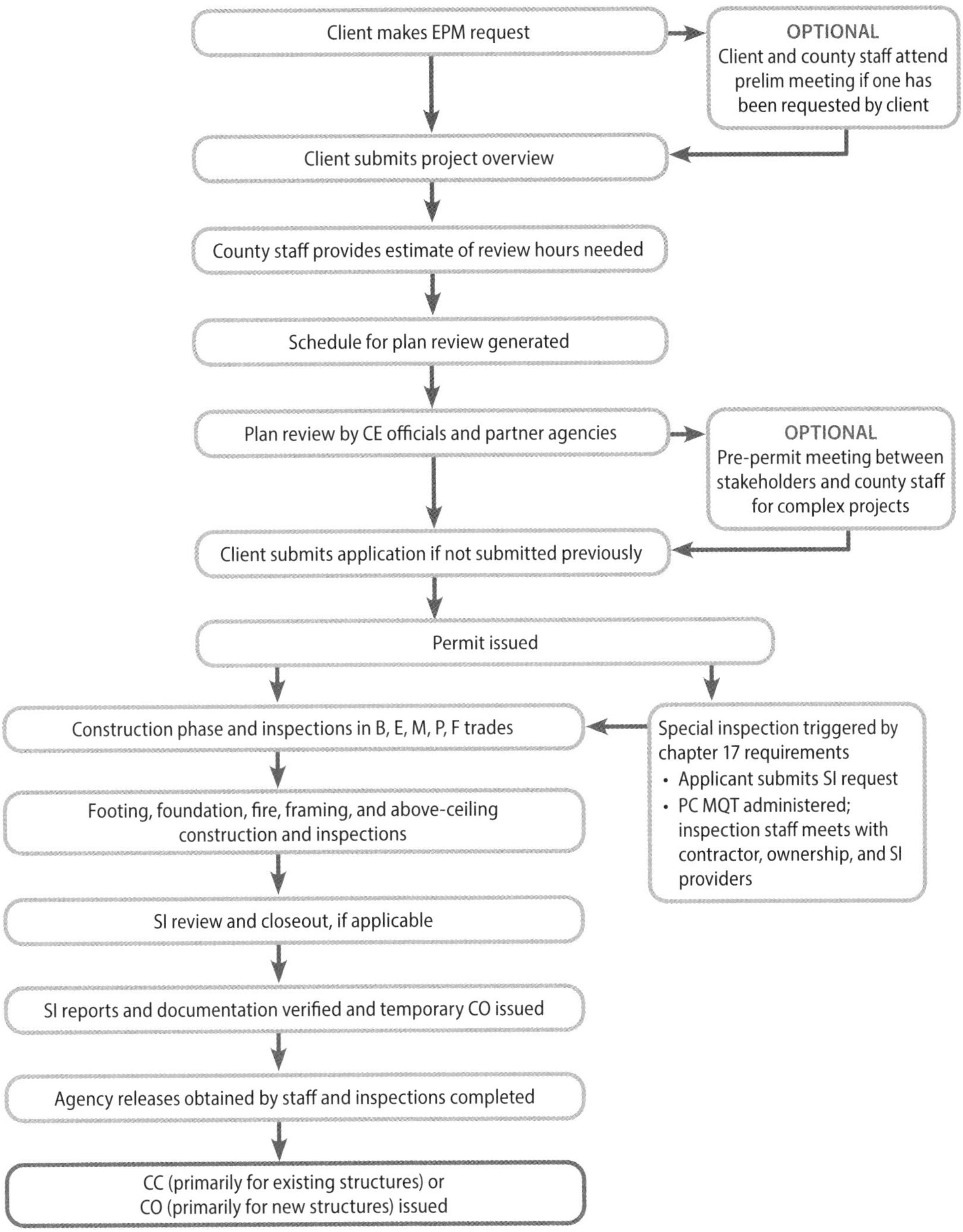

C5. Residential Permitting and Inspections Process for Mecklenburg County

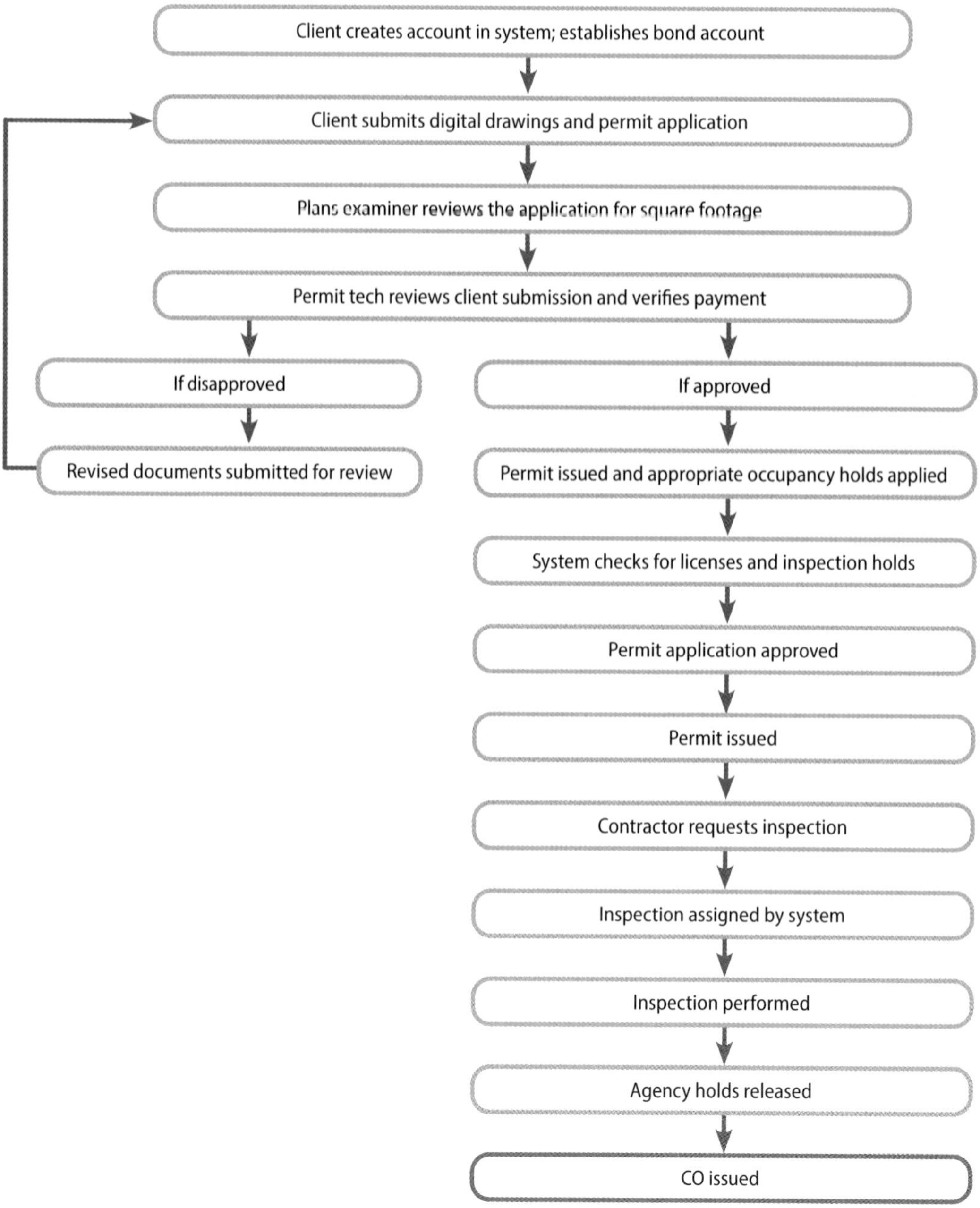

Appendix D

Sample Permit Applications

D1. Raleigh Nonresidential Permit Application

Non-Residential Permit Application

Planning and Development Customer Service Center | One Exchange Plaza, Suite 400 | Raleigh, NC 27601 | 919-996-2500

Raleigh

This form is required when seeking a non-residential building permit or zoning permit for development activity associated with apartments, offices, and commercial uses and Site Permit Review [Unified Development Ordinance (UDO) Section 10.2.8]. Submit applications by email to commercialbuilding@raleighnc.gov.

GENERAL INFORMATION	
Type of Review Service: ☐ Standard Review ☐ *Pony Review ☐ *Express Review	Application Date:
*Project Contact:	
Email:	Phone:
Property Owner:	
Email:	Phone:
*Pony and Express Review apply to certain types of projects and require additional fees. See Commercial Pony Express Review or Express Review for details. *The name listed as project contact will be the primary contact within the Permit and Development Portal for the submitted project.	

PROJECT INFORMATION	
Project Address:	Suite #:
Business or Tenant Name:	
Associated Site Permit Review (SPR) # if applicable:	Pin #:

Select the primary type of work:

☐ Accessory Structure	☐ *Change of Use	☐ Mass Grading Only	☐ Single Trade Permit
☐ Addition	☐ Demolition	☐ New Building	☐ Site Permit Review (SPR)
☐ Alteration/Repair	☐ *Fit-up Interior Completion	☐ Retaining Wall	☐ Other_____________

Provide a detailed project description:

*Change of use should be selected if a project is a change of building occupancy or change of zoning use based on Unified Development Ordinance (UDO) Chapter 6. See Change of Use to determine if your project qualifies.

*Fit-up interior completion should be selected when the project is a first-generation building (or built within the last 7 years). See Commercial Alteration or Repair for additional details.

Additional Information	
Does this project qualify as a frequent transit development option? ☐ Yes ☐ No	
Does this project involve Wake County Environmental Health? ☐ Yes ☐ No If yes, provide the HSIPOP #: ____________________	
List the property's current use(s) and proposed use(s) according to UDO chapter 6:	Current Use: Proposed Use:

Site Information		Building Information	
Zoning District:		Existing Building:	sq.ft.
Overlay District:		Proposed New Building:	sq.ft.
Total Project:	sq.ft.	Total Building:	sq.ft.
Maximum Parking:	spaces (UDO Sec. 7.1.2 C)	Proposed # of Stories:	
Proposed Parking:	spaces	☐ 2018 NC Code Building	
Land Disturbance:	sq.ft.	☐ 2018 Existing NC Building Code	

Cost Information	
Total Construction Cost: $	Total Electrical Cost: $

Revision 08-08-2024 raleighnc.gov 1

CONTRACTOR INFORMATION			
Contractors or contractor companies must be registered in the Permit and Development Portal before managing a project, paying fees, or scheduling inspections. See final review for project approval requirements. Use the Contractor Addendum Form if contractors are not listed on this application.			
Building			
*Contractor:		NC License #:	
Email:		Phone:	
Address:			
*NC law requires appointment of a lien agent for contractors/subcontractors when they are working on a project. Lien Agent appointments are not required for improvements under $40,000 or to the owner's existing residence, or for public building projects. www.liensnc.com			
Electrical			
Voltage: ☐ Over 600 ☐ 600 or less ☐ Low Voltage			
Contractor:		Low Voltage Contractor:	
Email:		Email:	
Address:		Address:	
NC License #:	Phone:	NC License #:	Phone:
Plumbing (For fuel piping work, fill out Mechanical)		**Plumbing Utility**	
Contractor:		Contractor:	
Email:		Email:	
Address:		Address:	
NC License #:	Phone:	NC License #:	Phone:
Mechanical			
Work Includes: ☐ Appliances ☐ Refrigeration ☐ Ducts ☐ Fuel Piping ☐ Hood ☐ VIMS/Radon ☐ Ventilation ☐ Other________			
HVAC		Refrigeration	
Contractor:		Contractor:	
Email:		Email:	
Address:		Address:	
NC License #:	Phone:	NC License #:	Phone:
Type of Heating: ☐ Electrical ☐ Gas ☐ Hot Water ☐ Oil ☐ Other__________		Hood	
		Contractor:	
Air Condition Size: tons		Email:	
*If work consists of replacement only, is the A/C unit:		Address:	
Same type (split or package) as existing? ☐ Yes ☐ No		NC License #:	Phone:
Same size or smaller than existing? ☐ Yes ☐ No		Fuel Piping	
Located in same location as existing? ☐ Yes ☐ No		Contractor:	
*If the scope of the proposed work consists of replacement of existing mechanical equipment only and the answer to ANY of the above questions is "No" then a tier one site plan is required.		Email:	
		Address:	
		NC License #:	Phone:
VIMS/Radon		Other: ________________	
Contractor:		Contractor:	
Email:		Email:	
Address:		Address:	
NC License #:	Phone:	NC License #:	Phone:
Fire			
Type of System(s): ☐ Emergency Responder Radio Coverage System ☐ Alternative Fire Extinguishing Systems (i.e., Hoods) ☐ Flammable/Combustible Liquids ☐ Fire Alarm ☐ Fire Sprinkler ☐ Hazardous Materials ☐ Manual Standpipe ☐ Private Fire Line ☐ Other____________			
Fire Sprinkler		Fire Alarm	
Contractor:		Contractor:	
Email:		Email:	
Address:		Address:	
NC License #:	Phone:	NC License #:	Phone:

Revision 08-08-2024 raleighnc.gov 2

Fire Suppression		Other: ________	
Contractor:		Contractor:	
Email:		Email:	
Address:		Address:	
NC License #:	Phone:	NC License #:	Phone:

Site/Zoning/Other	
Type of Work: ☐ Landscaping ☐ Parking Lot ☐ Swimming Pool ☐ Solid Waste/Recycling ☐ Other ________	
Contractor:	NC License #:
Email:	Phone:
Address:	

Grading	
Contractor:	
Email:	Phone:
Address:	

Right-of-Way		
Type of Work: ☐ Driveway: # of driveways		☐ Sidewalk: linear ft.
Contractor:		Permits for work in the right-of-way cannot be issued without bond. Is the Performance Bond and General Liability on file with the City? ☐ Yes ☐ No
Email:	Phone:	
Address:		

Utility: Meter			
Contractor:		Meter type: ☐ Individual	Select size in drop-down
Email:	Phone:	☐ Master Meter	Select size in drop-down
Address:		☐ Irrigation	Select size in drop-down
Service Type: ☐ Water ☐ Sewer ☐ Irrigation		☐ Other ________	Select size in drop-down

Utility: Stub	
Contractor:	NC License #:
Email:	Phone:
Address:	

Choose Type	Size	Proposed Stub Location
Select type in drop-down	Select size in drop-down	Is this stub in the right-of-way? ☐ Yes ☐ No
Select type in drop-down	Select size in drop-down	Is this stub in the right-of-way? ☐ Yes ☐ No
Select type in drop-down	Select size in drop-down	Is this stub in the right-of-way? ☐ Yes ☐ No
Select type in drop-down	Select size in drop-down	Is this stub in the right-of-way? ☐ Yes ☐ No

SIGNATURE

The undersigned applicant hereby authorizes the filing of this application (and any subsequent revisions thereto) and confirms having obtained permission from the property owner/occupant for the application and the City's entry onto the property, if applicable. Additionally, the undersigned authorizes City of Raleigh representatives to conduct inspections or evaluations to ensure compliance with relevant laws and rules.

Furthermore, the undersigned certifies that all information provided with this application and any attached documents is true, accurate, and complete to the best of their knowledge and belief. Any false information may result in rejection of the application or revocation of the permit or plan. The undersigned assumes sole responsibility for properly identifying and labeling all property lines and corners and ensuring site accessibility.

The undersigned acknowledges that the application and any resulting permits or communications are subject to disclosure under the North Carolina Public Records Act. Moreover, the undersigned confirms the property owner's awareness of the application and pledges adherence to submitted plans and specifications in accordance with the City of Raleigh Unified Development Ordinance. Lastly, pursuant to state law N.C.G.S. 143-755(b1), the undersigned acknowledges that failure to respond to city requests or holding the permit application on hold for six consecutive months or more will result in the cessation of review, requiring a new application under current regulations upon resumption of processing.

Additionally, by submitting this application, the undersigned confirms either being the property owner or an authorized party as defined by N.C.G.S. 160D-403(a), certifying the accuracy of the information provided. Acting as an authorized agent requires written permission from the property owner for the purposes of making this development approval and/or permit application. Written permission from the property owner to act as an authorized agent must be made available to the City of Raleigh upon request. False statements may lead to revocation of development approvals under N.C. Gen. Stat. § 160D-403(f).

Applicant Name:	
Email:	**Phone:**
Applicant Signature:	**Date:**

D2. Raleigh Residential Permit Application

Residential Permit Application

Planning and Development Customer Service Center | One Exchange Plaza, Suite 400 | Raleigh, NC 27601 | 919-996-2500

Raleigh

Submit this form to DowntownDS@raleighnc.gov when applying for select residential building or zoning permits for single-family or two-family homes. To find out if your project requires this application, refer to Residential Permits.

GENERAL INFORMATION	
*Project Contact:	Application Date:
Email:	Phone:
Property Owner:	
Email:	Phone:
*The name listed as project contact will be the primary contact within the Permit and Development Portal for the submitted project.	

PROJECT INFORMATION
Project Address:
Select the primary type of work: ☐ Accessory Structure **less than 12 ft. in any dimension** ☐ *Change of Use ☐ *Changeouts ☐ *Single Trade Permits ☐ Retaining Walls ☐ Water/Sewer Service ☐ Other: ____________
Provide a detailed project description:
*Select Change of Use if you are planning to convert a finished space, unfinished space, or existing detached garage to an Accessory Dwelling Unit (ADU). See ADU Change of Use to determine if your project qualifies.
*Use this application for changeouts and single trade permits only if the project is located in proximity to a flood-prone area. Please refer to the Permit and Development Portal to apply for all other permits.

Site Information		
Does this project qualify as a frequent transit development option? ☐ Yes ☐ No	*Will impervious surface change? ☐ Yes ☐ No	
	Existing Impervious Surface:	sq.ft.
Overlay District:	Proposed Total Impervious Surface:	sq.ft.
Need New Water Service? ☐ Yes ☐ No	Total Disturbed Area:	sq.ft.
*Any material that significantly reduces and prevents natural infiltration of water into the soil. For more information see Article 12.2 of the Unified Development Ordinance.		

Cost Information	
Total Construction Cost: $	Total Electrical Cost: $

CONTRACTOR INFORMATION

Contractors or contractor companies must be registered in the Permit and Development Portal before managing a project, paying fees, or scheduling inspections. See final review for project approval requirements. Use the Contractor Addendum Form if contractors are not listed on this application.

Building		**Site/Zoning/Other**	
*Contractor:		Contractor:	
Email:		Email:	
Address:		Address:	
NC License #:	Phone:	NC License #:	Phone:
*NC law requires the appointment of a lien agent for contractors/subcontractors when they are working on a project. Lien agent appointments are not required for improvements under $40,000, to the owner's existing residence, or for public building projects. For more information, visit www.liensnc.com.			

Electrical		**Plumbing Utility**	
Voltage: ☐ Over 600 ☐ 600 or less ☐ Low Voltage		Applicable to water/sewer from right-of-way to foundation	
Contractor:		Contractor:	
Email:		Email:	
Address:		Address:	
NC License #:	Phone:	NC License #:	Phone:

Plumbing (For fuel piping work, fill out Mechanical)		**Plumbing** (NFPA 13D Res Sprinklers)	
Contractor:		Contractor:	
Email:		Email:	
Address:		Address:	
NC License #:	Phone:	NC License #:	Phone:

Mechanical		
Work Includes: ☐ Appliances ☐ Ducts ☐ VIMS/Radon ☐ Fuel Piping ☐ Other______________		
Type of Heating: ☐ Electrical ☐ Gas ☐ Hot Water ☐ Oil ☐ Other___________	Air condition size: Tons	
Contractor:	NC License #:	
Email:	Phone:	
Address:		

Plumbing and Mechanical Changeout Questions	
*If work consists of an A/C unit or water heater replacement only, is either equipment:	*If the scope of the proposed work consists of replacement of existing plumbing or mechanical equipment only and the answer to ANY of the above questions is "No" then a tier one site plan is required.
The same type as existing? ☐ Yes ☐ No	
The same size or smaller than existing? ☐ Yes ☐ No	
Located in same location as existing? ☐ Yes ☐ No	

Utility: Meter			
This permit is for establishing new water or sewer service at a parcel that has not previously been served. The City will not install services where roadway width is greater than 45' or for new construction. Contractor installed connections require stub permits and may also require right-of-way permits. Complete the stop/start contract for meter service.			
Will this be a city-installed tap? ☐ Yes ☐ No			
Contact:		Meter Type	Meter Size
Email:	Phone:	☐ Individual	☐ ⅝ inch ☐ 1 inch ☐ Other
Address:		☐ Irrigation	☐ ⅝ inch ☐ 1 inch ☐ Other
Service Type: ☐ Water ☐ Sewer ☐ Irrigation ☐ Split		☐ Other ____________	☐ ⅝ inch ☐ 1 inch ☐ Other

Utility: Stub		
Contractor:	NC License #:	
Email:	Phone:	
Address:		
Choose Type	Size	Proposed Stub Location
☐ Water	☐ ¾ inch ☐ 1 inch ☐ Other	Is this stub in the right-of-way? ☐ Yes ☐ No
☐ Irrigation	☐ ¾ inch ☐ 1 inch ☐ Other	Is this stub in the right-of-way? ☐ Yes ☐ No
☐ Sewer	☐ 4 inches ☐ Other	Is this stub in the right-of-way? ☐ Yes ☐ No

SIGNATURE

The undersigned applicant hereby authorizes the filing of this application (and any subsequent revisions thereto) and confirms having obtained permission from the property owner/occupant for the application and the City's entry onto the property, if applicable. Additionally, the undersigned authorizes City of Raleigh representatives to conduct inspections or evaluations to ensure compliance with relevant laws and rules.

Furthermore, the undersigned certifies that all information provided with this application and any attached documents is true, accurate, and complete to the best of their knowledge and belief. Any false information may result in rejection of the application or revocation of the permit or plan. The undersigned assumes sole responsibility for properly identifying and labeling all property lines and corners and ensuring site accessibility.

The undersigned acknowledges that the application and any resulting permits or communications are subject to disclosure under the North Carolina Public Records Act. Moreover, the undersigned confirms the property owner's awareness of the application and pledges adherence to submitted plans and specifications in accordance with the City of Raleigh Unified Development Ordinance. Lastly, pursuant to state law N.C.G.S. 143-755(b1), the undersigned acknowledges that failure to respond to city requests or holding the permit application on hold for six consecutive months or more will result in the cessation of review, requiring a new application under current regulations upon resumption of processing.

Additionally, by submitting this application, the undersigned confirms either being the property owner or an authorized party as defined by N.C.G.S. 160D-403(a), certifying the accuracy of the information provided. Acting as an authorized agent requires written permission from the property owner for the purposes of making this development approval and/or permit application. Written permission from the property owner to act as an authorized agent must be made available to the City of Raleigh upon request. False statements may lead to revocation of development approvals under N.C. Gen. Stat. § 160D-403(f).

Applicant Name:	
Email:	**Phone:**
Applicant Signature:	**Date:**

Revision 01-08-2025 raleighnc.gov 2

Appendix E

Sample Building Code Enforcement Notices

E1. Raleigh Stop Work Order

Stop Work Order

Planning and Development Customer Service Center • One Exchange Plaza, Suite 400 | Raleigh, NC 27601 | 919-996-2500

Raleigh

STOP WORK ORDER

General Statute § 160D-404 & 160D-1114. A Stop Work Order violation shall constitute a Class 1 misdemeanor.

HOLDER OF DEVELOPMENT APPROVAL		
Name:	Date:	
Project Address:		
City:	State:	Zip Code:
Email:	Delivery method: ☐ By email ☐ Personal Delivery ☐ First-class mail	

PROPERTY OWNER IF NOT HOLDER OF DEVELOPMENT APPROVAL		
Name:	Date:	
Project Address:		
City:	State:	Zip Code:
Email:	Delivery method: ☐ By email ☐ Personal Delivery ☐ First-class mail	

PERSON DOING THE WORK OR ACTIVITY
Name:

The following work or activity has been undertaken in substantial violation of State and/or local laws, or in a manner that endangers life or property and, thus, City Inspection Staff hereby orders that the following work or activity be immediately stopped.

WORK TO STOP
1. Work or activity to be stopped:
2. Reason for Stop Work Order:
3. Work or activity may resume when:

Permits are available from the Planning and Development Customer Service Center
https://raleighnc-energovpub.tylerhost.net/apps/selfservice#/home

For Office Use Only	
Inspector:	Phone:

Page **1** of **1**

REVISION 01.09.24

raleighnc.gov

E2. Raleigh Stop Work Order Service Certification

STOP WORK ORDER
CERTIFICATE OF PROPER NOTICE

TO: City of Raleigh

FROM: Name:
Title:

RE: Stop Work Order at
Address:
Case #:

If serving by email

This is to certify that the above-referenced Stop Work Order has been properly delivered by electronically mailing a copy of the same to the following:

Name:

Email:

Holder of Development Approval:

Name:

Email:

Property Owner (if not the holder of the development approval):

If serving by first-class mail

This is to certify that the above-referenced Stop Work Order has been properly delivered by depositing a copy of the same in the United State mail, first-class, postage pre-paid, addressed to the following:

Name:

Address:

City: State: Zip:

Holder of Development Approval:

Name:

Address:

City: State: Zip:

Property Owner: (if not the holder of the development approval)

-1-

If serving by personal delivery

This is to certify that the above-referenced Stop Work Order has been properly delivered by personal delivery to the following:

Name:

Address:

City: State: Zip:

Holder of Development Approval:

Name:

Address:

City: State: Zip:

Property Owner: (if not the holder of the development approval)

This the ____ day of ___________, 20__.

Signed: ____

[TYPE NAME]

-2-

E3. Greenville Stop Work Order

CITY OF GREENVILLE, NC
PLANNING AND DEVELOPMENT SERVICES DEPARTMENT
INSPECTION DIVISION
252-329-4466

STOP WORK ORDER

Per the NC General Statutes & Administrative Code and Policies

TO PERSONS DOING WORK AT: ______________________________
Greenville, NC "City Limits or ETJ"

The building or structure at the location noted above is being:

- ❑ *Demolished*
- ❑ *Constructed*
- ❑ *Reconstructed*
- ❑ *Altered or repaired*

In:

- ❑ A hazardous manner
- ❑ Substantial violation of a state or local building law, in that

  ____.

- ❑ A manner that endangers life or property

  ____.

THE FOLLOWING WORK SHALL BE STOPPED IMMEDIATELY:

- ❑ All work
- ❑ The following described work: ______________________________

  ____

The conditions under which work may be resumed are:

____

____

______________________ ______________________
Building Official ***Date***

§ 160D-404. Enforcement.

(b)Stop Work Orders. – Whenever any work or activity subject to regulation pursuant to this Chapter or other applicable local development regulation or any State law delegated to the local government for enforcement purposes in lieu of the State is undertaken in substantial violation of any State or local law, or in a manner that endangers life or property, staff may order the specific part of the work or activity that is in violation or presents such a hazard to be immediately stopped. The order shall be in writing, directed to the person doing the work or activity, and shall state the specific work or activity to be stopped, the reasons therefor, and the conditions under which the work or activity may be resumed. A copy of the order shall be delivered to the holder of the development approval and to the owner of the property involved (if that person is not the holder of the development approval) by personal delivery, electronic delivery, or first-class mail. The person or persons delivering the stop work order shall certify to the local government that the order was delivered and that certificate shall be deemed conclusive in the absence of fraud. Except as provided by G.S. 160D-1112 and G.S. 160D-1208, a stop work order may be appealed pursuant to G.S. 160D-405. No further work or activity shall take place in violation of a stop work order pending a ruling on the appeal. Violation of a stop work order shall constitute a Class 1 misdemeanor.

160D-1114: Appeals of stop orders.

(a) The owner or builder may appeal from a stop order involving alleged violation of the North Carolina State Building Code or any approved local modification thereof to the State Fire Marshal or his or her designee within a period of five days after the order is issued. Notice of appeal shall be given in writing to the State Fire Marshal or his or her designee, with a copy to the local inspector. The State Fire Marshal or his or her designee shall promptly conduct an investigation, and the appellant and the inspector shall be permitted to submit relevant evidence. The State Fire Marshal or his or her designee shall as expeditiously as possible provide a written statement of the decision setting forth the facts found, the decision reached, and the reasons for the decision. Pending the ruling by the State Fire Marshal or his or her designee on an appeal, no further work shall take place in violation of a stop order. In the event of dissatisfaction with the decision, the person affected shall have the following options:

(1) Appealing to the Building Code Council or Residential Code Council.

(2) Appealing to the superior court as provided in G.S. 143-141.

(b) The owner or builder may appeal from a stop order involving alleged violation of a local development regulation as provided in G.S. 160D-405.

E4. Raleigh Notice of Building Code Violations

Raleigh

City of Raleigh

Notice of Building Code Violations

August 23, 2024

VIA US MAIL, CERTIFIED MAIL
RETURN RECEIPT REQUESTED
AND EMAIL TO: [ ]

Property Owner: [ ]
[ ]

Tenant: [ ] Owner/Operator, [ ]
[ ]
Raleigh, NC 27601

Re: 2018 NC Existing Building Code Violations at [ ]

Dear [ ]:

I am writing regarding on-going violations of the North Carolina Building Code at the property located at [ ] (the "Property"), which is used to operate [ ] As explained herein, and as I have previously informed [ ] is my determination that [ ] is operating as an unpermitted A-2 Nightclub, which, among other issues, creates serious concerns about the safety and welfare of the occupants and public. Pictures taken from the [ ] social media profiles and website showing nightclub activities at the Property are attached hereto.

As you know, I previously notified [ ] on February 7, 2024, that, per the City's records, [ ] was permitted as an A-2 Restaurant occupancy; however, it appears to currently operate as an A-2 Nightclub, which requires a change of use permit pursuant to the North

Page **1** of **3**

Carolina Building Code. A copy of my February 7, 2024 email is attached hereto. My February 7, 2024 email informed you that you must apply for and obtain a change of use permit to operate an A-2 Nightclub at the Property, and also stated that you may appeal this decision to the North Carolina Department of Insurance ("NC DOI"). You did not appeal or obtain a change of use permit and continued to operate an A-2 Nightclub at the Property.

Thereafter, on June 18, 2024, I sent a second notice to [ ], again notifying you of the violation and urging you to determine a path of compliance as soon as possible. A copy of my June 18, 2024 email is attached hereto. My June 18 email was prompted, in part, by a failed Fire Code inspection, a copy of which is also attached hereto. My June 18 email again provided you with a chance to remedy the violation or appeal my determination to NC DOI; however, no appeal was filed and you continued to operate an A-2 Nightclub at the Property.

Based on your on-going failure to resolve this violation, and the safety concerns and issues create by the operation of an unpermitted A-2 Nightclub at the Property, I am issuing you this Notice of Violation ("NOV") to provide one last opportunity to stop the unlawful activity and bring the Property into compliance before the City proceeds with further enforcement action. The specific nature of the violations are as follows:

1) A Change of Occupancy has been made to the [ ] without the required permitting and inspections or the required new Certificate of Occupancy for its current use. (Section 1001.2 of 2018 NC Existing Building Code)

2) Unapproved highly flammable finish materials have been added throughout the structure. (Section 302.3 and 302.4 of 2018 NC Existing Building Code)

3) Unclear path of egress travel. (Section 1003.6 of 2018 NC Building Code)

4) Inadequate Emergency/Exit lighting. (Section 1008.1 of 2018 NC Building Code)

As the property owner and tenant, it is your responsibility to immediately take corrective action to remedy the violations specified herein. See N.C. Gen Stat §160D-1118. Please contact the undersigned inspector as soon as possible to discuss what options may be considered to remedy these violations.

If you continue to operate an A-2 Nightclub at the Property, and a permit for the required Change of Occupancy has not been acquired and the other Building Code violations have not been remedied by September 13, 2024, the City will proceed with further enforcement action including, but not limited to, noticing and conducting an administrative hearing on the violations before the City Building Inspector, posting the Property as unsafe pursuant to N.C. Gen. Stat. § 160D-1119(a), obtaining an order for corrective action, and other enforcement remedies, as provided by law.

Please note that if you believe you have corrected the violations, the violations can only be considered corrected once you have contacted the undersigned building inspector and the facility has been inspected and deemed in compliance by the building inspector.

I can be reached at 919-996-2445 and [ ]

[ ] of **3**

Appendix F

Sample Compliance Forms

F1. Wilmington Code Enforcement Door Hanger

CITY OF WILMINGTON NORTH CAROLINA

Code Enforcement

Sorry I Missed You!

I stopped by to talk to you about a possible violation at this address. Please refer to the information below and contact me at the number listed so we can discuss the matter concerning:

Public Nuisance
Junk/Safety Vehicle
Zone Violation
Minimal Housing
University Parking
Sidewalk Furniture
Other ______________________

Non-Residential Structure
Domestic Fowl/ Livestock

Officer: ______________________
Phone: 910-______-__________
Date: ___/___/20___ Time: ___:____am pm

PUBLIC NUISANCE VIOLATION

Uncontrolled growth of vegetation, accumulation of animal/vegetative matter which is offensive by odor or inhabited by animals, accumulation of trash, garbage and debris; accumulation of old appliances, mattresses, tires, clothes, etc.; stagnant water; open storage such as furniture, glass, building materials or rubbish; etc.

MINIMAL HOUSING VIOLATION

Damaged interior walls, dangerous health and safety conditions such as dilapidation, decay or unsanitary conditions; inadequate ventilation, light, heating or sanitary condition; improper electrical or plumbing, deterioration of supporting outside walls, siding, or improperly distributed loads of floor or roof system.

F2. Wilmington Penalty Modification Request Form

CITY OF WILMINGTON NORTH CAROLINA

Housing and Neighborhood Services
Code Enforcement
929 N Front Street
PO Box 1810
Wilmington, NC 28402-810
910 341 3266
codeenforcement@wilmingtonnc.gov
Dial 711 TTY/Voice

Penalty Modification Request Form

Internal Use: Case# ________ Case Type ___ Customer# ____ CEO ________

In order to file a Penalty Modification Request, you must provide justification as to why a penalty modification should be granted. Please complete and submit the Penalty Modification Request form. The modification request shall be taken into consideration by the Division of Code Enforcement as the basis for recommendation to the City Manager.
Note: This form is a request for a review, and only a review, there is no guarantee the penalty will be modified.

A. Violation or Case Number:

____

D. I am the:

- ☐ Property Owner
- ☐ Heir
- ☐ Tenant
- ☐ Other

B. Citation Number and Amount:

____

E. Receive modification decision by:

- ☐ EMAIL
- ☐ MAIL

C. Contact Information:

Name: ____________________ **Mailing Address:** ____________________

E-mail: ____________________ ____________________

Phone: ____________________ ____________________

F. Please state why you feel that the penalty should be modified. Provide any details and reasoning that will support your modification request. You may also attach supplementary documentation that will aid your modification request.

____

____

____

____

____

____________**Signature:**____________________**Date:**________

City of Wilmington Code Enforcement Division
PO Box 1810; 929 N Front St. Wilmington NC 28402
Phone 910 341 3266 E-mail: codeenforcement@wilmingtonnc.gov

F3. Greensboro Housing and Neighborhood Code Brochure

Code Compliance & Our Code of Ordinances

One of the most comprehensive services the City's Housing and Neighborhood Development Department offers is Code Compliance enforcement. Cities, towns, states across the country enforce legal standards – or codes – by which all residential and commercial buildings and property must be maintained or the owners could be fined for failing to meet those standards.

In Greensboro, these are called the City's Code of Ordinances, which includes Minimum Housing Standards as well as various nuisance ordinances. More than 15 City staffers daily field reports and make on-site inspections of possible violations of these rules and work with property owners to resolve the issues.

The goal is to ensure safe and healthy places for all residents to live, work and play – whether they are homeowners or renters.

GREENSBORO
Housing & Neighborhood
Development

336-373-2111 • WWW.GREENSBORO-NC.GOV/CC

Tall Weeds & Grass

Failure to cut weeds or grass and overgrowth exceeding 12 inches on private property will result in a violation.

Neglect of Premise

Neglect of property is causing or allowing unsightly litter, tall weeds, and grass, yard waste, foul odor, dead animals, junk, unsecured appliances or potentially dangerous devices to remain on or emanate from a property.

You may receive a violation if you discard, abandon or cause these issues on public property, private property, vacant lots or any body of water or banks within city limits.

You may also receive a violation if property not enclosed within a building or dwelling is in a littered condition, such as dilapidated furniture, appliances, machinery, equipment, building materials, automotive parts, tires or any other items that are wholly or partially rusted, wrecked, junked, dismantled or inoperable.

Bulky & Junk Items

Call 336-373-CITY (2489) to schedule a pickup of eligible items. These items should not be placed at the curb prior to scheduling or any earlier than one day before the scheduled pickup date.

Questions? Complaints?
Call Code Compliance at 336-373-2111.

Abandoned Vehicles

Vehicles are in violation of the City's Junked and Abandoned Motor Vehicles Ordinance if they are on a public street or highway for longer than seven consecutive days.

Vehicles are also in violation of the ordinance if they appear to be abandoned on private property and have been so for longer than seven consecutive days.

Junked Vehicles

Any motor vehicle on private property without a valid license tag and that does not operate, is in violation of the City's Junked and Abandoned Motor Vehicles Ordinance. Also subject to a notice of violation are vehicles that are wrecked or dismantled or are worth less than $500.

Did you Know?

Parking in the front yard, or the front and side yards of a corner lot, is a code violation except if the vehicle is on an improved driveway or parking pad surfaced with gravel, concrete or asphalt.

GREENSBORO
Housing & Neighborhood Development

Code Compliance
Housing & Neighborhood Development Department
336-373-2111
www.greensboro-nc.gov/CC

Know the Codes

No one wants to be in violation of a code and be the target of complaining neighbors. And, no one wants to be the neighbor who calls the City over possible code infractions.

Regardless of what side of the fence you're on, you should be familiar with the City's codes.

Also, understand that fines vary depending on the infraction and additional fees may be added if a situation is not resolved in a timely matter.

Check out Greensboro's codes!

Yard Waste

Yard waste should not be placed at curbside any earlier than the day before your collection date. Tree and shrub limbs must be no longer than five feet and tied in bundles not to exceed 50 pounds. Leaves must be placed in cans or heavy duty clear plastic bags. Learn more at www.greensboro-nc.gov/YardWaste.

Did You Know?

During the winter Loose Leaf Collection program, leaves must be raked curbside by certain dates for pickup a few weeks later. Read up on this annual program's rules at www.greensboro-nc.gov/Leaves.

Appendix G

Sample Unsafe Structure and Enforcement Notices

G1. Raleigh Inspection Placards

Raleigh

INSPECTED

LAWFULLY OCCUPANCY PERMITTED

This structure has been inspected (as indicated below) and no apparent structural hazard has been found.

☐ **Inspected Exterior Only**

☐ **Inspected Exterior and Interior**

Report any unsafe condition to local authorities; reinspection may be required.

Inspector Comments:

____

____

____

Facility Name and Address:

____

____

____

Date: ____________________

Time: ____________________

(**Caution**: Aftershocks since inspection may increase damage and risk.)

This facility was inspected under emergency conditions for:

____

(Jurisdiction)

____

Inspector ID I Agency

____

____

____

Do Not Remove, Alter, or Cover this Placard until Authorized by Governing Authority

Raleigh

RESTRICTED USE

Caution: This structure has been inspected and found to be damaged as described below:

____

____

____

____

Entry, occupancy, and lawful use are restricted as indicated below:

☐ Do not enter the following areas: __________

☐ Brief entry allowed for access to contents: __________

☐ Other restrictions: __________

Facility name and address:

____

____

____

____

Date: __________

Time: __________

(**Caution:** Aftershocks since inspection may increase damage and risk.)

This facility was inspected under emergency conditions for:

____

(Jurisdiction)

Inspector ID I Agency

____

____

____

____

Do Not Remove, Alter, or Cover this Placard until Authorized by Governing Authority

Raleigh

UNSAFE

DO NOT ENTER OR OCCUPY
(THIS PLACARD IS NOT A DEMOLITION ORDER)

This structure has been inspected, found to be seriously damaged and is unsafe to occupy, as described below.

____

____

____

____

____

Do not enter, except as specifically authorized in writing by jurisdiction. Entry may result in death or injury.

Facility name and address:

____

____

____

____

Date: ______________________

Time: ______________________

This facility was inspected under emergency conditions for:

____

(Jurisdiction)

Inspector ID I Agency

____

____

____

____

Do Not Remove, Alter, or Cover this Placard until Authorized by Governing Authority

Raleigh

THIS STRUCTURE HAS BEEN
FOUND TO BE AN

UNSAFE BUILDING

By the Building & Safety Division This notice is to remain on this structure until it is repaired, vacated or demolished in accordance with the order which has been given to the owner, occupant, lessee, mortgagee, agent and all other persons having an interest in this building as shown by the records of the register of deeds of Wake County. It is unlawful to remove this notice.

AUTHORITY FOR ACTION: North Carolina General status 160D-1119.

DATE INSPECTOR

G2. Wilmington Nonresidential Structure Code Health and Safety Hazard Placard

CITY OF WILMINGTON MINIMUM HOUSING CODE

NON-RESIDENTIAL STRUCTURE CODE

HEALTH AND SAFETY HAZARD

THIS STRUCTURE IS UNFIT FOR ANY USE. THE USE OR OCCUPANCY OF THIS STRUCTURE FOR ANY PURPOSE IS PROHIBITED AND UNLAWFUL.

No person, firm or corporation shall remove any complaint, notice or order without written consent from the Inspector. Any person removing this notice shall be guilty of a misdemeanor. Any person who occupies or knowingly allows the occupancy of this structure shall be guilty of a misdemeanor.

______________________ Inspector

______________________ Date

North Carolina General Statues 160D-1203

Code Enforcement Division
codeenforcement@wilmingtonnc.gov
(910) 341-3266

G3. Greenville Notice of Hearing—Condemnation

(Date)

CERTIFIED MAIL / REGULAR MAIL

(Property Owner) *(Tenant)*

Subject: *Address* (Parcel #XXXXXX) Unsafe Building / Structure Condemned Notice of Hearing

Dear (Owner / Tenant):

As a result of recent concerns, the Inspections Division of the Planning and Development Services Department inspected the above subject property. Due to the condition, the building / structure has been deemed to be unsafe and in violation of the North Carolina State Building Code, Administrative Codes and Policies, General Statute 160D-1119 "Unsafe Buildings Condemned", therefore rendering the above-mentioned building / structure condemned. A condemned placard was posted on the above subject property on (date). Items resulting in the condemnation include:

- (*details of why the condemnation is taking place*)

Pursuant to G.S. 160D-1121, notice is hereby given:
(1) That the building or structure located at (Parcel #) is in a condition that appears to meet one or more of the following conditions:

a. Constitutes a fire or safety hazard.
b. Is dangerous to life, health, or other property.
c. Is likely to cause or contribute to blight, disease, vagrancy, or danger to children.
d. Has a tendency to attract persons intent on criminal activities or other activities that would constitute a public nuisance.

(2) That an administrative hearing will be held before me in the office of the Inspections Division, 201 W. 5th St., Greenville, North Carolina, on (***Date and Time not later than 10 days after the date of the notice***), at which time the owner will be entitled to be heard in person or by counsel and to present arguments and evidence pertaining to the matter.

(3) That following the hearing, the inspector may issue such order to repair, close, vacate, or demolish the building or structure as appears appropriate.

Your earliest attention to this matter will be appreciated, and should you have any questions, please contact our office at (xxx) xxx-xxxx, or me directly at (xxx) xxx-xxxx.

Respectfully,

(Building Official)
Title
Cc: *(City Attorney)*
(Supervisor)
(Applicable City Management)

G4. Greenville Order to Take Corrective Action—Condemnation

(Date)

CERTIFIED MAIL / REGULAR MAIL

(Property Owner) *(Tenant)*

Subject: ***Address*** **(Parcel #XXXXXX) Unsafe Building / Structure Condemned Order to Take Corrective Action**

Dear (Owner / Tenant):

As a result of recent concerns, the Inspections Division of the Planning and Development Services Department inspected the above subject property. Due to the condition, the structure has been deemed to be unsafe and in violation of the North Carolina State Building Code, Administrative Codes and Policies, North Carolina General Statute (NCGS) 160D-1119 "Unsafe Buildings Condemned", therefore rendering the above mentioned structure condemned. A condemned placard has been posted on the above subject property. Items resulting in the condemnation include:

- (*details of why the condemnation is taking place*)

In accordance with the provisions of NCGS 160D-1119, notice was given that a hearing was scheduled for (*Date*), in the office of the Inspections Division, 201 W. Fifth St., Greenville, North Carolina at (Time). Present at the hearing were: (*list those in attendance*). The following was presented and/or discussed at the hearing: (*List items presented and/or discussed*).

As a result of the hearing, it was found that the structure exhibited a condition as outlined in G.S. 160D-1121: *a condition that appears to meet one or more of the following conditions:*

a. Constitutes a fire or safety hazard.
b. Is dangerous to life, health, or other property.
c. Is likely to cause or contribute to blight, disease, vagrancy, or danger to children.
d. Has a tendency to attract persons intent on criminal activities or other activities that would constitute a public nuisance.

As a result, the following order to take corrective action is being made. You are notified pursuant to General Statute 160D-1122, you have until (*Date not less than 60 days unless imminent danger to life or other property exist*), to (*provide details, steps, or other orders to remedy the condition*). Further, if no substantial activity has taken place by (*Date listed above as deadline*), further enforcement actions by the City of Greenville may be warranted. Actions by the City could include enforcement measures as outlined in the NC General Statutes for failure to comply with this order. (*Refer to NCGS 160D-1124 and 1125*)

Please be advised that the building / structure must remain vacant and secure until corrective actions are taken. All proper permits must be obtained, and all appropriate inspections must be performed in the event repairs are made.

You have the right to appeal this order as outlined in NCGS:

> § 160D-1123. Appeal; finality of order if not appealed.
> Any owner who has received an order under G.S. 160D-1122 may appeal from the order to the governing board by giving notice of appeal in writing to the inspector and to the local government clerk within 10 days following issuance of the order. In the absence of an appeal, the order of the inspector is final. The governing board shall hear an appeal in accordance with G.S. 160D-406 and render a decision within a reasonable time. The governing board may affirm, modify and affirm, or revoke the order. (2019-111, s. 2.4; 2020-3, s. 4.33(a); 2020-25, ss. 34, 51(a), (b), (d).)

Your earliest attention to this matter will be appreciated, and should you have any questions, please contact our office at (252) 329-4466, or me directly at (252) xxx-xxxx.

Respectfully,

(Building Official)
Title

Cc: *(City Attorney)*
(Supervisor)
(Applicable City Management)

Appendix H

Sample Commercial Maintenance Code Documents and Enforcement Orders

H1. Wilmington Complaint and Notice of Hearing Before Nonresidential Structure Code Officer

COMPLAINT AND NOTICE OF HEARING
BEFORE NONRESIDENTIAL STRUCTURE CODE HEARING OFFICER

STATE OF NORTH CAROLINA	IN THE MATTER OF THE PROPERTY LOCATED AT
COUNTY OF NEW HANOVER	Wilmington, North Carolina Known as Map
CITY OF WILMINGTON	Block No. Lot No.

TO:

Please be advised that on or about , 20 the property located at , Wilmington, North Carolina, was inspected for conformance under the standards set forth by the City of Wilmington's Nonresidential Structure Code (Chapter 16, Article VII of the City Code). As a result of this inspection, the property located at the above address was found to be in violation of the following section(s) of the Nonresidential Structure Code:

SECTION: **16-310 – UNSAFE NONRESIDENTIAL STRUCTURES**

A copy of the **Violation Detail Report** on the above-mentioned property is attached hereto and made a part hereof. (A copy of the Nonresidential Structure Code is on file at the Code Enforcement Office, 929 North Front Street Street, Wilmington, North Carolina and is also available on the City's website at www.wilmingtonnc.gov under City Ordinances, Wilmington, NC, Chapter 16 Buildings and Building Regulations, Article VII).

You are further notified that a hearing will be held before the Nonresidential Structure Code Hearing Officer of the City of Wilmington, 929 North Front Street, Wilmington, NC on the **day of , 20 at o'clock .m.** for the purpose of determining whether the structure is in violation of the Nonresidential Structure Code and ordering an appropriate remedy. The owner(s) and the parties in interest may file an answer to this complaint and may appear at the hearing in person or by other means and give testimony and be represented by counsel if desired. The rules of evidence prevailing in courts of law or equity shall not be controlling.

If, after this hearing, the Nonresidential Structure Code Hearing Officer finds that the structure violates the Nonresidential Structure Code, the Hearing Officer shall make written findings of fact supporting those determinations and shall serve upon the owner(s) an Order requiring the owner(s) to remedy such conditions by repairing and improving the structure, vacating and closing it, and/or removing or demolishing it, within a specified time, and take such other steps as are authorized under the Nonresidential Structure Code and the General Statutes of North Carolina. A violation also subjects the offender to a civil penalty of $100.00 per day for each day that the violation continues.

If the structure is found to be a health and/or safety hazard, it shall be unlawful to occupy or allow occupancy of the structure after the time prescribed for its repair, alteration, or its vacating and closing.

Further information as to this matter may be obtained by contacting the undersigned.

This the day of , **20**

____

Code Enforcement Officer
Code Enforcement Division
Housing and Neighborhood Services Department
P.O. Box 1810
Wilmington, NC 28402
(910) 341-3266

Sworn to and subscribed before me this
_____ day of _____________, 20_____.

____
Notary Public

My Commission Expires: ______________

STATE OF NORTH CAROLINA
CITY OF WILMINGTON
NEW HANOVER COUNTY

AFFIDAVIT OF SERVICE

This is to certify that the foregoing "Complaint and Notice of Hearing" was duly served in accordance with the provisions of Wilmington City Code Sec. 16-316 and North Carolina General Stature Section 160D-1129 upon the owners and all parties in interest in the manner indicated below.

BEFORE ME, the undersigned Notary Public, personally came and appeared:

who being first duly sworn did depose and say that:

He is a Code Enforcement Officer, duly authorized to enforce the Code of Ordinance for the City of Wilmington, North Carolina.

are owners or parties in interest of the property located at .

On **,** a copy of the **Complaint and Notice of Hearing** was deposited in the U. S. Post Office for mailing by certified mail, return receipt requested and 1st Class Mail, to the owner(s) and party(ies) in interest of such property.

A copy of said Complaint and Notice was posted on the premises.

According to the information and belief of the Code Enforcement Officer, the whereabouts of are unknown and cannot be ascertained in the exercise of reasonable diligence.

Service of the **Complaint and Notice of Hearing** and other pleading must be made by publication in a newspaper having general circulation in the City as authorized by North Carolina General Statute Section 160D-1129. (Star News,)

This the day of ,

____
Code Enforcement Officer

Subscribed to and sworn before me this
the____ day of _____________, 20___.

____
Notary Public

My Commission Expires: _______________________

STATE OF NORTH CAROLINA

COUNTY OF NEW HANOVER

CITY OF WILMINGTON
BEFORE THE NONRESIDENTIAL
STRUCTURE HEARING OFFICER

IN THE MATTER OF THE)
PROPERTY LOCATED AT)
)
)
) **NOTICE OF LIS PENDENS**
AND OWNED BY)
)
)
)
)

This Notice of Lis Pendens, filed with the Clerk of Superior Court of New Hanover County, shows:

1. That the structure situated on the property located at in the City of Wilmington, and further described in Exhibit A attached hereto, has been inspected by the Code Enforcement Officer of the City of Wilmington and found to contain violations of the Nonresidential Structure Code, as set forth in Article VII of Chapter 16 of the Wilmington City Code (herein " Nonresidential Structure Code");

2. That the deed to the above-described property is recorded in the New Hanover County Registry in Book at Page , and that the parties in interest in said property, as shown by the public records of New Hanover County, are as follows:

3. That on , **20** the Code Enforcement Officer, on behalf of the City of Wilmington, instituted a proceeding under the Nonresidential Structure Code with respect to the above-described property, by causing a Complaint and Notice of Hearing to be served on the owner(s) and interested parties identified above; a copy of that Complaint and Notice of Hearing is attached hereto as Exhibit B;

4. That the purpose of said proceeding is to determine whether the structure on the above-described property is a health and/or safety hazard and deteriorated or dilapidated within the meaning of the Nonresidential Structure Code and to direct the owner or owners thereof to repair, vacate and close, or demolish said structure, as appropriate, in order to bring the structure and property into compliance with the Nonresidential Structure Code.

This Notice of Lis Pendens is filed in accordance with Wilmington City Code Sec. 16-314(2), adopted pursuant to the provisions of N.C. Gen. Stat. 160D-1129 and N.C. Session Laws 2007, c. 414 (Reg. Sess. 2007), and all persons shall hereby take notice of same.

This the ______ day of ____________________, 20___.

VERIFICATION

The undersigned, having been first duly sworn, deposes and says that she has read the foregoing "Notice of Lis Pendens" and that the matters and things alleged therein are true to the best of her knowledge, and that as to those things alleged on the basis of information and belief, she believes them to be true.

This the ______ day of __________________, 20___.

Subscribed to and sworn before me this
the_____ day of _______________, 20___.

____
Notary Public

My Commission Expires: ____________________________

CERTIFICATE OF SERVICE

This is to certify that the foregoing "Notice of Lis Pendens" was duly served in accordance with the provisions of Wilmington City Code Sec. 16-314 upon the owners and all parties in interest in the manner indicated below:

( ) by hand delivering a copy of same to _______________________ or his attorney at the following address:

( ) by first class and registered or certified mail by depositing a copy of same in an official depository of the United States Postal Service in an envelope with proper postage thereon, addressed as follows:

( ) by publication

( ) by the eCourts File & Serve platform, and will be electronically served to the counsel(s) by the system upon acceptance by the Clerk.

and that a copy of said Notice was posted on the premises.

This the _______ day of _________________, 20___.

____

H2. Wilmington Nonresidential Structure Finding of Fact and Order

FINDING OF FACT AND ORDER
NONRESIDENTIAL STRUCTURE CODE

STATE OF NORTH CAROLINA	IN THE MATTER OF THE PROPERTY LOCATED AT
COUNTY OF NEW HANOVER	**Wilmington, North Carolina**
	KNOWN AS MAP NO.
CITY OF WILMINGTON	BLOCK NO. **00** LOT NO.

TO:

The undersigned Hearing Officer of the City of Wilmington, North Carolina, pursuant to law conducted a hearing at 929 North Front Street, Wilmington, North Carolina as scheduled on the **day of 20 .** At or before said hearing an Answer filed by owners or parties in interest was included in the record.

The undersigned Hearing Officer, having reviewed the entire record considered any arguments or summaries of the owner(s) and parties in interest, their agents or attorneys does hereby find that the dwelling located at the above address violated the City Nonresidential Structure Code (Chapter 16, Article VII of the City Code) and the standards set forth therein, is a health and safety hazard. In support of said determination, the Hearing Officer makes the following:

FINDING OF FACT

1) The City of Wilmington, North Carolina, has jurisdiction over the owner(s), parties in interest, and subject matter of this proceeding.

2) The above-named owner(s) and parties in interest were duly served with a written Complaint and Notice of Hearing which alleged that the structure located at the above address is a health and safety hazard and violates the City Nonresidential Structure Code and fixed a time and place for a hearing upon such complaint as provided by law; the following owner(s), parties in interest, their agents or attorneys were present and were heard:

No one present

3) The Code Enforcement Officer was present and testified. The testimonies of the **Chief Code Enforcement Officer, , and Code Enforcement Officer** were heard and photographs showing the condition of the structure and the Code Enforcement case file for the property were admitted into evidence.

4) The Nonresidential Structure Case began with a complaint from as to the condition of the property.

5) At the time the Nonresidential Structure Case was opened, the structure was vacant.

6) The photographs taken of the structure during the Code Enforcement Officer inspections show the deterioration of the structure and the needed repairs to bring it into compliance with the Nonresidential Structure Code (paragraphs 7 through below).

7)

8)

9)

10)

11) Said structure fails to comply with the standards set forth in the Nonresidential Structure Code of the City of Wilmington, North Carolina, in the following respects:

Section 16-310. Unsafe Nonresidential Structures.

(1)*Access.* Access is not provided to all rooms within a structure such that reasonable exit is available if necessitated by circumstances; or all entrances and exits do not meet the standards set forth in the North Carolina State Building Code; or safe, continuous and unobstructed exit is not provided from the interior of the structure to the exterior at street or grade level; or platforms and steps are not provided, where appropriate, to serve exits or are not maintained in a safe condition.

(2) *Attachments, extensions, signs, etc.* Loose wood, loose or broken plastic or other dangerous objects or similar hazardous conditions; or loose and insufficiently anchored overhanging objects or attachments that are not safe to use, not kept in sound condition and in good repair, or which constitute a danger of falling on pedestrians or property, or objects and elements protruding from structure walls or roofs which are unsafe or that are not properly secured or which can create a hazard such as abandoned electrical boxes and conduits, wires, sign brackets and other brackets and similar objects; or canopies, metal awnings, standpipes, exhaust ducts, air conditioners, and similar overhanging extensions that are not maintained so as to be free of missing, defective, rotting or deteriorated foundations, supports, other members and basic structural elements; or improperly attached gutters or downspouts that are located so as to cause a hazard to pedestrians or property; or gutters and downspouts, if installed, that do not properly collect, conduct and discharge the water from the roof and away from the structure; or advertising signs attached or freestanding awnings, marquees and their supporting members or basic structural elements and other similar attachments that cause a safety hazard to the occupants or others.

(3) *Boarding.* All openings originally designed as windows, doors, loading docks, or other means of egress or ingress which have been temporarily closed by boarding or another manner that are not secure and might allow unauthorized admittance; or boarding that is not trim fit, sealed to prevent water intrusion, and painted or stained to properly conform with the other exterior portions of the structure; or boarding that is not maintained in a state that secures the structure from any unauthorized admittance of people, animals or birds.

(4) *Building code.* Possible violations of the North Carolina State Building Code and the North Carolina Rehabilitation Code, as amended from time to time and any new editions adopted by the North Carolina Structure Code Council, including general construction, electrical, plumbing, mechanical, and ventilation.

(5) *Chimneys.* Chimneys, flues, and vent attachments thereto which are not structurally sound; or chimneys, flues, gas vents, or other draft-producing equipment which are in use that do not provide sufficient draft to develop the rated output of the connected equipment, or are not structurally sound and safe, durable, smoke-tight and capable of withstanding the action of flue gases; or deterioration of external chimneys that causes leaning, sagging, splitting, listing or buckling.

(6) *Decay.* Rotting, holes and other forms of decay.

(7) *Doors, exterior and windows.* Broken or missing exterior doors or windows; or exterior doors or windows containing broken or cracked glass that could be in danger of falling or shattering; or exterior doors or windows with missing glass or their frames that are not weather-tight; or doors that are not tight-fitting with frames of proper size and design or not free from rotten wood; or windows without sashes of proper size and design, or not free from rotten wood, broken joints, or broken or loose mullions; or which have holes that might permit animals or birds to enter the structure; or defective protection or lack of weather protection for exterior doors or windows including lack of paint or weathering due to lack of paint or other protective covering.

(8) *Doors, interior.* Doors are not provided at all doorways leading to bathrooms.

(9) *Electrical, heating, plumbing.* Lack of proper electrical, heating or plumbing facilities which is unsafe or constitutes a health or safety hazard.

(10) *Exterior surfaces.* Exterior surfaces or finishes that are not weather-tight, watertight and painted or sealed with sufficient frequency to protect the underlying surface from deterioration; or are not maintained in such material or treated in such a manner as to prevent deterioration or crumbling; or are not repaired or replaced with like or similar material according to its original use; or have holes, cracks or rotted boards which permit outside air or water to penetrate rooms or animals or birds to enter; or exterior surfaces that have been painted which are not maintained generally free of peeling and flaking or that may cause unsafe conditions due to a lack of maintenance; or deterioration or crumbling of exterior stone, brick, plasters or mortars. (Where fifty (50) percent or more of the aggregate of any painted surface shall have peeling or flaking or previous paint worn away, the entire surface shall be repainted in order to prevent further deterioration.)

(11) *Feature, exterior.* Deterioration of any exterior feature, including but not limited to cornices, entablatures, wall facings and architectural details, so as to create or permit the creation of any hazardous or unsafe conditions; or that are deteriorated and causes delamination, instability, loss of shape and form or crumbling; or exterior features that are not structurally sound;

or that contain rotten or weakened portions requiring repair and/or replacement.

(12) *Fire, etc.* Such damage by fire, wind, or other causes so as to render the structure unsafe; or defects significantly increasing the hazards of fire, accident or other calamities; or inadequate facilities for egress in case of fire or panic.

(13) *Floors.* Floors that are not kept structurally sound or which have improperly distributed loads, which are overloaded, or which have insufficient strength to be reasonably safe for the purpose used; or deterioration of flooring, floor supports, horizontal members or basic structural elements that causes leaning, sagging, splitting, listing or buckling; or floors or flooring that are not maintained in a safe manner and have no defects; or which might admit rain or cause dampness in the walls or interior portion of the structure; or are not maintained by renewal, repair, waterproofing or other suitable means; or which have holes that might permit animals or birds to enter the structure.

(14) *Foundation.* Foundation walls, piers or other basic structural elements which are not maintained in a safe manner; or are not capable of supporting the load which normal use may cause to be placed thereon; or which have insufficient strength to be reasonably safe for the purpose used; or which are deteriorated, decayed or damaged to the extent that causes leaning, sagging, splitting, listing or buckling; or the structure's strength and soundness are questionable.

(15) *Porches, stairs, etc.* Exterior porches, landings, balconies, stairways, stairs or fire escapes which are not structurally sound or free of defects so as to be safe to use; or are incapable of supporting the load that normal use may cause to be placed thereon; or that do not have banisters or railings properly designed and maintained to minimize the hazard of falling.

(16) *Premises.* Structures including their premises that have insufficiently protected holes, excavations, breaks, projections, obstructions and other such dangerous impediments on and around walks, driveways, parking lots, alleyways and other areas which are accessible to and generally used by people on or around the premises; or heaving, subsidence or cracking of sidewalks, steps or pathways.

(17) *Roofs.* Roofs that are not kept structurally sound; or with improperly distributed loads, which are overloaded, or which have insufficient strength to be reasonably safe for the purpose used; or that are not supported properly or that have rafters that are rotted, broken, sagging or have improperly supported ends; or that are deteriorated or have horizontal members or other basic structural elements that cause leaning, sagging, splitting, listing or buckling; or that are not maintained in a safe manner; or are not maintained by renewal, repair, waterproofing or other suitable means; or with loose shingles that may fall on people or property; or that have defects which might admit rain or cause dampness in the walls or interior portion of the structure; or which have holes that might permit animals or birds to enter the structure.

(18) *Unsanitary, etc.* Structures with unsanitary conditions, dilapidation, decay, or disrepair which is unsafe or dangerous to the health and safety of the occupants or others; or structures including their premises that have accumulations of garbage, trash, or rubbish, which creates health and sanitation problems; or the collection of unreasonable or excessive amounts of garbage or rubbish in or near the structure which may attract rodents and insects or become breeding places for rodents and insects; or garbage and solid waste that is not placed in approved containers or stored in a safe and sanitary manner in the structure or on the premises.

(19)*Ventilation, etc.* Lack of adequate ventilation, light, heating or sanitary facilities so as to be unsafe or to endanger the health, safety or general welfare of the occupants or others.

(20) *Walls, exterior.* Exterior walls or vertical supports that are not structurally sound, or not maintained in sound condition and good repair and free from defects and damages, or are not capable of bearing imposed loads safely; deterioration of exterior walls or other vertical support that causes leaning, sagging, splitting, listing or buckling; or structural or load bearing walls that are bowed or out of plumb and not structurally sound; or exterior walls that are not substantially weather-tight and watertight or not impervious to the adverse effects of weather.

(21) *Walls, interior.* Interior walls, vertical studs, partitions, supporting members, sills, joists, rafters or other basic structural elements or members that list, lean, or buckle or are rotted, deteriorated or damaged to such an extent as to render the structure unsafe; or that have holes or cracks which might admit animals or birds; or structural or load bearing walls that are bowed or out of plumb and not structurally sound.

(22) Any combination of conditions which in the judgment of the public officer renders any structure unsafe or dangerous or injurious to the health, safety, or general welfare of the owners, occupants or others.

12) Said structure has not been properly maintained in accordance with the standards set forth in the Nonresidential Structure Code of the City of Wilmington, North Carolina, and constitutes a health and safety hazard to adjacent properties, occupants, and others.

13) The value of said structure is approximately **$**. The approximate cost of bringing the structure into compliance with the Nonresidential Structure Code is **$**. Therefore, the repair, alteration or improvement of this structure sufficient to bring it up to the standards set forth in the Nonresidential Structure Code is equal to **%** of the structure; and, the structure is (**dilapidated / deteriorated)** as defined by the Nonresidential Structure Code.

IT IS THEREFORE ORDERED that the owner(s) of the structure named and designated be and are hereby ordered and required to bring such structure into compliance with the Nonresidential Structure Code of the City of Wilmington, North Carolina, by repairing and improving the structure to remove the described Nonresidential Structure Code violations or demolishing and removing said structure from the property not later than the **day of 20 .**

If the owner(s) of the structure fail to bring such structure into compliance with the Nonresidential Structure Code as ordered by the date designated above, the offender shall be subject to a civil penalty of $100.00 per day for each day that the violation continues, The Code

Enforcement Officer may file a report with the City Council of the City of Wilmington which may, after hearing, cause the repair or demolition and removal of such structure to be done and the costs for same shall be a lien upon the property in accordance with Section 16-322 of the Nonresidential Structure Code.

IT IS FURTHER ORDERED that not later than the day of 20 , the owner(s) vacate and close the structure and secure the windows and doors of the structure until the dwelling complies with the Nonresidential Structure Code.

If the owner(s) of the structure fails to comply with the order to vacate, close and secure the structure, then the Code Enforcement Officer for the City of Wilmington may cause the dwelling to be vacated, closed and secured and the costs for same shall be a lien upon the property in accordance with Section 16-322 of the Nonresidential Structure Code.

Because the structure is found to be a health and safety hazard, it shall be unlawful to occupy or permit the occupancy of the same after ,20 unless the structure is found by the Code Enforcement Officer to be in compliance with the Nonresidential Structure Code.

The structure is subject to **quarterly periodic inspections** to determine compliance with this Order and the Nonresidential Structure Code.

Any appeals of this Finding of Fact and Order to the Housing Appeals Board must be taken within ten (10) days from rendering of the decision or service of the order and shall be taken by filing with the Nonresidential Structure Code Hearing Officer a Notice of Appeal that specifies the grounds upon which the appeal is made.

This is the day of ,

____

Hearing Officer

City of Wilmington, North Carolina

H3. Wilmington Nonresidential Structure Code Repair or Demolish Ordinance

..title

Ordinance Directing The Enforcement Officer To Vacate, Close And Repair Or Demolish The Nonresidential Structure at [ADDRESS] As A Health and Safety Hazard Pursuant To Article VII, Chapter 16 Of The City Code And Directing That A Notice Be Placed Thereon Prohibiting Its Use Or Occupancy

..body

LEGISLATIVE INTENT/PURPOSE:

WHEREAS, the City Nonresidential Structure Code enacted pursuant to Section 160D-1129 of the North Carolina General Statues authorizes the vacating, closing and the repair or demolition of nonresidential structures found to be health and safety hazards; and

WHEREAS, the City Council of the City of Wilmington finds that the property described herein is a health and safety hazard under the City Nonresidential Structure Code, and that all of the provisions of the City Nonresidential Structure Code have been complied with as a condition of the adoption of this ordinance; and

WHEREAS, said structure should be vacated, closed and repaired to meet the requirements of the City Nonresidential Structure Code, or demolished, as directed by the Enforcement Officer and should be placarded by placing thereon a notice prohibiting use or occupancy; and

WHEREAS, the owner of said structure has been given a reasonable opportunity to bring the structure up to the standards of the City Nonresidential Structure Code in accordance with N.C.G.S. Section 160D-1129(d) pursuant to an order issued by the Hearing Officer on **[FOF ISSUED DATE]**, and the owner having failed to comply with the order; and

WHEREAS, N.C.G.S. Section 160A-193 provides cities with the authority to summarily remove, abate, or remedy everything in the city limits that is dangerous or prejudicial to the public health or public safety; and

WHEREAS, the City Council has determined that the condition of the structure at **[ADDRESS]** constitutes a danger to the public safety and should be immediately repaired or removed.

NOW, THEREFORE, BE IT ORDAINED

Section 1. That the Enforcement Officer is hereby authorized and directed to place on the structure bearing the postal enumeration: **[ADDRESS]** a placard containing the legend:

"This building is unfit for any use; the use or occupation of this building for any purpose is prohibited and unlawful."

The realty upon which said structure is situated is more particularly described as follows:

[FULL LEGAL DESCRIPTION]

Parcel ID: **[PARCEL NUMBER]**

Section 2. That it shall be unlawful for any person to remove or cause to be removed said placard from any structure to which it is affixed. It shall likewise be unlawful for any person to occupy or to permit the occupancy of any structure therein declared to be unfit for human habitation. Occupation of a building so posted shall constitute a Class 3 misdemeanor.

Section 3. That the owners and/or parties in interest of the structure herein above described are hereby ordered to vacate and close the subject structure found by the Enforcement Officer to be a health and safety hazard, and to repair or demolish the subject structure within **[ADDITIONAL COMPLIANCE PERIOD GRANTED BY COUNCIL IF ANY]** days from the date of adoption of this ordinance to meet the requirements of the City Nonresidential Structure Code. If the owners and/or parties in interest fail to have the structure vacated, the Enforcement Officer is hereby authorized to commence summary ejectment proceedings pursuant to 160D-1129(j).

If the owner and/or parties in interest shall fail or refuse to vacate, close and repair or demolish said structure within the time allowed, then the Enforcement Officer is hereby authorized and directed to proceed to vacate, close and repair or demolish the above-described structure in accordance with this ordinance and order to the owner thereof dated **[FOF ISSUED DATE],** pursuant to Section 16-317 of the Nonresidential Structure Code and N.C.G.S. Section 160D-1129. The cost of any such repairs, alterations, demolition, or improvements, and vacating and closing, by the Enforcement Officer shall be a lien against the real property upon which the cost was incurred as provided in Section 16-322 of the Nonresidential Structure Code and N.C.G.S. Section 160D-1129(i).

Section 4. That the Enforcement Officer is further directed and authorized to take such other and further action and exercise such other powers with respect to said structure as may be necessary or convenient to carry out and effectuate the provisions of the Nonresidential Structure Code of the City of Wilmington.

Section 5. That the City Clerk is hereby directed to record a certified copy of this ordinance in the office of the New Hanover County Register of Deeds and see that it is properly indexed in the name of the property owner(s) in the grantor index.

Section 6. That any person violating the provisions of the ordinance shall be subject to the penalties set forth in Section 16-1 of the City Code. If the violation is continued, each day's violation shall be a separate offense.

Section 7. That this ordinance may be enforced by an appropriate equitable remedy including but not limited to an injunction or order of abatement issued from any court or competent jurisdiction pursuant to N.C.G.S. Section 160D-1129 or by receivership pursuant to N.C.G.S. Section 160D-1130.

Section 8. That this ordinance may be enforced by any, all, or a combination of the remedies as authorized and prescribed above and by law.

Section 9. That all ordinances or parts of ordinances in conflict with this ordinance are hereby repealed to the extent of such conflict.

Section 10. That if any section, subsection, paragraph, sentence, clause, phrase or portion of this ordinance is for any reason held invalid or unconstitutional by any court of competent jurisdiction, such portion shall be deemed severable and such holding shall not affect the validity of the remaining portions hereof.

Section 11. That the owner(s) of the property described herein is **[OWNER NAME]**.

Section 12. That the City Attorney is authorized to proceed with in rem foreclosure proceedings to collect taxes and liens owed for the property.

Section 13. This ordinance shall become effective upon its adoption.

Appendix I

Sample Housing Enforcement Documents

I1. Wilmington Courtesy Notice Housing and Neighborhood Services Code Enforcement

CITY OF WILMINGTON
NORTH CAROLINA

Courtesy Notice
Housing and Neighborhood Services
Code Enforcement

Case Number:
Case Type: CE - Structure Codes - Minimum Housing Requirements
Violation Notice
Date of Inspection: 10/02/2024
Date of Next Inspection:

Property Owner:

Mailing Address

Courtesy Notice for the following location:

Address **Parcel**

Violation: -

PLEASE CORRECT THE ITEMS WE TALKED ABOUT AT THE INSPECTION . I WILL BE RE-INSPECTING THE PROPERTY NOV 2024.IF YOU HAVE ANY QUESTIONS PLEASE CALL ME AT 910-341-7814

The purpose of this letter is to inform you that a City of Wilmington Code Enforcement Officer recently inspected the property located at the above referenced address. The inspection resulted in the violations referenced above in this letter.

Currently, the above noted concerns DO NOT rise to the level set by the Minimum Housing Code as Unfit for Human Habilitation.

The Code Enforcement Office is requesting that these issues be addressed to prevent further deterioration to your property. Again, no Minimum Housing Code case is open at this time.

Failure to make repairs may lead to additional issues in the future, including further violations of the Minimum Housing Code which could result in the dwelling being determined to be Unfit for Human Habitation.

There are Housing Rehabilitation assistance programs available for low-to-moderate income owner-occupants in need of repairs.

More information about these housing repair programs can be found by calling Community Development at (910) 341-7836, or by visiting www.wilmingtonnc.gov/departments/community-services/housing

Thank you,

City of Wilmington Code Enforcement
PO Box 1810, 2nd Floor, 929 N Front St.
Wilmington, NC 28402
(910) 341-3266
CodeEnforcement@wilmingtonnc.gov

Code Enforcement Officer
(910) 341-7814

Printed: 10/3/24

Page 1 of 1

CITY OF WILMINGTON NORTH CAROLINA

Courtesy Notice
Housing and Neighborhood Services
Code Enforcement

Case Number:

Case Type: CE - Structure Codes - Minimum Housing Requirements

Violation Notice

Date of Inspection: 10/02/2024

Date of Next Inspection:

Mailing Address

Current Occupant

Couresty Notice for the following location:

Address **Parcel**

Violation: -

The purpose of this letter is to inform you that a City of Wilmington Code Enforcement Officer recently inspected the property located at the above referenced address. The inspection resulted in the violations referenced above in this letter.

Currently, the above noted concerns DO NOT rise to the level set by the Minimum Housing Code as Unfit for Human Habilitation.

The Code Enforcement Office is requesting that these issues be addressed to prevent further deterioration to your property. Again, no Minimum Housing Code case is open at this time.

Failure to make repairs may lead to additional issues in the future, including further violations of the Minimum Housing Code which could result in the dwelling being determined to be Unfit for Human Habitation.

There are Housing Rehabilitation assistance programs available for low-to-moderate income owner-occupants in need of repai

More information on housing repair programs can be found by calling Community Development at (910) 341-7836, or by visiting www.wilmingtonnc.gov/departments/community-services/housing

No response to this letter is required.

Thank you,

Code Enforcement Officer
(910) 341-7814

City of Wilmington Code Enforcement
PO Box 1810, 2nd Floor, 929 N Front St.
Wilmington, NC 28402
(910) 341-3266
CodeEnforcement@wilmingtonnc.gov

Printed: 10/3/24 **Page 1 of 1**

I2. Raleigh Unfit Hearing Letter

City of Raleigh
North Carolina

February 26, 2025

RE:
PIN#:
REID#:

To:

The City of Raleigh is concerned about the health, safety and welfare of every citizen. As part of this concern, many years ago the City Council adopted a Minimum Housing Code. These provisions deal with keeping our homes in a safe and sanitary condition. The specific standards set forth are not excessive but rather very basic to good housekeeping and general maintenance. One of the responsibilities of the Code Enforcement Division of the Housing & Neighborhoods Department is to inspect dwellings within the city's jurisdiction and enforce the code as it applies to the structure, the occupants, and the owners.

An inspection of the above referenced address was made 08/15/2023 and violations (Article 11.6 of the Housing Code) as listed on the enclosed Housing Report were observed and are causing this dwelling to be unfit. So that we may review these matters, discuss City procedures and what corrections need to be made, a hearing has been scheduled on at . You may appear in person or send a representative to this hearing which will be held at 421 Fayetteville Street, Suite 1200, Raleigh, North Carolina 27601.

In accordance with Section 11.6.17 of the Housing code the owner of a dwelling shall be assessed a Three Hundred Twenty-Five Dollars ($325.00) administrative fee associated with this inspection upon the scheduled hearing date if the repairs have not been completed and approved by the Code Enforcement Division prior to the hearing. You are thereby encouraged to make repairs or corrections to the dwelling(s) prior to the hearing. Please obtain all permits necessary to make the repairs <u>prior</u> to beginning work. If you are uncertain that a permit is necessary, please contact our Permit Office, (919) 996-2495 or the Code Enforcement Inspector for guidance.

This is part of the continuing effort Raleigh is making to improve living conditions for its citizens. Your cooperation and support will help us achieve this goal.

Sincerely,

Senior Multi-Trades Housing Inspector II
919-632-0408

Case#:
Enclosure
cc: Executive Director
Historic Districts Commission

605 Bragg Street Land Trust, Party of Interest

Housing & Neighborhoods, Code Enforcement Division - 421 Fayetteville Street, Suite 1200, Raleigh, NC 27601 (919) 996-2444

City of Raleigh
North Carolina

February 26, 2025

Violation Details

City Ordinance violations and details:

Location: /Location 01/General Statement
Date Reported: 08/15/2023 **Active?** ☑ **Date Corrected:**
Permits - Mechanical permit required. (City of Raleigh Code Article 11.6.1.C & NC State Building Code: Administrative Code & Policies)
Notes:

Location: /Location 01/General Statement
Date Reported: 08/15/2023 **Active?** ☑ **Date Corrected:**
Permits - Plumbing permit required. (City of Raleigh Code Article 11.6.1.C & NC State Building Code: Administrative Code & Policies)
Notes:

Location: /Location 01/General Statement
Date Reported: 08/15/2023 **Active?** ☑ **Date Corrected:**
Permit required - City of Raleigh Electrical Permit required prior to work commencing. (NC State Building Co(Administrative Code & Policies)
Notes:

Location: /Location 01/General Statement
Date Reported: 08/15/2023 **Active?** ☑ **Date Corrected:**
Permits - Building permit required. (City of Raleigh Code Article 11.6.1.C & NC State Building Code: Administrative Code & Policies)
Notes:

Location: /Location 01/General Statement
Date Reported: 08/15/2023 **Active?** ☑ **Date Corrected:**
Violations must be corrected to meet the City of Raleigh's Housing Code. (City of Raleigh Code Article 11.6)
Notes:

Housing & Neighborhoods, Code Enforcement Division - 421 Fayetteville Street, Suite 1200, Raleigh, NC 27601 (919) 996-2444

13. Wilmington Complaint and Notice of Hearing Before Minimum Housing Code Officer

COMPLAINT AND NOTICE OF HEARING
BEFORE MINIMUM HOUSING CODE HEARING OFFICER

STATE OF NORTH CAROLINA	IN THE MATTER OF THE PROPERTY LOCATED AT
COUNTY OF NEW HANOVER	Wilmington, North Carolina Known as Map
CITY OF WILMINGTON	Block No. Lot No.

TO:

Please be advised that on or about , 20 the property located at , Wilmington, North Carolina, was inspected for conformance under the standards set forth by the City of Wilmington's Minimum Housing Code (Chapter 16, Article V of the City Code). As a result of this inspection, the property located at the above address was found to be in violation of the following section(s) of the Minimum Housing Code:

☐ **SECTION: 16-229 - RESIDENTIAL BUILDING UNFIT FOR HUMAN HABITATION**
☐ **SECTION: 16-266 - GENERAL**
☐ **SECTION: 16-267 - LIGHT; VENTILATION**
☐ **SECTION: 16-268 - ELECTRICAL SYSTEMS**
☐ **SECTION: 16-269 - EXTERIOR AND INTERIOR STRUCTURES GENERALLY**
☐ **SECTION: 16-270 - SPACE AND USE**
☐ **SECTION: 16-271 - SANITATION**

A copy of the **Violation Detail Report** on the above-mentioned property is attached hereto and made a part hereof. (A copy of the Minimum Housing Code is on file at the Code Enforcement Office, 929 North Front Street, Wilmington, North Carolina and is also available on the City's website at www.wilmingtonnc.gov under City Ordinances, Wilmington, NC, Chapter 16 Buildings and Building Regulations, Article V.)

You are further notified that a hearing will be held before the Minimum Housing Hearing Officer of the City of Wilmington, 929 North Front Street, Wilmington, NC on the **day of , 20 at .m.** for the purpose of determining whether the dwelling is in violation of the Minimum Housing Code and unfit for human habitation, and ordering an appropriate remedy. The owner(s) and the parties in interest may file an answer to this complaint and may appear at the administrative hearing in person or by other means and give testimony and be represented by counsel if desired. The rules of evidence prevailing in courts of law or equity shall not be controlling.

If, after this hearing, the Minimum Housing Hearing Officer finds that the dwelling violates the Minimum Housing Code and is unfit for human habitation, the Hearing Officer shall make written findings of fact supporting those determinations and shall serve upon the owner(s) an Order requiring the owner(s) to remedy such conditions by repairing and improving the dwelling, vacating and closing it, posting and/or removing or demolishing it, within a specified time, and take such other steps as are authorized under the Minimum Housing Code and the General Statutes of North Carolina. A violation also subjects the offender to a civil penalty of $100.00 per day for each day that the violation continues.

If the dwelling is found to be unfit for human habitation, it shall be unlawful to receive rents and/or to occupy or allow occupancy of the dwelling.

Further information as to this matter may be obtained by contacting the undersigned.

This the day of , **20**

____

Housing Inspector/Code Enforcement Officer
Code Enforcement Division
Housing and Neighborhood Services Department
P.O. Box 1810
Wilmington, NC 28402
(910) 341-3266

Sworn to and subscribed before me this
_____ day of _____________, 20_____.

____
Notary Public

My Commission Expires: ______________

STATE OF NORTH CAROLINA
CITY OF WILMINGTON
NEW HANOVER COUNTY

AFFIDAVIT OF SERVICE

This is to certify that the foregoing "Complaint and Notice of Hearing" was duly served in accordance with the provisions of Wilmington City Code Sec. 16-234 and North Carolina General Statute Section 160D-1206 upon the owners and all parties in interest in the manner indicated below.

BEFORE ME, the undersigned Notary Public, personally came and appeared:

who being first duly sworn did depose and say that:

He is a Code Enforcement Officer, duly authorized to enforce the Code of Ordinance for the City of Wilmington, North Carolina.

is owner or party in interest of the property located at .

On , a copy of the **Complaint and Notice of Hearing** was deposited in the U. S. Post Office for mailing by certified mail, return receipt requested and 1st Class Mail, to the owner(s) and party(ies) in interest of such property.

A copy of said Complaint and Notice was posted on the premises.

According to the information and belief of the Code Enforcement Officer, the whereabouts of are unknown and cannot be ascertained in the exercise of reasonable diligence.

Service of the **Complaint and Notice of Hearing** and other pleading must be made by publication in a newspaper having general circulation in the City as authorized by North Carolina General Statute Section 160D-1206. (Star News,)

This the _______ day of _______________, 20___.

____
Code Enforcement Officer

Subscribed to and sworn before me this
the____ day of _____________, 20___.

____
Notary Public

My Commission Expires: _______________________

I4. Raleigh Unfit Repair Order

City of Raleigh
North Carolina

February 26, 2025

RE:
PIN#:
REID#:

Dear

A hearing was held on to review the list of repairs or corrections, that need to be made to the above address in order to bring it into compliance with the City's Minimum Housing Code.

The violations of Section 11.6.3 and 11.6.4 of the Housing Code as listed on the enclosed Housing Report were discussed at the hearing.

Your cooperation in bringing this dwelling into compliance with the Housing Code in one of the following ways on or before 05/27/2025 is appreciated:

1. Make repairs as outlined:

If you choose to make the repairs, please be certain you have the proper permits. You may call our Permits Office ((919) 996-2495) or the Code Enforcement Inspector for these requirements. If a dwelling becomes vacant and the Housing & Neighborhoods Department has declared that the structure must be repaired or demolished, then it is against the law for anyone to live in the unit until the conditions have been corrected and the Housing & Neighborhoods Department has issued a Certificate of Housing Code Compliance. It is also against the law to rent or offer to rent a dwelling on which .

In accordance with City Code Section 11.6.17, as applicable, an Administrative Inspection Fee of One Hundred Seventy-Five Dollars ($175.00) is hereby assessed and enclosed with this order relating to violations of City Minimum Housing Code standards Section.

Under the provisions of the Code, you have a right to appeal these findings to the Raleigh Housing Appeals Board if you feel the violation was wrongly found. The administrative fee is due and payable unless you prevail in an appeal of the determination that the condition violated the Code. The appeal must be submitted in writing to the Housing & Neighborhoods Department, c/o Code Enforcement Administrator within ten (10) days of the date this order was served on you. Please state clearly the grounds upon which the appeal is based.

Any owner of a dwelling who fails to comply with a notice to repair, vacate and close, or demolish any dwelling determined unfit for human habitation according to Sections 11.6.7 and 11.6.8, or who permits the reoccupancy of an unfit dwelling in violation of Section 11.6.6 shall be subject to a civil penalty of Five Hundred Dollars ($500.00) on the first day following the expiration of the notice or a determination of reoccupancy. In each instance, a One Hundred Dollars ($100.00) per day penalty will be imposed for each subsequent day that the unfit dwelling remains in violation. If a person fails to pay the civil penalty within thirty (30) days after being notified of the amount due, the City may recover the penalty together with all costs by filing a civil action in the general court of justice.

Any owner of a dwelling who fails to comply with an order to repair, vacate and close or demolish any dwelling determined unfit for human habitation pursuant to provisions of Section 11.6.12 and 11.6.13 of City Code shall be subject to an additional civil

Housing & Neighborhoods, Code Enforcement Division - 421 Fayetteville Street, Suite 1200, Raleigh, NC 27601 (919) 996-2444

City of Raleigh
North Carolina

February 26, 2025

penalty of One Thousand Dollars ($1,000.00) upon the first day following the effective date of a City Council Ordinance declaring said dwelling to be unfit for human habitation or ordering it to be repaired or demolished. A penalty of Two Hundred Fifty Dollars ($250.00) per day shall be imposed for each subsequent day that the unfit dwelling remains in violation of the Ordinance or remains unlawfully occupied.

It is our belief that by working together we can maintain a healthy, safe environment for all citizens. Please call me if you have any questions or concerns regarding this matter between Office hours of 8:00 am and 4:15 p.m., and I will endeavor to assist you.

Sincerely,

Administrative Assistant
919-996-2174

Case #:
cc:

Housing & Neighborhoods, Code Enforcement Division - 421 Fayetteville Street, Suite 1200, Raleigh, NC 27601 (919) 996-2444

City of Raleigh
North Carolina

February 26, 2025

Violation Details

City Ordinance violations and details:

Location: Violations
Date Requested: 09/09/2024 **Active?** ☐ **Date Corrected:** 10/22/2024
Any junk or concentration of litter. City Code Section 12-6002 (k)
Notes:

Location: Violations
Date Requested: 09/09/2024 **Active?** ☐ **Date Corrected:** 10/22/2024
A dense growth of weeds and grasses except ornamental grasses over 8 inches in height are to be cut which: (1 lies less than one hundred (100) feet from any abutting street or (2) lies less than one hundred (100) feet from a adjoining property which contains a dwelling or commercial building or (3) lies less than fifty (50) feet from a dwelling or commercial building. City of Raleigh Code Section 12-6002 (b) (1), (2) and (3)
Notes:

Housing & Neighborhoods, Code Enforcement Division - 421 Fayetteville Street, Suite 1200, Raleigh, NC 27601 (919) 996-2444

Case Number:	
Invoice Date:	02/26/2025
Amount Due:	$1,132.00
Due Date:	03/28/2025

City of Raleigh

City of Raleigh
Housing & Neighborhoods
Department
Code Enforcement Division
PO Box 590
Raleigh NC 27602-0590

(919) 990-2444
housing.inspections@raleighnc.gov

Re: HS - Public Nuisance

Code Enforcement Assessed Fees

Please be advised that you are or have been in violation of Part 10A of the City of Raleigh's Unified Development Ordinance, Chapter 11, Code entitiled "Building & Housing Code".

According to Section 11.6.16 entitled Penalty and Section 11.6.17 entitled "Administrative Fee" of the Raleigh City Code, you are hereby cited for this violation and issued a civil penalty and an administrative fee. The total amount of the civil penalty and administrative fee must be paid in full within thirty (30) days.

Failure to make payment within thirty (30) days will result in the referral of the charges for collection action.

CASE NUMBER	DESCRIPTION	AMOUNT
	HS - Cost of Abatement	$357.00
	PN - Administrative Fee	$100.00
	PN - Civil Citation - Subsequent Violations	$500.00
	HS - Abatement Admin Fee	$175.00
	AMOUNT DUE AS OF 03/28/2025	$1,132.00

The City of Raleigh charges a $35.00 fee for returned checks

DETACH AND RETAIN THIS PORTION FOR YOUR RECORDS

Housing & Neighborhoods, Code Enforcement Division - 421 Fayetteville Street, Suite 1200, Raleigh, NC 27601 (919) 996-2444

15. Wilmington Citation and Fees

CITY OF WILMINGTON NORTH CAROLINA

Housing and Neighborhood Services
Code Enforcement

Case Number:

Civil Citation

Case Type: CE - Structure Codes - Minimum Housing Requirements

Date of Inspection: 11/13/2024

Date of Next Inspection: 12/18/2024

Other Contact: STATE EMPLOYEES CREDIT UNION C/O

Mailing Address

Notice of Civil Citation for the following location:

Address **Parcel**

FAILURE TO COMPLY WITH FINDING OF FACT AND ORDER ISSUED MARCH 11, 2024; EXPIRED JUNE 11, 2024. $15,000 CITATION. INVOICE ATTACHED.

Violation: 16-229 (a) (2) - Residential Buildings Unfit for Human Habitation: Supporting Members, Nonsupporting or Outside Walls Unsafe
Supporting member or members which show thirty-three (33) percent or more damage or deterioration or nonsupporting enclosing or outside walls or covering which shows fifty (50) percent or more of damage or deterioration.

Corrective Action: Please correct the items listed.

Violation: 16-229 (a) (3) - Residential Buildings Unfit for Human Habitation: Floors or Roofs Unsafe
Floors or roofs which have improperly distributed loads, which are overloaded or which have insufficient strength to be reasonably safe for the purpose used.

Corrective Action: PLEASE REPLACE, REPAIR ENTIRE KITCHEN, BATHROOM FLOORING SYSTEM VERY UNSAFE CONDITIONS.

Compliance Date: 02/19/2023

Violation: 16-229 (a) (5) - Residential Buildings Unfit for Human Habitation: Dangerous, Unsafe Conditions, Unsanitary Health and Safety
Dilapidation, decay, unsanitary conditions or disrepair which is dangerous to the health, safety or welfare of the occupants or other people in the city.

Corrective Action: Please correct the items listed.

Violation: 16-229 (a) (6) - Residential Buildings Unfit for Human Habitation: Egress
Inadequate facilities for egress in case of fire or panic.

Corrective Action: Please correct the items listed.

Violation: 16-229 (a) (7) - Residential Buildings Unfit for Human Habitation: Risk, Hazard of Fire
Defects significantly increasing the hazards of fire, accident or other calamities.

Corrective Action: Please correct the items listed.

Violation: 16-229 (a) (8) - Residential Buildings Unfit for Human Habitation:Ventilation, Light, Heating, Sanitary. Health and Safety
Lack of adequate ventilation, light, heating or sanitary facilities to such extent as to endanger the health, safety or general welfare of the occupants or other residents of the city.

Corrective Action: Please correct the items listed.

Violation: 16-229 (a) (9) - Residential Buildings Unfit for Human Habitation: Lack of Electrical, Heating, Plumbing Health and Safety
Lack of proper electrical, heating or plumbing facilities required by this chapter which constitutes a health or a definite safety hazard.

Corrective Action: PLEASE REPLACE,REPAIR ALL NON WORKING OUTLETS, SWITCHES, NON WORKING LIGHTING FIXTURES.

Compliance Date: 02/19/2023

Printed: 11/14/24

Page 1 of 4

CITY OF WILMINGTON NORTH CAROLINA

Housing and Neighborhood Services
Code Enforcement

Case Number:

Civil Citation

Case Type: CE - Structure Codes - Minimum Housing Requirements

Date of Inspection: 11/13/2024

Date of Next Inspection: 12/18/2024

Violation: 16-266 (1) - Minimum Standards for Equipment and Facilities: General, Sanitary Facilities
Sanitary facilities—Required. Every dwelling unit shall contain not less than a kitchen sink, lavatory, tub or shower, and a water closet, all in good working condition and properly connected to an approved water and sewer system. Every plumbing fixture and water and waste pipe shall be properly installed and maintained in good sanitary working condition, free from defects, leaks and obstructions.
Corrective Action: Please correct the items listed.

Violation: 16-266 (2) - Minimum Standards for Equipment and Facilities: General, Sanitary Facilities Location
Same—Location. All required sanitary facilities shall be located within the dwelling unit and shall be accessible to the occupants of same. The water closet, tub or shower, and lavatory in at least one (1) bathroom shall be located in a room affording privacy to the user and such rooms shall have a minimum floor space of thirty (30) square feet.
Corrective Action: Please correct the items listed.

Violation: 16-266 (4) - Minimum Standards for Equipment and Facilities: General, Heating Faciltiies
(a) Every dwelling unit shall have heating facilities which are properly installed, are maintained in safe and good working condition and are capable of safely and adequately heating all habitable rooms, bathrooms and water closet compartments in every dwelling unit therein to a temperature of at least sixty-eight (68) degrees Fahrenheit at a distance three (3) feet above the floor during ordinary minimum winter conditions. (b) Where a gas or electric central heating system is not provided, each dwelling unit shall be provided with sufficient fireplaces, chimneys, flues or gas vents, whereby heating appliances may be connected so as to furnish a minimum temperature of sixty-eight (68) degrees Fahrenheit measured to a point three (3) feet above the floor during ordinary minimum winter conditions, and in safe and proper working order.
Corrective Action: PLEASE INSTALL CENTRAL HEATING SYSTEM , REMOVE SPACE UNSAFE SPACE HEATERS.
Compliance Date: 02/19/2023

Violation: 16-267 (2) - Minimum Standards for Equipment and Facilities: Light; Ventilation, Habitable Rooms - Ventiliation
Same—Ventilation. Every habitable room shall have at least one (1) window or skylight which can be safely opened, or such other device as will adequately ventilate the room. The total of openable window area in every habitable room shall be equal to at least forty-five (45) percent of the minimum window area size or minimum skylight-type size, as required, or the room shall have other approved equivalent ventilation.
Corrective Action: Please correct the items listed.

Violation: 16-267 (3) - Minimum Standards for Equipment and Facilities: Light; Ventilation, Bathroom
Bathroom. Every bathroom shall comply with the light and ventilation requirements for habitable rooms except that no window or skylight shall be required in adequately ventilated bathrooms equipped with an approved ventilation system.
Corrective Action: Please correct the items listed.

Violation: 16-267 (4) - Minimum Standards for Equipment and Facilities: Light; Ventilation, Electrical Lights and Outlets
Electric lights and outlets. Every dwelling shall be adequately and safely wired for electric lights and convenience receptacles. Every habitable room and hallway shall have provisions for adequate lighting and other necessary electrical service.
Corrective Action: Please correct the items listed.

Violation: 16-268 (1) - Minimum Standards for Equipment and Facilities: Electrical Systems, Fixtures, Wiring
All fixtures, receptacles, equipment and wiring shall be maintained in a state of good repair, safe, capable of being used and installed and connected to the source of electric power in accordance with the adopted electrical code of the city.
Corrective Action: Please correct the items listed.

Violation: 16-268 (2) - Minimum Standards for Equipment and Facilities: Electrical Systems, Capacity, Service, Disconnect Switch, Load
The minimum capacity of the service supply and the main disconnect switch shall be sufficient to adequately carry the total load required in accordance with the electrical code of the city.
Corrective Action: Please correct the items listed.

Violation: 16-269 (1) - Minimum Standards for Equipment and Facilities: Exterior and Interior of Structures Generally, Foundation
Foundation. The building foundation walls, piers or other elements shall be maintained in a safe manner and capable of supporting the load which normal use may cause to be placed thereon.

Printed: 11/14/24 **Page 2 of 4**

CITY OF WILMINGTON NORTH CAROLINA

Housing and Neighborhood Services
Code Enforcement

Case Number:

Civil Citation

Case Type: CE - Structure Codes - Minimum Housing Requirements

Date of Inspection: 11/13/2024

Date of Next Inspection: 12/18/2024

Corrective Action: KITCHEN, BATHROOM

Compliance Date: 02/19/2023

Violation: 16-269 (10) - Minimum Standards for Equipment and Facilities: Exterior and Interior of Structures Generally, Hardware Doors
Hardware. Every exterior door shall be provided with proper hardware and maintained in good condition.

Corrective Action: Please correct the items listed.

Violation: 16-269 (11) - Minimum Standards for Equipment and Facilities: Exterior and Interior of Structures Generally, Door Frames
Door frames. Every exterior door shall fit reasonably well within its frame so as to substantially exclude rain and wind from entering the dwelling building.

Corrective Action: PLEASE REPLACE OR REPAIR FRONT ,REAR DOOR UNSAFE CONDITIONS,REPLACE ALL LOCKS.

Violation: 16-269 (12) - Minimum Standards for Equipment and Facilities: Exterior and Interior of Structures Generally, Screens Windows, Doors
Screens. Every door opening directly from a dwelling unit to outdoor space shall have screens and a self-closing device; and every window or other device with opening to outdoor space, used or intended to be used for ventilation, shall likewise have screens, tightfitting, free of holes and not nailed to the window frame or sash. Dwellings containing central heating furnaces and adequate cooling equipment for mechanically ventilating the building year around are not required to have screens on door or window openings.

Corrective Action: Please correct the items listed.

Violation: 16-269 (14) - Minimum Standards for Equipment and Facilities: Exterior and Interior of Structures Generally, Interior Floors, Walls, Partions, Ceilings.
Interior floors, walls, partitions, ceilings. Every floor, wall, partition and interior ceiling shall be substantially rodent proof, shall be kept in sound condition and good repair and shall be safe to use and capable of supporting the load which normal use may cause to be placed thereon.

Corrective Action: Please correct the items listed.

Violation: 16-269 (15) - Minimum Standards for Equipment and Facilities: Exterior and Interior of Structures Generally, Structural Supports
Structural supports. Every structural element of the dwelling shall be structurally sound and show no evidence of deterioration which would render it incapable of carrying loads which normal use may cause to be placed thereon.

Corrective Action: Please correct the items listed.

Violation: 16-269 (16) - Minimum Standards for Equipment and Facilities: Exterior and Interior of Structures Generally, Protective Railings
Protective railings. Protective railings shall be required on any unenclosed structure over thirty (30) inches above adjacent finish grade or on any steps exceeding four (4) risers. Interior stairs and stairwells more than four (4) risers high shall have handrails located in accordance with requirements of the building code. Handrails or protective railings shall be capable of bearing normally imposed loads and shall be maintained in good condition.

Corrective Action: Please correct the items listed.

Violation: 16-269 (2) - Minimum Standards for Equipment and Facilities: Exterior and Interior of Structures Generally, Exterior Walls
Exterior walls. The exterior walls shall be substantially weathertight and watertight, and shall be made impervious to the adverse effects of weather and be maintained in sound condition and good repair

Corrective Action: Please correct the items listed.

Violation: 16-269 (3) - Minimum Standards for Equipment and Facilities: Exterior and Interior of Structures Generally, Roofs
Roofs. Roofs shall be maintained in a safe manner and have no defects which might admit rain or cause dampness in the walls or interior portion of the building

Corrective Action: Please correct the items listed.

Violation: 16-269 (5) - Minimum Standards for Equipment and Facilities: Exterior and Interior of Structures Generally, Stairs
Stairs. Every inside and outside stair shall be safe to use and capable of supporting the load that normal use may cause to be

Printed: 11/14/24 **Page 3 of 4**

CITY OF WILMINGTON NORTH CAROLINA

Housing and Neighborhood Services
Code Enforcement

Case Number:

Civil Citation

Case Type: CE - Structure Codes - Minimum Housing Requirements

Date of Inspection: 11/13/2024

Date of Next Inspection: 12/18/2024

placed thereon; and shall be kept in sound condition and good repair.

Corrective Action: Please correct the items listed.

Violation: 16-269 (6) - Minimum Standards for Equipment and Facilities: Exterior and Interior of Structures Generally, Porches and Appurtenances
Porches and appurtenances. Every outside porch and any appurtenance thereto shall be safe to use and capable of supporting the load that normal use may cause to be placed thereon; and shall be kept in sound condition and good repair.

Corrective Action: Please correct the items listed.

Violation: 16-269 (7) - Minimum Standards for Equipment and Facilities: Exterior and Interior of Structures Generally, Windows and Doors Generally
Windows and doors generally. Every window, exterior door and basement or cellar door and hatchway shall be substantially weathertight, watertight and rodent proof; and shall be kept in sound working condition and good repair.

Corrective Action: PLEASE REPLACE ALL NON MECHANICAL WINDOWS.

Compliance Date: 02/19/2023

Violation: 16-269 (8) - Minimum Standards for Equipment and Facilities: Exterior and Interior of Structures Generally, Windows to be Glazed
Windows to be glazed. Window panes or an approved substitute shall be maintained without cracks or holes which allow passage of air.

Compliance Date: 02/19/2023

Violation: 16-269 (9) - Minimum Standards for Equipment and Facilities: Exterior and Interior of Structures Generally, Window Sash
Window sash. Window sash shall be properly fitted and weathertight within the window frame.

Corrective Action: Please correct the items listed.

Pursuant to above identified section(s) of the Wilmington City Code, a civil penalty has been assessed for the above described violation(s). This penalty must be paid within ten (10) days of receipt of this citation or the City may seek to collect it by a civil action in the nature of a debt. This civil penalty may be paid as follows:

Mail to:
City of Wilmington-Collections Office
P.O. Box 1810
Wilmington, NC 28402

In Person:
City of Wilmington Collection
929 N Front St.
Wilmington, NC 28401

If paying by mail, send a check or money order made payable to the City of Wilmington. Do not send cash. Include this citation and invoice, or copies, with your payment and indicate the Invoice number on your check. If you have any questions regarding this matter; call the undersigned Officer at their number or contact the Department below.

City of Wilmington Code Enforcement
PO Box 1810, 929 N Front St.
Wilmington, NC 28402
(910) 341-3266
www.wilmingtonnc.gov
Dial 711 TTY

Printed: 11/14/24

Page 4 of 4

16. Wilmington Minimum Housing Code Finding of Fact and Order

FINDING OF FACT AND ORDER
MINIMUM HOUSING CODE

STATE OF NORTH CAROLINA	IN THE MATTER OF THE PROPERTY LOCATED AT
COUNTY OF NEW HANOVER	**Wilmington, North Carolina**
	KNOWN AS MAP NO.
CITY OF WILMINGTON	BLOCK NO. LOT NO.

TO:

The undersigned Hearing Officer of the City of Wilmington, North Carolina, pursuant to law conducted a hearing at 929 North Front Street, Wilmington, North Carolina as scheduled on the **(date of hearing)** . At or before said hearing an Answer filed by owners or parties in interest was included in the record.

The undersigned Hearing Officer, having reviewed the entire record considered any arguments or summaries of the owner(s) and parties in interest, their agents or attorneys does hereby find that the dwelling located at the above address violated the City Minimum Housing Code (Chapter 16, Article V of the City Code) and the standards set forth therein, is unfit for human habitation and dilapidated. In support of said determination, the Hearing Officer makes the following:

FINDING OF FACT

1) The City of Wilmington, North Carolina, has jurisdiction over the owner(s), parties in interest, and subject matter of this proceeding.

2) The above-named owner(s) and parties in interest were duly served with a written Complaint and Notice of Hearing which alleged that the dwelling located at the above address is unfit for human habitation and violations the City Minimum Housing Code and fixed a time and place for a hearing upon such complaint as provided by law; the following owner(s), parties in interest, their agents or attorneys were present and were heard:

   (Those present and how they are connected to the property)

3) The Code Enforcement Officer/Housing Inspector was present and testified. The testimony of the **Code Enforcement Officer (Name)** was heard and photographs showing the condition of the dwelling and the Minimum Housing case file for the property were admitted into evidence.

4) The Minimum Housing Case began with a complaint from neighbors as to the condition of the property.

FFO_MHC_
Page 1 of 3

5) At the time the Minimum Housing Case was opened, the dwelling was being rented by the owners to **tenants (or change language if vacant).**

6) The photographs taken of the dwelling during the Code Enforcement Officer inspections show the deterioration of the dwelling and the needed repairs to bring it into compliance with the Minimum Housing Code (paragraphs # through # below).

7) **(description of the violations)**
8)
9)
10)
11)
12)
13)
14) Said dwelling fails to comply with the standards set forth in the Minimum Housing Code of the City of Wilmington, North Carolina, in the following respects:

* * *

15) Said dwelling is unfit for human habitation in accordance with the standards set forth in the Minimum Housing Code of the City of Wilmington, North Carolina.

16) The value of said dwelling is approximately . The approximate cost of bringing the dwelling into compliance with the Minimum Housing Code is . Therefore, the repair, alteration or improvement of this dwelling sufficient to bring it up to the standards set forth in the Minimum Housing Code is to % of the dwelling; and, the dwelling is *(dilapidated/ deteriorated)* as defined by the Minimum Housing Code.

IT IS THEREFORE ORDERED that the owner(s) of the dwelling named and designated be and are hereby ordered and required to bring such dwelling into compliance with the Minimum Housing Code of the City of Wilmington, North Carolina, by repairing and improving the dwelling to render it fit for human habitation or demolishing and removing said dwelling from the property not later than the day of , 20 .

If the owner(s) of the dwelling fail to bring such dwelling into compliance with the Minimum Housing Code as ordered by the date designated above, the offender shall be subject to a civil penalty of $100.00 per day for each day that the violation continues, The housing inspector shall file a report with the City Council of the City of Wilmington which may, after hearing, cause the repair or demolition and removal of such dwelling to be done and the costs for same shall be a lien upon the property in accordance with Section 16-232 of the Minimum Housing Code.

IT IS FURTHER ORDERED that not later than the day of , 20 , the owner(s) vacate and close the dwelling and secure the windows and doors of the dwelling until the dwelling complies with the Minimum Housing Code.

If the owner(s) of the dwelling fails to comply with the order to vacate, close and secure the dwelling, then the housing inspector for the City of Wilmington may cause the dwelling to be vacated, closed and secured and the costs for same shall be a lien upon the property in accordance with Section 16-232 of the Minimum Housing Code.

Because the dwelling is found to be unfit for human habitation, it shall be unlawful to receive rents, offer for rent or occupy the dwelling after unless the dwelling is found by the housing inspector to be in compliance with the Minimum Housing Code.

The dwelling is subject to **quarterly periodic inspections** to determine compliance with this Order and the Minimum Housing Code.

Any appeals of this Finding of Fact and Order to the Housing Appeals Board must be taken within ten (10) days from rendering of the decision or service or the order and shall be taken by filing with the Minimum Housing Hearing Officer a Notice of Appeal that specifies the grounds upon which the appeal is made.

This is the day of ,

____

Hearing Officer

City of Wilmington, North Carolina

FFO_MHC_
Page 3 of 3

17. Raleigh Lis Pendens

NORTH CAROLINA
WAKE COUNTY

A MATTER BEFORE THE HOUSING AND NEIGHBORHOODS DEPARTMENT OF THE CITY OF RALEIGH

CITY OF RALEIGH)
)
Plantiff,)
)
v.) NOTICE OF LIS PENDENS
)
[ ], (Building and Housing Code)
owner
)
)

THIS NOTICE OF LIS PENDENS, filed with the Wake County Clerk of Superior Court, shows as follows:

1. A complaint containing a Notice of Hearing was served upon the Defendant(s) on advising the Defendant(s) of the Defendant's right to show cause why the dwelling located at [ ] should not be deemed unsafe for human habitation under the Housing Code of the City of Raleigh, Raleigh City Code § 11.5, et seq.

2. The purpose of the Complaint and Notice of Hearing is to inform the Defendant(s) of the conditions of the dwelling that may render it unfit for human habitation and afford Defendant(s) an opportunity to be heard in this matter.

3. The property is described at Pin No.[ ], Real Estate ID No[ ], located at [ ] in the City of Raleigh (or its extra-territorial Jurisdiction), Wake County, North Carolina.

4. An order has been issued directing the Defendant(s) to comply with the Housing Code within a prescribed time period. Failure to comply with this order shall result in the assessment of a civil penalty and may, depending upon the condition of the dwelling, result in the demolition of the dwelling.

5. A copy of the Order is attached and incorporated by reference as if fully set forth herein.

This Notice of Lis Pendens is filed under the provisions of §1-120.2 of the General Statutes of North Carolina and Section 11.5.9 of the Raleigh City Code, and all persons shall take notice of the same.

This the 26th day of February, 2025

____
Name ______________________________
Title ______________________________

City Attorney's Office
P.O. Box 590
Raleigh, NC 27602-0590
****
NORTH CAROLINA

VERIFICATION

WAKE COUNTY

__________________, being duly sworn, deposes and says that (s)he is an Inspector and an agent of the Plaintiff named in the foregoing Notice of Lis Pendens, that the facts set forth herein are true of his/her own knowledge, except as to those matters set forth upon information and belief, and as to those matters, (s)he believes them to be true.

____

Sworn to and subscribed
Before me this 26th day of
February, 2025.

____
NOTARY PUBLIC

(SEAL)

My commission expires:________________.

I8. Wilmington Dismissal of Lis Pendens

STATE OF NORTH CAROLINA

COUNTY OF NEW HANOVER

CITY OF WILMINGTON
BEFORE THE MINIMUM HOUSING
HEARING OFFICER

IN THE MATTER OF THE
PROPERTY LOCATED AT

AND OWNED BY

NOTICE OF VOLUNTARY DISMISSAL AND CANCELLATION OF NOTICE OF LIS PENDENS

On day of 20 , the City of Wilmington filed a Notice of Lis Pendens in regards to the above referenced property, file number .

The City of Wilmington hereby given notice of voluntary dismissal in this proceeding as to all owners and parties in interest and cancels the Notice of Lis Pendens.

This the _____ day of ___________________, 20___.

____

Subscribed to and sworn before me this
the____ day of ______________, 20___.

____
Notary Public

My Commission Expires: __________________________

I9. Raleigh Unfit Council Notice

City of Raleigh
North Carolina

RE: Housing -
REID NO:

Dear :

The City of Raleigh is concerned about the health, safety and welfare of every citizen. As part of this concern, many years ago the City Council adopted a Minimum Housing Code. The provisions deal with keeping our homes in a safe and sanitary condition. The specific standards set forth are not excessive but rather very basic to good housekeeping and general maintenance. One of the responsibilities of the Code Enforcement Division of the Housing & Neighborhoods Department is to inspect dwellings within the City's jurisdiction and enforce the code as it applies to the structure, the occupants and the owners.

An inspection of the above-referenced address was made on 09/09/2024 and the Inspector saw Housing Code violations (Part 10A, Chapter 11, Article 11.6 and Sections 11.6.3 and 11.6.4 of the Unified Development Ordinance Code of the City of Raleigh) and listed them in his Housing Report, which was previously served. A hearing was held on to review the violations, discuss City procedure and determine the corrections that needed to be made.

An order was subsequently entered requiring that you bring this dwelling into compliance with the Housing Code in one of the following ways on or before 09/19/2024.

1. Make repairs as outlined.
2. Vacate the building and secure against unauthorized entry.

A copy of that order is enclosed. Inspection of this structure on by Code Enforcement Inspections Staff found that you had elected to vacate and close this building. A recent inspection determined that the structure remained vacant and closed.

According to Part 10A, Chapter 11, Article 11.6, Section 11.6.8(D) of the Unified Development Ordinance Code of the City of Raleigh, the City Council can order the repair, demolition, or both, of certain dwellings that remain vacant and closed for a period of more than one (1) year. The Housing & Neighborhoods Department believes that your property is subject to such an order under Section 11.6.8(D).

The above-captioned dwelling has been vacant and closed for a period of time in excess of one year and it appears to the Housing & Neighborhoods Department that each of the criteria set out in Section 11.6.8(D) exists. We will, therefore, be asking the City Council to enact an ordinance requiring you to repair or demolish the dwelling within 90 days and to allow us to demolish it if you do not do so as ordered. You have the right to appear before the Council and present evidence or testimony to it. **The Council will hear this matter on** . The meeting is scheduled for in

Housing & Neighborhoods, Code Enforcement Division - 421 Fayetteville Street, Suite 1200, Raleigh, NC 27601 (919) 996-2444

City of Raleigh
North Carolina

the Council Chambers, 222 W Hargett Street, Raleigh, NC 27601. Your case will be heard according to its placement on the Council agenda. If you do not appear, the Council will hear the case without you being present.

The Housing & Neighborhoods Department will request that the City Council adopt an ordinance authorizing the demolition of this unfit building within ninety (90) days if the repairs necessary to render the dwelling fit for human habitation are not made by the owner. If the structure is demolished by the City, the costs will be confirmed as a lien against the property and collected as taxes.

If I can be of any help to you or provide you with additional information, please advise.

Sincerely,

Code Enforcement Administrator
City of Raleigh Housing & Neighborhoods Department
919-996-2450

Case #:

cc:

Housing & Neighborhoods, Code Enforcement Division - 421 Fayetteville Street, Suite 1200, Raleigh, NC 27601 (919) 996-2444

I10. Wilmington Notice of Public Hearing

CITY OF WILMINGTON NORTH CAROLINA

Housing and Neighborhood Services
Community Development
Code Enforcement
929 North Front Street
PO Box 1810
Wilmington, NC 28402-1810
910 341 3266
codeenforcment@wilmingtonnc.gov
wilmingtonnc.gov
Dial 711 TTY/Voice

January 29, 2025

RE: Notice of Public Hearing

Legal Description:

The Wilmington City Council will consider the ordinances to vacate, close and repair or demolish the dwellings located at , and **Street.** This letter is being sent to you because you are the record owner of the property, or you may have an interest in the referenced property.

Should you wish to make any comments concerning these ordinances, you are invited to attend the **February 18, 2025,** City Council meeting to be held at **6:30 p.m.** in the City Council Chambers, City Hall, Third and Princess Streets, 102 North 3rd Street. Wilmington, NC.

All materials and supplementary materials related to these items are available for public inspection and review at the office of the City of Wilmington Code Enforcement Division located on the second floor at 929 N Front Street by appointment during regular working hours between 8:00 a.m. to 5:00 p.m., Monday through Friday.

If you have any questions regarding this ordinance, please call the Code Enforcement Division at (910) 341-3266, email: codeenforcement@wilmingtonnc.gov

Sincerely,

Chief Code Enforcement Officer
January 29, 2025

CITY OF WILMINGTON NORTH CAROLINA

Housing and Neighborhood Services
Community Development
Code Enforcement
929 North Front Street
PO Box 1810
Wilmington, NC 28402-1810
910 341 3266
codeenforcment@wilmingtonnc.gov
wilmingtonnc.gov
Dial 711 TTY/Voice

STATE OF NORTH CAROLINA
CITY OF WILMINGTON
NEW HANOVER COUNTY

AFFIDAVIT OF SERVICE

This is to certify that the foregoing "Notice of Public Hearing" was duly served in accordance with the provisions of Wilmington City Code Sec. 16-234 and North Carolina General Statute Section 160D-1206 upon the owners and all parties in interest in the manner indicated below.

BEFORE ME, the undersigned Notary Public, personally came and appeared:

[ ]

who being first duly sworn did depose and say that:

He is a Code Enforcement Officer, duly authorized to enforce the Code of Ordinance for the City of Wilmington, North Carolina.

All Lawful Heirs of [ ] are the owners or parties in interest of the properties located at [ ], and [ ].

On January 29, 2025, a copy of the Notice of Public Hearing was deposited in the U. S. Post Office for mailing by certified mail, return receipt requested and 1st Class Mail, to the owner(s) of such property.

A copy of said Notice of Public Hearing was posted on the premises.

Notice of Public Hearing and other pleadings have been made by publication in a newspaper having general circulation in the City.

This the _______ day of ________________, 2025.

____
Chief Code Enforcement Officer

Subscribed to and sworn before me this
the_____ day of _______________, 20___.

____
Notary Public

My Commission Expires: ____________________________

I11. Raleigh Unfit for Human Habitation

Raleigh

[ADDRESS OF PROPERTY]
RALEIGH, NC [ZIP]

THIS BUILDING IS

UNFIT FOR HUMAN HABITATION;

The USE or OCCUPATION of this building for human habitation is PROHIBITED and UNLAWFUL.

This placard is being posted in accordance with Ordinance No. [ORDINANCE NO.] which was adopted by the City of Raleigh pursuant to N.C.G.S. § 160D-1201 et seq. and Chapter 11, Article 11.6 of the City of Raleigh's Unified Development Ordinance (the "UDO"). Unauthorized removal of this placard is unlawful per UDO Sec. 11.6.12.

WARNING: Use or occupation of this building constitutes a Class I Misdemeanor per N.C.G.S. § 160D-1203(4).

____
City of Raleigh Minimum Housing
Public Officer

____
Date

I12. Wilmington Minimum Housing Code Repair or Demolish Ordinance

..title

Ordinance Directing The Housing Inspector To Vacate, Close And Repair Or Demolish The Dwelling At [ADDRESS] As Unfit For Human Habitation Pursuant To Article V, Chapter 16 Of The City Code And Directing That A Notice Be Placed Thereon Prohibiting Its Use Or Occupancy

..body

LEGISLATIVE INTENT/PURPOSE:

WHEREAS, the City Minimum Housing Code ("MHC") enacted pursuant to Section 160D-1203 of the North Carolina General Statues authorizes the vacating, closing and the repair or demolition of dwellings found unfit for human habitation; and

WHEREAS, the City Council of the City of Wilmington ("Council") finds that the property described herein, located at **[ADDRESS]** and having owners identified as **"[OWNER NAME]"** ("Owners"), is unfit for human habitation under the MHC, and that all of the provisions of the MHC have been complied with as a condition of the adoption of this ordinance; and

WHEREAS, said dwelling should be vacated, closed and repaired to meet the requirements of the MHC, or demolished, as directed by the Housing Inspector and should be placarded by placing thereon a notice prohibiting use for human habitation; and

WHEREAS, the Owners of said dwelling have been given a reasonable opportunity to bring the dwelling up to the standards of the MHC, in accordance with N.C.G.S. Section 160D-1203(3), and pursuant to an order issued by the Hearing Officer on **[FOF ISSUED DATE],** and the Owners having failed to comply with the order; and

WHEREAS, N.C.G.S. Section 160A-193 provides cities with the authority to summarily remove, abate, or remedy everything in the city limits that is dangerous or prejudicial to the public health or public safety; and

WHEREAS, the Council has determined that the condition of the dwelling at **[ADDRESS]** constitutes a danger to the public safety and should be immediately repaired or removed.

NOW, THEREFORE, BE IT ORDAINED

Section 1. That the Housing Inspector is hereby authorized and directed to place on the dwelling bearing the postal enumeration **[ADDRESS]** a placard containing the legend:

"This building is unfit for human habitation; the use or occupation of this building for human habitation is prohibited and unlawful."

Section 2. The realty upon which said dwelling is situated is more particularly described as follows:

[FULL LEGAL DESCRIPTION]

Parcel ID: **[PARCEL NUMBER]**

Section 3. It shall be unlawful for any person to remove or cause to be removed said placard from any dwelling to which it is affixed. It shall likewise be unlawful for any person to occupy or to permit the occupancy of any dwelling therein declared to be unfit for human habitation. Occupation of a building so posted shall constitute a Class 1 misdemeanor.

Section 4. The Owners and/or parties in interest of the dwelling herein above described are hereby ordered to vacate and close the subject dwelling found by the Housing Inspector to be unfit for human habitation from the date of adoption of this ordinance, and to repair or demolish the subject dwelling within **[ADDITIONAL COMPLIANCE PERIOD GRANTED BY COUNCIL IF ANY]** days from the date of adoption of this ordinance to meet the requirements of the MHC.

Section 5. If the owners and/or parties in interest fail to have the dwelling vacated, the Housing Inspector is hereby authorized to commence summary ejectment proceedings pursuant to 160D-1203(8).

Section 6. If the owner and/or parties in interest shall fail or refuse to vacate, close and repair or demolish said dwelling within the time allowed, then the Housing Inspector is hereby authorized and directed to proceed to vacate, close and repair or demolish the above-described dwelling in accordance with this ordinance and order to the Owners thereof, dated **[FOF ISSUED DATE],** pursuant to Section 16-232 of the MHC and N.C.G.S. Section 160D-1203. The cost of any such repairs, alterations, demolition, or improvements, and vacating and closing, by the Housing Inspector shall be a lien against the real property upon which the cost was incurred as provided in Section 16-232 of the MHC and N.C.G.S. Section 160D-1203(7).

Section 7. The Housing Inspector is further directed and authorized to take such other and further action and exercise such other powers with respect to said dwelling as may be necessary or convenient to carry out and effectuate the provisions of the MHC.

Section 8. The City Clerk is hereby directed to record a certified copy of this ordinance in the office of the New Hanover County Register of Deeds and see that it is properly indexed in the name of the property owner(s) in the grantor index.

Section 9. Any person violating the provisions of the ordinance shall be subject to the penalties set forth in Section 16-1 of the City Code. If the violation is continued, each day's violation shall be a separate offense.

Section 10. This ordinance may be enforced by an appropriate equitable remedy, including but not limited to an injunction or order of abatement issued from any court of competent jurisdiction, pursuant to N.C.G.S. Section 160D-1208 or by receivership pursuant to N.C.G.S. Section 160D-1130.

Section 11. This ordinance may be enforced by any, all, or a combination of the remedies as authorized and prescribed above and by law.

Section 12. All ordinances or parts of ordinances in conflict with this ordinance are hereby repealed to the extent of such conflict.

Section 13. If any section, subsection, paragraph, sentence, clause, phrase or portion of this ordinance is for any reason held invalid or unconstitutional by any court of competent jurisdiction, such portion shall be deemed severable and such holding shall not affect the validity of the remaining portions hereof.

Section 14. The Owner of the property described herein are **[OWNER NAME]**.

Section 15. That the City Attorney is authorized to proceed with in rem foreclosure proceedings to collect taxes and liens owed for the property.

Section 16. This ordinance shall become effective upon its adoption.

I13. Wilmington Sample Demolition Ordinance

Ordinance

City Council
City of Wilmington
North Carolina

Introduced By: , City Manager **Date:** 3/18/2025

Ordinance Directing The Housing Inspector To Vacate, Close And Repair Or Demolish The Dwelling At As Unfit For Human Habitation Pursuant To Article V, Chapter 16 Of The City Code And Directing That A Notice Be Placed Thereon Prohibiting Its Use Or Occupancy

LEGISLATIVE INTENT/PURPOSE:

WHEREAS, the City Minimum Housing Code ("MHC") enacted pursuant to Section 160D-1203 of the North Carolina General Statues authorizes the vacating, closing and the repair or demolition of dwellings found unfit for human habitation; and

WHEREAS, the City Council of the City of Wilmington ("Council") finds that the property described herein, located at and having owners identified as ("Owners"), is unfit for human habitation under the MHC, and that all of the provisions of the MHC have been complied with as a condition of the adoption of this ordinance; and

WHEREAS, said dwelling should be vacated, closed and repaired to meet the requirements of the MHC, or demolished, as directed by the Housing Inspector and should be placarded by placing thereon a notice prohibiting use for human habitation; and

WHEREAS, the Owners of said dwelling have been given a reasonable opportunity to bring the dwelling up to the standards of the MHC, in accordance with N.C.G.S. Section 160D-1203(3), and pursuant to an order issued by the Hearing Officer on May 1, 2023, and the Owners having failed to comply with the order; and

WHEREAS, N.C.G.S. Section 160A-193 provides cities with the authority to summarily remove, abate, or remedy everything in the city limits that is dangerous or prejudicial to the public health or public safety; and

WHEREAS, the Council has determined that the condition of the dwelling at constitutes a danger to the public safety and should be immediately repaired or removed.

NOW, THEREFORE, BE IT ORDAINED

Section 1. That the Housing Inspector is hereby authorized and directed to place on the dwelling bearing the postal enumeration [ ]reet a placard containing the legend:

"This building is unfit for human habitation; the use or occupation of this building for human habitation is prohibited and unlawful."

Section 2. The realty upon which said dwelling is situated is more particularly described as follows:

Beginning at a point in the eastern line of [ ] 33 feet southwardly from the intersection of the eastern line of [ ]; runs thence eastwardly and parallel with [ ] 155 feet more or less to the western line of [ ]; thence southwardly along the western line of [ ] 33 feet; thence westwardly and parallel with [ ] 155 feet more or less to the eastern line of [ ]; thence northwardly along the eastern line of [ ] 33 feet to the point of beginning. Same being southwestern one fourth of [ ], according to the official plan of the City of Wilmington, North Carolina.

Parcel ID: [ ]

Section 3. It shall be unlawful for any person to remove or cause to be removed said placard from any dwelling to which it is affixed. It shall likewise be unlawful for any person to occupy or to permit the occupancy of any dwelling therein declared to be unfit for human habitation. Occupation of a building so posted shall constitute a Class 1 misdemeanor.

Section 4. The Owners and/or parties in interest of the dwelling herein above described are hereby ordered to vacate and close the subject dwelling found by the Housing Inspector to be unfit for human habitation from the date of adoption of this ordinance, and to repair or demolish the subject dwelling within **90** days from the date of adoption of this ordinance to meet the requirements of the MHC.

Section 5. If the owners and/or parties in interest fail to have the dwelling vacated, the Housing Inspector is hereby authorized to commence summary ejectment proceedings pursuant to 160D-1203(8).

Section 6. If the owner and/or parties in interest shall fail or refuse to vacate, close and repair or demolish said dwelling within the time allowed, then the Housing Inspector is hereby authorized and directed to proceed to vacate, close and repair or demolish the above-described dwelling in accordance with this ordinance and order to the Owners thereof, dated May 1, 2023, pursuant to Section 16-232 of the MHC and N.C.G.S. Section

160D-1203. The cost of any such repairs, alterations, demolition, or improvements, and vacating and closing, by the Housing Inspector shall be a lien against the real property upon which the cost was incurred as provided in Section 16-232 of the MHC and N.C.G.S. Section 160D-1203(7).

Section 7. The Housing Inspector is further directed and authorized to take such other and further action and exercise such other powers with respect to said dwelling as may be necessary or convenient to carry out and effectuate the provisions of the MHC.

Section 8. The City Clerk is hereby directed to record a certified copy of this ordinance in the office of the New Hanover County Register of Deeds and see that it is properly indexed in the name of the property owner(s) in the grantor index.

Section 9. Any person violating the provisions of the ordinance shall be subject to the penalties set forth in Section 16-1 of the City Code. If the violation is continued, each day's violation shall be a separate offense.

Section 10. This ordinance may be enforced by an appropriate equitable remedy, including but not limited to an injunction or order of abatement issued from any court of competent jurisdiction, pursuant to N.C.G.S. Section 160D-1208 or by receivership pursuant to N.C.G.S. Section 160D-1130.

Section 11. This ordinance may be enforced by any, all, or a combination of the remedies as authorized and prescribed above and by law.

Section 12. All ordinances or parts of ordinances in conflict with this ordinance are hereby repealed to the extent of such conflict.

Section 13. If any section, subsection, paragraph, sentence, clause, phrase or portion of this ordinance is for any reason held invalid or unconstitutional by any court of competent jurisdiction, such portion shall be deemed severable and such holding shall not affect the validity of the remaining portions hereof.

Section 14. The Owner of the property described herein are ______________ ________.

Section 15. That the City Attorney is authorized to proceed with in rem foreclosure proceedings to collect taxes and liens owed for the property.

Section 16. This ordinance shall become effective upon its adoption.

Adopted at a ________________ meeting

On ____________________ 2025

____
[ ], Mayor

Attest:

____
[ ], City Clerk

Approved As To Form:

____
City Attorney

I14. Wilmington Demolition Lien

STATE OF NORTH CAROLINA

LIEN NOTICE

CITY OF WILMINGTON

TO: CITY-COUNTY TAX COLLECTOR

Under and by virtue of the authority vested in the City or Wilmington, North Carolina, by reason of North Carolina General Statutes Section 160D-1203; and pursuant to notice duly given in accordance with Chapter 16 Article V of the Code of the City of Wilmington, North Carolina, the said City of Wilmington, North Carolina claims a lien upon the real estate listed upon the tax records in the name(s) of;

and described as;

Situs Address:
Legal Description:
Parcel Number:
Case Number:
Lien Identifier: MHC - Demolition
Lien Details: DEMOLITION

said lien being in the amount of $ together with interest at the rate of eight percent annum from date; the same representing the cost incurred by the said City for the removal of the dwelling or structure from said property. Signed on this day of .

____
, Mayor

ATTEST:

____
, City Clerk (SEAL)

I15. Wilmington Appeal of Minimum Housing, Nonresidential

Application No. ______________________ Page 1 of 2

CITY OF WILMINGTON
STATE OF NORTH CAROLINA

APPLICATION FOR APPEAL FROM A DECISION OF THE MINIMUM HOUSING/ NONRESIDENTIAL STRUCTURES/ABANDONED STRUCTURES HEARING OFFICER

TO THE BUILDING APPEALS BOARD/BOARD OF ADJUSTMENT:

I, ____, hereby appeal to the Building Appeals Board/Board of Adjustment from the following adverse decision of a Minimum Housing/ Nonresidential Structures/Abandoned Structures Hearing Officer of the City of Wilmington: (State the decision)

____
____
____
____

This adverse decision was made with respect to property described herein or on the attached sheet.

____
____
____

Also known as Tax Parcel No. ___________________________

STATEMENT BY THE APPELLANT

In the space provided below or on a separate sheet of paper, present your reasons for appeal. In addition, state what facts you are prepared to prove to the Building Appeals Board that should lead the Board to conclude that the decision of the Hearing Officer was erroneous. Include a copy of the Findings of Fact and Order from the Hearing Officer, with the decision you are appealing.

____
____
____
____
____
____
____
____
____
____

Application No. ______________________ Page 2 of 2

Should the applicant choose to retain legal representation, an agent form must be completed and submitted as part of the application. Failure to notify staff of legal representation may result in a continuance of the case to allow city staff time to secure outside legal representation.

I certify that all of the information presented by me in this Application is true and correct to the best of my knowledge, information and belief.

______________________ ______________________________________

Date Signature of Applicant

Mailing address: ______________________________________

Telephone number: ______________________________________

Email Address: ______________________________________

Appendix J

Sample Nuisance Code Notices

J1. Raleigh Public Nuisance Notice of Violation

City of Raleigh
North Carolina

February 26, 2025

Previous Offenses in last 12 months: 3
Case#:

RE:

Dear

The City of Raleigh is committed to providing a clean, safe and healthy environment for its citizens. The Code Enforcement Division of the Housing & Neighborhoods Department enforces the Health, Sanitation and Public Nuisance provisions (Part 12, Chapter 6) of the Raleigh City Code. Under this code, each property owner is responsible for maintaining their property in a safe, clean and uncluttered condition. When a Housing Inspector identifies a public nuisance, the property owner is notified of the type of nuisance and requested to take actions necessary to correct the violation.

NOTICE OF VIOLATION

During an inspection of the above referenced property on 09/09/2024 conditions defined by City Code Section 12-6001-12-6004 and identified on the attached Notice of Violations form were observed and determined to constitute a Public Nuisance Code violation. According to the City or County tax records, you are the owner or manager of this property. Your cooperation in removing or correcting this public nuisance on or before 03/08/2025 is requested.

Failure to remove or correct the nuisance violation on or before the above date will result in the City of Raleigh abating the public nuisance. When the City of Raleigh abates a nuisance on your property, you will be charged both for the costs incurred in the abatement and an additional One Hundred Seventy Five Dollars ($175.00) administrative fee. If these expenses are not paid promptly after the demand for payment, a lien could be placed against the property.

If the Public Nuisance Code violation on your property consists of, or includes, items that do not qualify for pick up by normal Solid Waste Services such as household furniture, appliances, yard waste, you may arrange for a Special Load or Bulky Load pick up by the City. You may call the City of Raleigh for more detailed information about these services at telephone number (919) 996-3245 or obtain additional information by visiting the City of Raleigh web page http://www.raleighnc.gov.

ADMINISTRATIVE FEE

In accordance with City Code Section 12-6006 ADMINISTRATIVE FEE any owner of a property that is notified pursuant to Code Section 12-6003 of a public nuisance violation on their property as defined by the City of Raleigh Health, Sanitation and Public Nuisance Code Section 12-6001-12-6004 shall be subject to an administrative fee assessment of One Hundred Dollars ($100.00) upon a SECOND nuisance notice of violation occurring within twelve (12) months of a first nuisance notice. For each subsequent nuisance notice of violation occurring prior to the expiration of a twelve (12) month period following the first public nuisance notice the owner will also be subject to assessment of an administrative fee of One Hundred Dollars ($100.00).

CIVIL PENALTY

In accordance with City Code Section 12-6005 CIVIL PENALTY any owner of a property that is notified pursuant to Code Section 12-6003 of a public nuisance violation on their property as defined by the City of Raleigh Health, Sanitation and Public Nuisance Code Section 12-6001-12-6004 shall be subject to a civil penalty of Two Hundred and Fifty Dollars ($250.00) upon a

Housing & Neighborhoods, Code Enforcement Division - 421 Fayetteville Street, Suite 1200, Raleigh, NC 27601 (919) 996-2444

City of Raleigh
North Carolina

February 26, 2025

SECOND nuisance notice of violation occurring within twelve (12) months of a first nuisance notice. For each subsequent nuisance notice of violation occurring prior to the expiration of a twelve (12) month period following the first public nuisance notice the owner will also be subject to a civil penalty of Five Hundred Dollars ($500.00).

If this is a second or subsequent notice of violation within twelve (12) months at this address, the number of previous offenses is noted at the top of the first page of this notice, an administrative fee and civil penalty is enclosed with this notice.

APPEALS

Under the provisions of City Code, you have a right to appeal the Housing & Neighborhoods Department public nuisance findings described on the attached Notice of Violations to the Code Enforcement Administrator. If the appellant is not satisfied with the Code Enforcement Administrator's decision, the appellant may request that the appeal be heard by the Raleigh City Council. Appeal of a Notice of Public Nuisance must be written and received by the Code Enforcement Administrator at the address shown below within ten (10) calendar days from the mailing of this notice. A notice of appeal will stay abatement of the nuisance by the Housing & Neighborhoods Department.

Under the provisions of City Code Section 12-6008 any person assessed a civil penalty or an administrative fee may appeal by filing a written notice of appeal with the Housing & Neighborhoods Director c/o Code Enforcement Administrator, 421 Fayetteville Street, Suite 1200, P.O. Box 590, Raleigh, NC 27602-0590 within ten (10) days after service of the assessment. The written notice of appeal shall provide the reasons that the petitioner contends that the assessment was wrongly applied and any supporting documentation. The failure to file a notice of appeal within this time period shall constitute a waiver of the right to contest the civil penalty or administrative fee.

While it is not the City's intention to cause undue hardship, we are concerned about the health, safety and welfare of all Raleigh citizens and therefore again ask for your cooperation in correcting the violations listed on this notice. Additional information pertaining to conditions that create a public nuisance may be obtained by visiting the City of Raleigh Housing & Neighborhoods Department web site, http://www.raleighnc.gov. It is our belief that by working together we can improve the quality of life and environment of our City. Please call me if you have any questions or concerns regarding this matter or the City of Raleigh Public Nuisance Code between 8:00 a.m. and 4:15 p.m.and I will endeavor to assist you.

Sincerely,

Housing & Neighborhoods, Code Enforcement Division - 421 Fayetteville Street, Suite 1200, Raleigh, NC 27601 (919) 996-2444

City of Raleigh
North Carolina

February 26, 2025

Violation Details

City Ordinance violations and details:

Location: Violations
Date Reported: 09/09/2024 **Active?** ☐ **Date Corrected:** 10/22/2024
Any junk or concentration of litter. City Code Section 12-6002 (k)

Notes:

Location: Violations
Date Reported: 09/09/2024 **Active?** ☐ **Date Corrected:** 10/22/2024
A dense growth of weeds and grasses except ornamental grasses over 8 inches in height are to be cut which: (1) lies less than one hundred (100) feet from any abutting street or (2) lies less than one hundred (100) feet from any adjoining property which contains a dwelling or commercial building or (3) lies less than fifty (50) feet from any dwelling or commercial building. City of Raleigh Code Section 12-6002 (b) (1), (2) and (3)

Notes:

Housing & Neighborhoods, Code Enforcement Division - 421 Fayetteville Street, Suite 1200, Raleigh, NC 27601 (919) 996-2444

Case Number:	
Invoice Date:	02/26/2025
Amount Due:	$1,132.00
Due Date:	03/28/2025

City of Raleigh

City of Raleigh
Housing & Neighborhoods Department
Code Enforcement Division
PO Box 590
Raleigh NC 27602-0590

(919) 996-2444
housing.inspections@raleighnc.gov

Code Enforcement Assessed Fees

Please be advised that you are or have been in violation of Part 12, Chapter 6 of the Raleigh City Code entitled "Health, Sanitation and Public Nuisances".

According to Section 12-6005 entitled Civil Penalty and Section 12-6006 entitled "Administrative Fee" of the Raleigh City Code, you are hereby cited for this violation and issued a civil penalty and an administrative fee. The total amount of the civil penalty and administrative fee must be paid in full within thirty (30) days.

Failure to make payment within thirty (30) days will result in the referral of the charges for collection action.

CASE NUMBER	DESCRIPTION	AMOUNT
	HS - Cost of Abatement	$357.00
	PN - Administrative Fee	$100.00
	PN - Civil Citation - Subsequent Violations	$500.00
	HS - Abatement Admin Fee	$175.00
	AMOUNT DUE AS OF 03/28/2025	$1,132.00

The City of Raleigh charges a $35.00 fee for returned checks

DETACH AND RETAIN THIS PORTION FOR YOUR RECORDS

PLEASE RETURN THIS PORTION WITH YOUR PAYMENT

CASE NUMBER	ACCOUNT CODE	DUE DATE	AMOUNT	AMOUNT PAID
	0025	03/28/2025	$532.00	
	AR 300	03/28/2025	$100.00	
	AR 306	03/28/2025	$500.00	
	AMOUNT DUE AS OF 03/28/2025		$1,132.00	

CUSTOMER:
VIOLATION ADDRESS:

Mail Payment & Stub To:

City of Raleigh
Revenue Services - AR
PO Box 590
Raleigh NC 27602-0590

To Pay by Credit Card:

Call (919) 996-3200 and Select Option #4

Pay in Person:
222 W Hargett St
Revenue Services Lobby

J2. Wilmington Notice of Violation Posting

Housing & Neighborhood Services
Code Enforcement
929 N Front Street
PO Box 1810
Wilmington, NC 28402-1810
910 341 3266
wilmingtonnc.gov/code

CITY OF WILMINGTON NORTH CAROLINA

Notice of Violation

Case #__________________

The purpose of this notice is to inform you of a Public Nuisance violation on your property at ____. An inspection of the above referenced property was conducted on or about ______________________ the inspection revealed condition(s) that are in violation of the Wilmington City Code, Chapter 10, Sections 10-18 and 10-28. Please see the following for a summary of the violation(s) that were found, the applicable code section(s), and the necessary corrective action(s) required for compliance with the Code. You have until ______________________ to complete the corrective action(s) needed to abate the violation. Failure to correct the violation(s) will result in further actions, including civil citations, abatement by the city, and/or a court ordered injunction.

Violations

___**Sec 10-18 (a)** It shall be unlawful for the owner, lessee, or occupant of any property to create, maintain, permit or fail to abate any public nuisance as defined in this code on such property. **(b)** Every owner, lessee or occupant of any property within the city shall keep the same clean and clear of weeds, bushes and any wild growth thereon, including grass over eight (8) inches in height. Every owner lessee or occupant shall also keep such property free and clear of all filth, open wells or containers, and all refuse materials of every kind and description. **(c)** As provided in section 11-42 of this code, the obligations set forth shall extend to the area between the property line of a lot and the curb line or edge of the roadway.

____**Sec 10-28(a)(1)** The uncontrolled growth of weeds or grass to a height of eight (8) inches or more within one hundred (100) feet of any principal structure or public right of way.
Corrective action: Cut grass and weeds.

____ **Sec 10-28(a)(2)** Accumulation of animal or vegetable matter that is offensive by virtue of odors or vapors or which is inhabited by rats, mice, snakes, or vermin of any kind which is or may be dangerous or prejudicial to the public health.
Corrective action: Remove animal/vegetable matter from property.

_____ **Sec 10-28(a)(3)** Accumulation of trash, garbage or other waste not in compliance with provisions of this chapter.
Corrective actions: Remove waste consisting of ____

_____ **Sec 10-28(a)(4)** Accumulation of hazardous refuse or concentration of combustible items such as mattresses, boxes, paper, Automobile tires, old clothes, or any other combustible materials or objects of a like nature.
Corrective action: Remove hazardous/combustible items: ____

_____ **Sec 10-28(a)(5)** Open wells.
Corrective action: Appropriately fill pits, wells, and other excavations.

_____ **Sec 10-28(a)(6)** Any Accumulation of stagnant water causing or threatening to cause the inhabitation thereof by mosquitoes.
Corrective action: Remove accumulation of standing water.

_____ **Sec 10-28(a)(7)** The open storage of any items detrimental to the public health or safety including but not limited to, any furniture, appliances, ice box, stove, glass, building material or building rubbish.
Corrective action: Remove or properly store items within an enclosure.

_____ **Sec 10-28(a)(8)** Any condition detrimental to the public health which violates the rules and regulations of the New Hanover County Health Department.

_____ **Sec 10-28(a)(9)** The presence of any debris from the demolition of any structure on the property, including but not limited to, partially demolished walls, foundation, basements, building materials and rubbish, after the cessation of all active demolition activity on the property.
Corrective action: Properly dispose of demolition materials.

_____ **Sec 10-28(a)(10)** Unsecured and deteriorated windows, doors or other openings in dwellings or structures that (a) do not have water or other utility services, or (b) are used or have been used by persons, not residents, as living quarters in the absence of sanitary facilities, or (c) are used or have been used for criminal activity.
Corrective action: Board and/or secure all openings on dwelling; restore utility services.

_____ **Sec 10-28(a)(11)** Graffiti, which is defined as any unauthorized inscription, word, figure, painting or other defacement that is written, marked, etched, scratched, sprayed, drawn, painted, or engraved on or otherwise affixed to any surface of public or private property by any implement, to the extent that the graffiti was not authorized in advance by the owner or occupant of the property, or despite advance authorization, is otherwise deemed a public nuisance.
Corrective action: Remove or cover graffiti.

Severe Nuisances Public Right-of-Way
_____ **Sec 10-28(b)(1)** Any accumulation of animal or organic matter that is offensive by virtue of odors or which is inhabited by rats, mice, snakes or vermin which may be dangerous to the public health.

_____ **Sec 10-28(b)(2)** Any accumulation of trash, garbage or other waste not in compliance with the provisions of this chapter.

_____ **Sec 10-28(b)(3)** Any accumulation of hazardous refuse or concentration of combustible items such as mattresses, boxes, paper, housewares, tires, clothes, or furniture.

_____ **Sec 10-28(b)(4)** Any accumulation of appliances, glass, building materials, demolition materials or rubbish.

Sidewalks

_____ **Sec 11-42** Keep the sidewalk in front of such lot and the area between the property line and the curb line or edge of the roadway clean and clear of all weeds and other vegetation, shall keep any grass thereon cut and shall keep street drains and street gutters open and free from obstruction.

Code Enforcement Officer: ______________ **Email:** _________________________ **Phone Number:** ___________________

J3. Wilmington Notice of Violation Transmittal Letter

CITY OF WILMINGTON NORTH CAROLINA

City Code Violation
Housing and Neighborhood Services
Code Enforcement

Case Number:

Case Type: CE - Public Nuisance

Violation Notice

Date of Inspection: 10/16/2024

Date of Next Inspection: 11/04/2024

Property Owner:

Mailing Address

Notice of Violation for the following location:

Address **Parcel**

Overgrowth of grass/weeds and scattered trash throughout the lot and in the right of way. Also, there is furniture and mattresses towards the rear of the lot.

Violation: 10-18 (c) Right-of-way Responsibility - Creation of Public Nuisancces Unlawful As provided in section 11-42 of this Code, the obligations set forth in this section shall extend to the area between the property line of a lot and the curb line or edge of the roadway.
Corrective Action: Please correct the items listed.
Compliance Date: 11/03/2024

Violation: 10-28 (a) (1) Grass and Weeds - Public Nuisances Enumerated: Tall Grass and Weeds The uncontrolled growth of weeds or grass to a height of eight (8) inches or more within one hundred (100) feet of any principal structure or public right-of-way;
Corrective Action: Please correct the items listed.
Compliance Date: 11/03/2024

Violation: 10-28 (a) (3) Trash, Garbage, Other Wastes - Public Nuisances Enumerated: Trash, Garbage, Other Wastes, Tree Debris, Yard Waste Any accumulation of trash, garbage or other waste not in compliance with the provisions of this chapter;
Corrective Action: Please correct the items listed.
Compliance Date: 11/03/2024

Violation: 10-28 (a) (4) Hazardous Refuse, Combustible Items - Public Nuisances Enumerated: Hazardous Refuse or Combustible Items, Mattresses, Tires Any accumulation of hazardous refuse or concentration of combustible items such as mattresses, boxes, paper, automobile tires, old clothes, or any other combustible materials or objects of a like nature;
Corrective Action: Please correct the items listed.
Compliance Date: 11/03/2024

Violation: 10-28 (a) (7) Open Storage - Public Nuisances Enumerated: Open Storage, Furniture, Applicances, , Building Materials or Rubbish The open storage of any item detrimental to the public health or safety including, but not limited to, any furniture, appliance, ice box, stove, glass, building material or building rubbish;
Corrective Action: Please correct the items listed.
Compliance Date: 11/03/2024

Printed: 10/17/24 **Page 1 of 2**

CITY OF WILMINGTON NORTH CAROLINA

City Code Violation
Housing and Neighborhood Services
Code Enforcement

Case Number:

Violation Notice

Case Type: CE - Public Nuisance
Date of Inspection: 10/16/2024
Date of Next Inspection: 11/04/2024

If you would like to request an extension, please contact the Code Enforcement Officer below or the Code Enforcement Office at (910) 341-3266 or email us at CodeEnforcement@WilmingtonNC.gov.

If not resolved, action may be taken to include civil penalties and abatement. The costs to the City for abatement may be placed as a lien against the property. The City may take other action as permitted by law which may result in additional costs or fees. Continued violations may be considered as a Chronic Violator. Appeals of whether a violation exists can be made in writing to the City Manager's Office within fifteen (15) days of the date of this letter.

Se encontró una violación de molestias públicas en esta propiedad. Por favor resuelve el problema. Comuníquese con CodeEnforcement@wilmingtonnc.gov o 910-341-3266 si tiene preguntas.

If the violation(s) has already been corrected, or if you have any questions or concerns, please contact the City Code Enforcement Officer below. Staff is here to assist you.

Thank you for your cooperation and for helping to make the City of Wilmington an even more beautiful place to live.

Sincerely,

City of Wilmington Code Enforcement
PO Box 1810, 929 N Front St.
Wilmington, NC 28402
(910) 341-3266
www.wilmingtonnc.gov
Dial 711 TTY

Printed: 10/17/24

Page 2 of 2

J4. Wilmington Chronic Violator Letter

CITY OF WILMINGTON NORTH CAROLINA

Housing and Neighborhood Services
Code Enforcement
PO Box 1810
Wilmington, NC 28402-1810
910 341 3266
codeenforcement@wilmingtonnc.gov

January 7, 2025,

RE: NOTICE OF CHRONIC VIOLATOR

Dear OWNER:

The purpose of this notice is to inform you that in the calendar year 2024, you were notified at least three (3) times of Public Nuisance conditions on the above listed property that violate the Wilmington City Code, Chapter 10, Sections 10-18 and 10-28. You are a chronic violator as defined under Section 10-1 of the City Code.

Per Section 10-29(d) of the Wilmington City Code, if your property is found to be in violation of Sections 10-18 and/or 10-28 of the City Code, the City shall, without further notice this calendar year, take action to remedy the public nuisance violations and the expense of the action shall become a lien upon your property and shall be collected as unpaid taxes.

Your cooperation to maintain your property and prevent further enforcement actions is very much appreciated. Please call the undersigned at (910) 341-3266 or email us at codeenforcement@wilmingtonnc.gov if you have any questions or concerns.

Sincerely,

Neighborhood Compliance Manager/Chief Code Enforcement Officer
Housing and Neighborhood Services
CodeEnforcement@wilmingtonNC.gov

J5. Raleigh Public Nuisance Lien Confirmation Notice

City of Raleigh
North Carolina

December 20, 2024

RE: Public Nuisance Abatement

Dear Property Owner(s):

Due to the failure or inability to remove the public nuisance on your property described in a prior letter and enclosed description of violations, City of Raleigh Health, Sanitation and Public Nuisance Code, Part 12, Chapter 6, the City has had the matter abated by City forces. Payment of the expenses to have the City remove a public nuisance must be paid by the property owner as stated in Part 12, Chapters 1 and 6 of the Raleigh City Code.

The cost to remove this nuisance was $532.00 and includes a $175.00 administrative fee. If the expenses are not paid to the City by 12:00 Noon on the City Council will be requested at a hearing to be held on this date at or sometime thereafter at 222 W Hargett Street, Raleigh, NC 27601 in the Council Chambers to confirm a lien on your property for $532.00. Any objections which you may have in our handling of your case can be heard at this time.

To be heard at City Council regarding this issue, we ask that you sign up for this public hearing in advance. You may sign up to speak by filling out the online form with the City Clerk's office at www.raleighnc.gov/public-hearings-city-council or by calling 919-996-3040 during the two weeks prior to and up until 5pm on the Monday before the scheduled City Council meeting.

If you choose to make payment this action will not occur or the Council will be so advised and your case will be withdrawn. Payment may be made to the City of Raleigh Revenue Services, Revenue Services Lobby, First Floor, Raleigh Municipal Building, or by mailing payment to the City of Raleigh, Revenue Services -25, P. 0. Box 590, Raleigh, NC 27602-0590. A self-addressed envelope has been enclosed for your convenience in submitting payment. Please attach a copy of this letter in order that the proper account can be credited.

If I may be of any assistance regarding this matter, please do not hesitate to call me at the number below.

Sincerely,

Code Enforcement Administrator
919-996-2450

Case #:
cc:

Housing & Neighborhoods, Code Enforcement Division - 421 Fayetteville Street, Suite 1200, Raleigh, NC 27601 (919) 996-2444

City of Raleigh
North Carolina

December 20, 2024

Violation Details

City Ordinance violations and details:

Location: Violations
Date Reported: 09/09/2024 **Active?** ☐ **Date Corrected:** 10/22/2024
Any junk or concentration of litter. City Code Section 12-6002 (k)
Notes:

Location: Violations
Date Reported: 09/09/2024 **Active?** ☐ **Date Corrected:** 10/22/2024
A dense growth of weeds and grasses except ornamental grasses over 8 inches in height are to be cut which: (1) lies less than one hundred (100) feet from any abutting street or (2) lies less than one hundred (100) feet from any adjoining property which contains a dwelling or commercial building or (3) lies less than fifty (50) feet from any dwelling or commercial building. City of Raleigh Code Section 12-6002 (b) (1), (2) and (3)
Notes:

Housing & Neighborhoods, Code Enforcement Division - 421 Fayetteville Street, Suite 1200, Raleigh, NC 27601 (919) 996-2444

Case Number:	
Invoice Date:	12/20/2024
Amount Due:	$1,132.00
Due Date:	01/21/2025

City of Raleigh

City of Raleigh
Housing & Neighborhoods Department
Code Enforcement Division
PO Box 590
Raleigh NC 27602-0590

(919) 996-2444
housing.inspections@raleighnc.gov

Re: HS - Public Nuisance -

Administrative Fee/Civil Penalty

Please be advised that you are or have been in violation of Part 12, Chapter 6 of the Raleigh City Code entitled "Health, Sanitation and Public Nuisances".

According to Section 12-6005 entitled Civil Penalty and Section 12-6006 entitled "Administrative Fee" of the Raleigh City Code, you are hereby cited for this violation and issued a civil penalty and an administrative fee. The total amount of the civil penalty and administrative fee must be paid in full within thirty (30) days.

You have the right to contest this action by filing a written appeal with the City of Raleigh Housing and Neighborhoods Department, Code Enforcement Division. Your appeal must be sent to the above address and received no later than 10 days from the date of service of this notice.

Failure to make payment within thirty (30) days or file an appeal within ten (10) days will result in the referral of the charges for collection action.

CASE NUMBER	DESCRIPTION	AMOUNT
	HS - Cost of Abatement	$357.00
	PN - Administrative Fee	$100.00
	PN - Civil Citation - Subsequent Violations	$500.00
	HS - Abatement Admin Fee	$175.00
	AMOUNT DUE AS OF 01/21/2025	$1,132.00

The City of Raleigh charges a $35.00 fee for returned checks

DETACH AND RETAIN THIS PORTION FOR YOUR RECORDS

PLEASE RETURN THIS PORTION WITH YOUR PAYMENT

CASE NUMBER	ACCOUNT CODE	DUE DATE	AMOUNT	AMOUNT PAID
	0025	01/21/2025	$532.00	
	AR 300	01/21/2025	$100.00	
	AR 306	01/21/2025	$500.00	
		AMOUNT DUE AS OF 01/21/2025	$1,132.00	

CUSTOMER:
VIOLATION ADDRESS:

Mail Payment & Stub To:

City of Raleigh
Revenue Services - AR
PO Box 590
Raleigh NC 27602-0590

To Pay by Credit Card:

Call (919) 996-3200 and Select Option #4

Pay in Person:
222 W Hargett St
Revenue Services Lobby

Indexes

Case Index

North Carolina Supreme Court

North Carolina Court of Appeals

Table of Statutes and Regulations

North Carolina General Statutes

North Carolina Administrative Code and Policies

North Carolina Session Laws

Federal Statutes and Regulations

United States Code

Code of Federal Regulations

Subject Index

F

G

M

N

O